D0765230

Transportation for the Elderly

Transportation
for the Elderly

Changing Lifestyles, Changing Needs

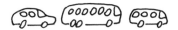

Martin Wachs

University of California Press
Berkeley · Los Angeles · London

In loving memory of Lillian Margolis,
from whom I learned so much about
growing old gracefully.

University of California Press
Berkeley and Los Angeles, California
University of California Press, Ltd.
London, England
Copyright © 1979 by
The Regents of the University of California
ISBN 0-520-03691-3
Library of Congress Catalog Card Number: 78-63091
Printed in the United States of America

1 2 3 4 5 6 7 8 9

Contents

CHAPTER 1
The Changing Elderly and the
Diversity of Their Lifestyles
PAGES 1–26

CHAPTER 4
Current Transportation Services for the Elderly
PAGES 68–91

CHAPTER 5
The Changing Social Setting of the Elderly
PAGES 92–151

CHAPTER 6

The Future Population and
Residential Location of the Elderly

PAGES 152–177

CHAPTER 7

The Future Travel
Patterns of the Elderly

PAGES 178–207

CHAPTER 8

Meeting the Changing Transportation
Needs of Older Americans

PAGES 208–256

List of Tables and Figures

Tables

Figures

Acknowledgements

*T*his book is the result of a two-year study performed at the School of Architecture and Urban Planning of the University of California, Los Angeles, under research contract DOT-OS-50109, awarded by the Program of University Research, United States Department of Transportation. The objective of the study was to develop a methodology for determining the future mobility needs of the elderly as a function of their future locational patterns and travel behavior. Although I am listed as the author of this book, the work is actually the joint product of a team of researchers, including several outstanding research assistants who worked with me at various stages of the project. Although I was responsible for the overall management of the project, and for the compilation and editing of this volume, my research assistants participated in every phase of the work, including formulating research strategy, collecting and analyzing data and drafting the research results. Robert D. Blanchard, now with the Transportation and Urban Analysis Department of the General Motors Research Laboratories in Warren, Michigan, helped to formulate the concept of lifestyle and the basic research design. His doctoral dissertation was completed as part of this project and gave rise to much of the material included in Chapters 2 and 5. Chapter 1 is based upon a paper that Dr. Blanchard and I presented at the 1976 Annual Meeting of the Transportation Research Board. James B. Bunker, now with the System Development Corporation in Santa Monica, California, was responsible for most of the computer analysis performed on the census data covering 1940 through 1970, as well as the home interview data for 1967 from the Los Angeles Regional Transportation Study (LARTS). Chapter 3 of this book is a distillation of Mr. Bunker's master's thesis. Karen Jones, presently employed by PBQ&D, a planning and engineering firm in Santa Ana, California, collected and analyzed the data concerning existing transportation services for the elderly in Los Angeles County. Chapter 4 of this book is drawn from her master's thesis. Paul Matsuoka, presently on the staff of Kaiser Foundation Health Plan, and Don H. Pickrell, currently a doctoral student in Urban Planning at UCLA, conducted the forecasts of population and travel that form the basis of Chapters 6 and 8. Mr. Pickrell also prepared the first draft of many of the policy recommendations included in the final chapter. Marilyn Westfall, now on the transportation planning staff of the Southern California Association of Governments (SCAG), also participated in many phases of the research, especially in the longitudinal analysis. Carrie Chassin, currently a member of the staff of Los Angeles City Councilman Marvin Braude, assisted in drafting the research proposal which resulted in the contract under which this study was conducted. Jacqueline Gillan, now with the Federal Highway Administration, worked with me on some of the earliest investigations of the travel patterns of the elderly in Los Angeles which ultimately gave rise to the design of this study. Jennifer Shoho, an undergraduate at UCLA, participated in the telephone survey of providers of special transportation services.

The completion of this project would not have been possible without the support and cooperation of many persons in transportation, gerontology, and public service agencies. In the data collection and data base design phases, Thomas Smuczynski, William Diemer, Robert Mullens, and Ralph Carlson of the Los Angeles Community Analysis Bureau contributed both data and their time to the research as well as continuing advice on technical and statistical matters. Data from the Bureau were the basis for the longitudinal sections of the study. Several people provided assistance in collecting health data. Professor Anne

Coulson, of the School of Public Health at UCLA, compiled health statistics and assisted in obtaining their release to the project. Sol Roschal and Pat Van Doren of the Los Angeles County Department of Health Services compiled mental health statistics. Leo Schuerman and Wayne Hansen, demographers with the Program for Data Research, University of Southern California, provided advice regarding reconciliation of census tracts and data over several census periods, as well as tract correspondence tables. W. A. V. Clark of the Geography Department at UCLA provided acreages for the 1970 census tracts. Travel data from LARTS were provided by Karl Wellisch. Terry Blank of the LARTS staff provided liaison during the data collection phase. Norman Roy of LARTS provided travel inventory data and advice on the trip generation forecasting procedures. Joe Sanchez, of the California Department of Transportation, commented upon the research plan and the draft report.

Staff members of the Los Angeles City and County Agencies on Aging identified for us other researchers in the Los Angeles area whose work was helpful; Jay Glassman of the County Agency and Carmela LaCayo of the City Agency were especially helpful. Pat Sennett, of the Los Angeles Area Agency on Aging, provided useful suggestions and a great deal of information about existing programs serving the elderly. Richard Kawasaki, of the Regional Planning Organization of Los Angeles County, assisted in assembling data used in the population forecasts. Steve Parry, of the Southern California Rapid Transit District (SCRTD), provided estimates of elderly ridership of public transit in Los Angeles County. A special tabulation compiled by Larry Carbaugh and his staff of the United States Bureau of the Census provided data that could not be obtained from any other source.

A number of people on the staff of SCAG contributed technical reports and information used in the forecasts of population and travel, and in the compilation of the inventory of existing transport service for the elderly. In particular, Louise Manuel provided housing inventory data,

Irving Jones provided information on the distribution of existing public transportation services in the SCAG region, Marilyn Westfall supplied the initial list of social service agencies providing specialized transportation service, and Mark Zerkin provided information on transit service policy. R. David MacDonald of SCAG served as an advisor and critic of this research for the two years of the project and helped to introduce us to the many sources of information and assistance available from his organization. Figure 1 was provided by the Regional Planning Commission of Los Angeles County.

Throughout the project, we have had constant guidance and assistance from our project monitors in the United States Department of Transportation. During the first year of the study Joseph Meck, of the Office of the Secretary, gave prompt and helpful support. During the second year Barbara Reichart, of the Federal Highway Administration, continued to meet the high standard initially set by Mr. Meck. They both provided creative and helpful suggestions and responded promptly to all of our inquiries.

Although the bulk of the research was conducted at UCLA with the support of the United States Department of Transportation, the final manuscript was prepared during the fall of 1977 while I was on sabbatical leave at the Transport Studies Unit of Oxford University, in England. I am grateful to the Unit and its director, Ian Heggie, for providing me with the pleasant environment in which it was possible to complete this research. A fellowship from the John Simon Guggenheim Memorial Foundation provided the travel and expense support necessary to complete this manuscript while on sabbatical.

Laurel Kelly typed the early manuscript virtually flawlessly and made a great contribution to the style and format of the document, as well as the compilation of the bibliography. Barbara Haynie typed the final manuscript. Vanessa Dingley played an important role in the entire project. She managed the typing and assembly of the final manuscript in my absence from UCLA, carefully proofread several drafts of the manuscript, compiled tables and figures, and made both stylistic and substantive suggestions for the improvement of the manuscript. Special thanks are also due to Catherine Kroger, who recently retired as an administrative analyst in the Urban Planning Program at UCLA. Since the inception of this project she managed the grant. In this capacity she helped to develop the budget for each year's study, participated in the development of the research plan, and managed the research and clerical personnel actions associated with the project.

Martin Wachs   *Oxford, England*
                                                   March, 1978

Chapter 1

The Changing Elderly
and the Diversity
of Their Lifestyles

*M*obility is critical to the physical, social, and psychological well-being of the elderly. Physical health depends upon access to medical facilities and other social services. The ability to maintain an active social life in old age depends upon accessibility to family and friends as well as recreational and cultural activities. Key ingredients of psychological health which are enhanced by mobility are freedom from isolation and the ability to choose one's range of activities. Because of its central role in American life, mobility has become an explicit element of national policy on aging. In 1970 Congress mandated ". . . the national policy that elderly and handicapped persons have the same right as other persons to utilize mass transportation facilities and services."[1] In response to this policy, many programs have been instituted to provide improved transportation for the elderly. Reduced fares for senior citizens on public transportation systems are now universal, and steps are being taken to remove architectural barriers which interfere with the ability of many disabled persons, including millions of senior citizens, to use transport vehicles. Specialized paratransit systems for the elderly

1. U.S. Congress, Senate, Special Committee on Aging, *Transportation and the Elderly: Problems and Progress*, 93rd Cong., 2d. sess., 1974, Report No. 34–273.

also have been instituted in many locations to enable elderly persons to avail themselves of many private and public social service programs.

Because this emphasis upon meeting the mobility needs of the elderly is relatively new, it is understandable that transportation officials have concentrated upon meeting immediate requirements of the elderly and have had neither the resources nor the time to consider possible long-run changes in transportation needs of the elderly. Simple methods of analysis and planning have been employed, and resources have been expended in such ways as to initiate programs for the elderly as quickly as possible. While enormous progress has been made, it is appropriate to question whether the programs now in operation will be adequate to meet the changing needs of the elderly over the coming decades. A commitment has been made to provide transportation services to the elderly, and because a significant start has been made at overcoming current barriers to their mobility, this is an appropriate time to estimate what the travel needs and patterns of the elderly might be in coming years. It is particularly important to look forward because many programs and projects have long lead times and service lives. By the time many systems now being planned are in service, today's elderly will be dead. It should not be assumed that the elderly of the future will have needs similar to those of today. If succeeding generations of the elderly are to have significantly different styles of living and travel patterns, they should now be identified and incorporated into planning goals.

There is evidence to suggest that living patterns and transportation requirements of older people are indeed shifting. By the year 2000 they may differ substantially from the requirements of the 1970s. Early transportation programs for senior citizens were based upon an image of higher density living by a fairly homogeneous group of elderly persons in central-city locations, many of whom were non-drivers. The elderly of the future, however, will be more heterogeneous, more affluent, more highly educated, dispersed in a variety of living environments, and more likely to drive. The trend for the last twenty years has been toward lower density living and increasing reliance on the automobile by senior citizens, and it is probable that this will continue as those who moved to suburban areas after World War II reach retirement age.

This book contains the results of a two-year research project concerning the future transportation needs of the elderly. The research is based upon the premise that the elderly include people of many different lifestyles giving rise to different travel demands. While it has not yet been possible to tailor transportation services to the diverse lifestyles of older Americans, planning should proceed in order that the design of future transportation systems meet these differing needs. In a case study in Los Angeles County, this research demonstrated that among the elderly there were seven groups with significantly different life-styles and that these groups differed from one another in terms of social patterns, living conditions, residential locations, and travel habits. The investigation also showed that transportation services currently available to the elderly population did not vary systematically with these different lifestyles and travel patterns and thus were not as closely tailored to the needs of the clients as such services should be. The investigation also included an analysis of probable changes in the living and travel patterns of the elderly by the turn of the next century, in addition to an explicit forecast, for Los Angeles County, of the population distribution and travel patterns of the elderly in 1990 and 2000. The research shows that membership of the different lifestyle groups will change significantly during the remainder of this century, and that their travel needs will not be adequately met by the transportation services presently available. Based upon these findings, the final chapter recommends some policy directions better suited to meeting the needs of tomorrow's elderly.

It is, of course, important to question the generality of conclusions which arise from a case study involving only one city, especially a city internationally known for its uniqueness. Are the findings that emerged in Los Angeles likely to be equally applicable in Chicago, New York, or

Boston? In those cities auto ownership rates are lower, climates are more severe, transit systems are more fully developed, and ethnic and cultural patterns are quite distinct from those characterizing Los Angeles. The question has a two-fold answer. One of the most significant purposes of the research was, simply, to demonstrate that the elderly are more heterogeneous than current transportation policy recognizes, and that statistical techniques and data sets are available which permit the analysis and understanding of this heterogeneity. There is thus reason to believe that the outcomes of this study are transferable to other settings. The specific cultures and behavior patterns found among the elderly of Los Angeles are, however, undoubtedly unique and not matched by those of other places. The presence of large numbers of older persons of Spanish-American heritage, and their consequent emergence as one of the major lifestyle groups, is but one dimension that might be unique to this study. Another might be the greater reliance in Los Angeles upon automobiles for travel, even among senior citizens. It is hoped that readers of this book will be sufficiently interested in the generality of the rationale and research approach so as to conduct similar analyses in other geographic settings, perhaps even with groups other than the elderly. Through such additional research, we can determine how more detailed findings apply to other locales and population groups. Furthermore, it is recognized that, based upon this research, conclusions relating to policy cannot be assumed to be directly applicable to other settings. Yet issues raised by the findings are so critical to current policymaking that they are addressed in the last chapter. They must, however, be considered preliminary until findings from other locales either prove or disprove their generality.

The Place of the Elderly in Future Transportation Policy

Thirty years ago transportation planning and programming did not include the elderly as an identifiable group worthy of special study and unique programs. It is a basic premise of this study, however, that thirty years from now current interest in programs for the elderly will continue to characterize transportation policymaking. There are at least four reasons for believing that current interest in senior citizens will not be short-lived, soon to subside when current programs are fully implemented. Borrowing terms used by Gold, Kutza, and Marmor, the reasons may be characterized to include economic, political, psychosocial, and ethical-philosophical factors.[2] Together these factors help to explain why public investment in transportation programs for the elderly is currently substantial and why few other age groups have such a large range of social programs directed toward them. These factors also explain why public interest in this group of people will remain high over the next several decades.

Economic Factors

Special programs for the elderly are usually predicated on the observation that the elderly are economically disadvantaged and can benefit greatly by subsidy, particularly for the purchase of essential goods and services. During the past thirty years mobility has clearly become an essential service and thus a focus for public involvement. Although income among senior citizens can be expected to improve during the coming decades because of improved pension programs, expenses for housing, health care, and transportation can also be expected to increase significantly. While not all elderly persons will be economically disadvantaged during the coming decades, the elderly will continue to be a group having relative economic need. The price of purchasing, maintaining, and operating automobiles is increasing faster than that of many other goods and services and may continue to do so for some time. Similarly, it can be anticipated that the providers of

2. Byron Gold, Elizabeth Kutza, and Theodore R. Marmor, "United States Social Policy on Old Age: Present Patterns and Predictions," in Bernice L. Neugarten and Robert J. Havighurst, eds., *Social Policy, Social Ethics, and the Aging Society* (Washington, D.C.: U.S. Government Printing Office, 1976), pp. 9–21.

public transportation will experience cost increases which directly relate to the provision of service for senior citizens. The extension of bus or specialized services into new areas is costly, largely because the amount of labor expended is great and the demand for such services is low. Service to senior citizens is, however, usually provided at fares far lower than the actual costs. Fuel costs have risen more than 10 percent per year since 1973, and ancillary transportation services provided under Title VII of the Older Americans Act have already been cut back in order to keep within relatively constant annual budget allocations.[3] Over the next thirty years it would appear that the costs of private transportation will keep pace with or outstrip increases in the income of senior citizens, and the recent rapid expansion of public transportation service will not be able to be sustained without financial crisis.

Political Factors

In a country having a representative form of government, public programs are usually tailored to meet the needs of particular constituencies having power and influence. Political salience can often be more important in determining public action than the severity of the problem that the action is intended to remedy. The elderly are an increasingly powerful political constituency. In 1976 there were 22 million elderly persons in the United States, and there will be nearly 27 million by the end of the century.[4] Furthermore, a larger proportion of the elderly than of any other age group cast votes in each election, and the elderly are becoming politically organized to lobby more effectively for their interests. While persons over the age of 65 constitute some 10 or 11 percent of the American population, it has been recently estimated that they constitute 47 percent of all people having handicaps related to trans-

3. Ibid., p. 15.
4. Bernice L. Neugarten and Robert J. Havighurst, "Aging and the Future," in Neugarten and Havighurst, eds., *Social Policy, Social Ethics, and the Aging Society*, pp. 3–7.

portation.[5] In combination these facts imply that for decades to come we can expect the elderly and their transportation needs to command attention.

Psycho-Sociological Factors

A third type of explanation for the growth of programs for senior citizens is offered by Gold, Kutza, and Marmor. They suggest that continuing emphasis upon providing for the needs of older people is a means of assuaging societal guilt. While denying the work role to the elderly because of retirement practices, modern mobility, and the dominance of the nuclear family we also deny them many family roles. To compensate, it is argued, we employ government programs to provide for such basic needs as mobility, while in an earlier day such needs might have been viewed as the responsibility of an extended family whose members lived in proximity to one another. It is possible to state a similar argument in more positive terms, by viewing such social programs as an intergenerational transfer wherein "one generation agrees to provide for the preceding one under an implicit guarantee that the succeeding generation will, in turn, provide for its elders."[6] Those who are currently middle-aged are paying the costs of providing mobility to those who are now elderly. During the next thirty years the middle-aged will join the ranks of

5. This proportion of transportation handicapped persons among the elderly is based upon preliminary results of a study entitled "Incidence Counts of Transportation Handicapped People," being conducted by the Grey Marketing and Research Department for the Urban Mass Transportation Administration. The figures were presented at a Transportation Research Board Workshop on Transportation for the Disadvantaged, held at Belmont, Maryland, in September 1977. They incorporate a fairly broad definition of handicaps related to transportation. For example, "use of a hearing aid," "difficulty in standing," and "difficulty in waiting," during the past twelve months as reported by respondents in a nationwide survey of 15,700 households, was sufficient to classify them among the transportation handicapped.

6. Gold, Kutza, and Marmor, "United States Social Policy on Old Age," p. 19.

the elderly and will expect to receive similar benefits. The expectation that these programs will give future benefits to their current financial contributors will make it increasingly difficult to discontinue such programs.

Ethical-Philosophical Factors

Americans are increasingly coming to believe that the elderly are "worthy" of public support. The elderly, it is felt, deserve special programs because of their past contributions to society, in both economic and more personal terms. Recent literature as well as television programs indicate that Americans are collectively beginning to grant recognition to older persons for sustaining the society through the children they have raised and the work they have done. In an era when the social and cultural contributions of many minority groups are beginning to be recognized, the attention which we are beginning to lavish upon our elders is parallel and related to the civil rights movement. Because transportation will continue to be central to American life in the last decades of the twentieth century, it is inconceivable that this movement will ignore mobility as it gains momentum in other areas of social concern.

Demographic and Social Changes Among the Elderly

In addition to the philosophical or ideological issues which will continue to underlie the provision of transportation services for the elderly, the demographic and social changes which are occurring in America will also strongly influence the nature of the required programs over the next decades.

It was estimated that in 1975 there were 8.9 million men and 12.8 million women aged 65 and older in the United States. If present trends in age-specific mortality rates continue, there will be about 10.2 million men and 16.3 million women in this age group by the turn of the century. While this will represent an increase of approximately 22 percent over the current elderly population, there will be a much less dramatic increase in the proportion of the total United States population which will be elderly. If present trends continue, the elderly population will increase from about 10 percent to between 11 and 12 percent by the year 2000.[7]

The 1970 census showed that three-quarters of all Americans aged 65 and older resided in urban areas. It seems likely that this trend toward concentration in metropolitan areas will continue, although the elderly appear to be decentralizing within metropolitan areas.

With the number of the elderly increasing by over one-fifth, principally in urban areas, it would seem that increased services of the types being offered today might be adequate to meet the needs of the elderly twenty years hence. Several social trends already well underway, however, are likely to bring about significantly different life patterns for older Americans in the 1990s.

Improved Health

There is a tendency to associate old age with a reduced capacity for movement and with increased disabilities of various types. Physical and psychological changes do accompany the aging process, but more than 80 percent of the elderly have no health-related limitations on mobility, and many of the remaining 20 percent are quite mobile.[8] While approximately half of those Americans having handicaps related to transportation are elderly, it is erroneous to conclude that most of the elderly are limited in their mobility because of handicaps.

Increasing survival into old age, the major factor which will bring about an increase in the number of elderly during the next decades, might imply either increased or decreased proportions who are handicapped, disabled, or otherwise immobile. If increased longevity is associated with survival of illnesses which were previously fatal,

7. Bernice L. Neugarten, "The Future and the Young-Old," *The Gerontologist* 15 (February 1975), p. 5.

8. U.S. Department of Health, Education, and Welfare, *Facts on Aging* (Washington, D.C.: U.S. Government Printing Office, May 1970).

more disabled persons might be expected. If increases in longevity are associated with generally improved health, then we will have larger numbers of healthy senior citizens comprising the older population in the year 2000.

Because the relationships between morbidity, mortality, and life expectancy are complex, it is difficult to predict the health status of tomorrow's elderly. Yet, two major subpopulations, which have been termed the "young-old" and the "old-old," seem to be emerging.[9] At retirement (presently around age 65 but probably at more varied ages in future years) people may be expected to have relatively few disabilities which limit their mobility or impact lifestyles or travel patterns. As aging continues, however, young-old persons will become "old-old." Those surviving to age 80 and beyond may be expected to have health conditions which limit physical mobility and living patterns. Significant increases can be expected, however, in the numbers of young-old persons capable of relatively vigorous activity with relatively few constraints on mobility.

Independent Living Arrangements

An increasing number of young-old persons will reinforce the recent trend toward an elderly population living in separate households, independent of relatives and institutions. Today, even among persons over age 75, 80 percent of all women and 90 percent of all men are living alone or with a spouse.[10] Women tend to outlive men, and the 1970 census showed that 72.4 percent of all men aged 65 and over were married, while only 36.5 percent of women in the same age group were married. Among those not married there were many more elderly women living alone than men, since 52.2 percent of women over

9. Bernice L. Neugarten, "Age Groups in American Society and the Rise of the Young-Old," *Annals of the American Academy of Political and Social Science* (September 1974), pp. 187–98.
10. Neugarten, "Future and Young-Old."

age 65 were widowed, while only 17.1 percent of the men in this age group were widowed.[11]

These statistics demonstrate that the vast majority of elderly persons live in small and independent households. This trend is likely to continue unless housing costs force older persons to double up or to move in with younger relatives. Neugarten anticipates an increase in the number of old-old persons with children who are young-old.[12] This may give rise to larger intergenerational family units of elderly within the basic trend of independent living.

Improved Economic Welfare

Understanding of the economic situation of the aged has improved a great deal in recent years. It is now realized that the typically low monetary income of the elderly serves as an inadequate indicator of the economic welfare of this group. In addition to pensions and social security payments, some elderly persons have accumulated economic assets which are as important in determining their living patterns as are flows of dollar income into their households. For example, it is estimated that 80 percent of the elderly households in the United States are living in owner-occupied dwelling units.[13] These units, more frequently owned "free and clear" than is the case for other age groups, constitute one of the most important economic resources of the elderly. Similarly, savings and investments are important sources of economic security. If both current income and accumulated assets are considered, then, as Havighurst states:

. . . it can be predicted with relative assurance that dire poverty among the elderly will be practically eliminated before the year

11. Martin Wachs, ed., *Transportation Patterns and Needs of the Elderly Population in Los Angeles* (Los Angeles: School of Architecture and Urban Planning, University of California, 1974), p. 27.

12. Neugarten, "Future and Young-Old."

13. Henry D. Sheldon, "The Changing Demographic Profile," in Clark Tibbetts, ed., *Handbook of Social Gerontology* (Chicago: University of Chicago Press, 1960), pp. 27–61.

2000. The major step has already been taken in this direction, in principle, by the Federal government provision for Supplementary Security Income (SSI), which replaces the varied state Old Age Assistance programs of the recent past. Payments from Federal funds for SSI will probably increase, to compensate for increased cost of living.[14]

Statements such as this are not intended to assert that the elderly will enjoy a standard of living which is high in comparison to that of younger population groups. Rather, Havighurst is concluding that fewer old people will live below a minimal acceptable level of financial security than is presently the case. Although inflation will continue to eat away at the value of accumulated savings and pension programs, social services programs, property tax relief, income supplements, and similar programs will insure that fewer elderly persons are in deep financial difficulty.

Improved Educational Levels

Today, of every 100 persons aged 65 and over, eight men and eight women have had less than five years of schooling and are, therefore, classified as functionally illiterate. The 1970 census showed that more than half of those over age 65 had an educational background which included only elementary school, while more than half of those under age 65 had educations which included at least some high school attendance. It is clear that major advances have taken place in the public education system during the life span of today's elderly, and those who approach old age by the year 2000 will in general be educated to an extent far beyond that of the present elderly population.[15]

Consequences of Social and Demographic Changes Among the Elderly

Although the elderly of today are probably more heterogeneous than current transportation programs and

14. Robert J. Havighurst, "The Future Aged: The Use of Time and Money," *The Gerontologist* 15 (February 1975), p. 11.

15. U.S. Department of Health, Education, and Welfare, *Facts on Aging*.

planning methods would imply, it appears that old people will become even more diverse during the coming decades. Improved health, greater economic resources, and improved education will result in increased varieties of lifestyles among the elderly. These lifestyles will be drawn from more diverse experiences in younger life as well as from greater freedom of choice in retirement. Denis Johnston, among others, sees the future elderly in neither the "blue" world of the work ethic nor the "green" world of the leisure ethic, but in a "turquoise" world in which new concepts of work and flexible lifestyles will appear, providing more opportunity for personal growth and fulfillment.[16] Some persons will select dense urban environments while others will seek out free-standing retirement villages. The majority may continue to inhabit the suburbs which they helped to create and populate during their younger years. Just as different communities of younger people are based upon lifestyle variables of culture, ethnicity, and socioeconomic class, these variables will play a larger role than age itself in identifying communities of the elderly during the coming decades.

One important aspect of the probable proliferation of lifestyles among the elderly is of special relevance to transportation planners. It is likely that an increasing proportion of the elderly population will reside in lower density areas than they do at present. Such a trend is already evident. Table 1 shows that among elderly whites in the United States the proportion dwelling in rural areas declined from 35 percent to 27 percent between 1950 and 1970, while the proportion dwelling in the central cities increased by only 1 percent (from 32 to 33 percent of the total) in the same period. The proportion living on the "urban fringe," however, increased from 13 percent to 22 percent. Thus, the largest increase occurred in locations of relatively low density. Among the nonwhite elderly, a slightly different pattern was observed. For this group, presumably more constrained by income and education as

16. Denis F. Johnston, "The Future of Work: Three Possible Alternatives," *Monthly Labor Review* (Washington, D.C.: U.S. Department of Labor, May 1972).

Table 1. Shifting Patterns of Residence
Among the Elderly, 1950–1970

	White Elderly Population		Non-White Population	
	1950	1970	1950	1970
% Rural	35	27	43	24
% Central City	32	33	34	51
% Urban Fringe	13	22	5	10
% Other Urban	20	18	18	15

Source: Stephen M. Golant, "Residential Concentration of the Future Elderly," The Gerontologist, Vol. 15 (February 1975), pp. 16-23.

well as residential segregation, the largest shift was from rural to central-city areas, where more than half of the elderly nonwhite now reside. In addition, however, the proportion of the nonwhite elderly living on the urban fringe has doubled from 5 percent to 10 percent.[17]

There is reason to believe that such trends will continue. It was mentioned earlier that the vast majority of the elderly occupy dwellings which they own. Thus, the present elderly are found in high density communities largely because they have grown old with those communities where they have long been residents. While increased income and better education and health will permit greater freedom to relocate in the future, it may also be observed that the suburbanization which accelerated after World War II may induce many to remain in the homes they acquired in the 1950s and 1960s. These individuals will become a major component of the elderly population by the turn of the century.

Further, it should be noted that many states have instituted policies of granting property tax relief to elderly persons owning their homes. Such programs will, if continued, provide added incentive for couples to remain in the suburbs when children leave and retirement approaches. Based upon similar reasoning, Butler and Lewis have written that "there are relatively few suburban elderly but it is projected that twenty years from now the

17. Stephen M. Golant, "Residential Concentrations of the Future Elderly," *The Gerontologist* 15 (February 1975), pp. 16–23.

suburbs may be predominantly elderly."[18] Gelwicks was rather pessimistic about this prospect when he wrote that "tomorrow's elderly will be left in declining suburbs; will suffer from too low a density to maintain social interaction and widely dispersed vital services without public transportation."[19]

Examination of 1970 census data for Los Angeles County showed that many elderly are already residing at extremely low densities. Approximately half were found residing at densities lower than 14 persons per gross acre and 30 percent at densities below 10 persons per gross acre. Thus, while it is true that half of the elderly population is residing on the most densely populated 5 percent of the land, it is also true that the other half is scattered at much lower densities on no less than 95 percent of the land.[20] Public transportation services are being significantly improved in areas of dense concentration of the elderly, but even now these improvements do not reach a large proportion of people residing at lower densities, and the costs of such improvements are becoming prohibitive. In a study conducted for the Urban Mass Transportation Administration, the Regional Plan Association of New York estimated that local bus transit was economically feasible only in areas having population densities in excess of 15 dwelling units (between 30 and 40 persons) per gross acre, and that dial-a-bus service required about five dwelling units (10 to 15 persons) per acre.[21] It is clear that the trend toward lower density living by senior citizens presents some significant difficulties for those who hope to meet the transportation needs of the elderly predominantly through public modes of transport.

18. Robert M. Butler and Myrna I. Lewis, *Aging and Mental Health: Positive Psychological Approaches* (St. Louis: C.V. Mosby, 1970), p. 6.

19. Lewis Gelwicks, "Planning for the Elderly," paper presented at the Conference of the American Society of Planning Officials, Los Angeles, California, 1973.

20. Wachs, ed., *Transportation Patterns and Needs of the Elderly.*

21. New York Regional Plan Association, "Where Transit Works: Urban Densities for Public Transportation," *Regional Plan News* 99 (August 1976), pp. 1–23.

Anticipated Changes in Mobility and Tripmaking Among the Elderly

Statistics related to auto ownership and drivership show conclusively that the elderly are currently much less mobile than are younger-age cohorts. There is reason to believe, however, that these data are being interpreted improperly with respect to the implications which they hold for future generations of the elderly. Table 2 shows national data on car ownership by age of head of household.[22] These data indicate that the proportion of households without cars is dramatically higher for those with household heads over 65 than for those from other age groups. Nearly half of the households headed by senior citizens owned no cars, while only about one-fifth of the immediately younger cohort (aged 55–64) and one-tenth of households headed by those in their thirties and forties had no cars. Similarly, data on the possession of a driver's license indicate large disparities between the elderly and younger-age cohorts. Olsen reported that in Florida only 58 percent of those aged 65 to 75 and 30 percent of those over age 75 were licensed to drive, in comparison with 83 percent of those in age groups 25 through 64.[23] Similar patterns were found in the city of Los Angeles. Here only 65 percent of those aged 65 through 70, 51 percent of those aged 70 through 74, and 30 percent of those over 75 were found to possess a driver's license, in comparison with more than 90 percent of the population in age groups 35 through 45 who possess licenses.[24] In response to these findings, Olsen and other authors describe a "serious loss of mobility for the elderly," implying that the process of

22. Automobile Manufacturers' Association, *Automobile Facts and Figures: 1971* (Detroit: Economics Research and Statistics Department, Automobile Manufacturers' Association, 1971).

23. U.S. Congress, Senate, Special Committee on Aging, *Transportation and the Elderly.*

24. Jacqueline Gillan and Martin Wachs, "Lifestyles and Transportation Needs Among the Elderly of Los Angeles County," *Transportation* 5 (March 1976), pp. 45–61.

**Table 2. Automobile Ownership in the United States
by Age of Head of Household**

Age of Household Head	Percent of Households Owning	
	No Car	At Least One Car
Under 25	19.3	80.7
25–34	12.0	88.0
35–44	11.6	88.4
45–54	13.6	86.4
55–64	19.7	80.3
65 and over	44.9	55.1

Source: Automobile Manufacturers' Association, Automobile
Facts and Figures: 1971. (Detroit: Economics
Research and Statistics Department, Automobile
Manufacturers Association, 1971).

aging is itself causally related to reduced mobility.[25] The
implication of this view is that elderly persons today are
"mobility dependent" as an inevitable outgrowth of the
process of aging and will continue to be so in the future.
This may be an exaggeration. Car ownership varies with
income for all groups in the United States. Table 3 shows
that low-income groups own fewer cars than upper-
income groups. In 1970 nearly 60 percent of all households with incomes below $3,000 per year and 30 percent
of households with incomes between $3,000 and $5,000
did not own cars. Only 4 percent of households with
incomes in excess of $15,000 per year, however, were
without cars.[26] Since the elderly are still found dispropor-
tionately among the lower-income groups, it may be that
elderly persons are less likely to possess automobiles
because they have limited incomes, and that lack of financial resources contributes as much to low car-ownership
rates as does physical aging. This interpretation is upheld
by Markovitz in studies in the New York area.[27]

We should bear in mind that Markovitz used figures on
car availability rather than car ownership, and that Tables

25. U.S. Congress, Senate, Special Committee on Aging, *Transportation and the Elderly.*

26. Automobile Manufacturers' Association, *Automobile Facts and
Figures: 1971.*

27. Joni K. Markovitz, "Transportation Needs of the Elderly," *Traffic
Quarterly* 25 (April 1971), pp. 237–53.

Table 3. Automobile Ownership in the United States
by Household Income Level

Household Income	Percent of Households Owning	
	No Car	At Least One Car
Under $3,000	57.5	42.5
$3,000 - $4,999	30.8	69.2
$5,000 - $7,499	13.6	86.4
$7,500 - $9,999	8.4	91.6
$10,000 - $14,999	4.1	95.9
$15,000 and over	3.8	96.2

Source: Automobile Manufacturers' Association, Automobile
          Facts and Figures: 1971. (Detroit: Economics
          Research and Statistics Department, Automobile
          Manufacturers' Association, 1971).

3 and 4 are not directly comparable because cars may be available to households but not owned by their members. It is nevertheless interesting to note from Table 4 that Markovitz found that among the elderly auto availability varied significantly with income. While more than four-fifths of elderly households with incomes below $3,000 per year had no autos available, only one-fifth of elderly households with incomes over $10,000 per year had no autos available to them. Thus, taking income into account, it would appear that the elderly are more similar to other age groups in terms of car availability than is generally thought. Conclusions about increases in income among the elderly during the next generation imply that it is reasonable to expect future senior citizens to possess and use automobiles at higher rates than they do today.

Data cited earlier show that the elderly are much less likely than younger persons to possess drivers' licenses. In part, this decline is due to the process of aging, which often brings about a reduction in visual acuity, hearing ability, and physical strength. In response, some people voluntarily give up driving, and others forego driving because of physicians' instructions or because they become unable to qualify for a license. It is an exaggeration, however, to explain the decline in license possession solely in terms of the physical processes of aging. It is, in fact, likely that many of today's elderly *never* possessed drivers' licenses. Many of the elderly of the 1970s were teenagers

**Table 4. Automobile Availability Among the Elderly
in the New York Metropolitan Region**

Household Income	Percent of Elderly Households with Zero Auto Availability
$0 - $2,999	83.7
$3,000 - $5,999	58.2
$6,000 - $9,999	29.6
Greater than $10,000	20.6

Source: Joni K. Markovitz, "Transportation Needs of the
          Elderly," Traffic Quarterly, Vol. 25 (April 1971),
          pp. 237-53.

during and immediately after World War I. In 1920 it was less common for young people to learn to drive. It was especially unlikely that young women would learn to drive. It is not surprising, therefore, that in Los Angeles, among men over age 65, 74 percent were licensed drivers while only 39 percent of women in the same age group possessed licenses. Among the very old, the disparity was even greater. While more than half (53 percent) of the men aged 75 and older had licenses, only 18 percent of the women in this age group had them.[28] Although data are not available, it is likely that in these age groups many never drove and that the statistics reflect the living patterns of earlier years to a greater extent than the explanation that the decline of driving principally reflects old age. Added support is given to this reasoning when the ratio of males to females with drivers' licenses is examined in detail. In California, according to data from the Department of Motor Vehicles, only four women possess drivers' licenses for every ten men having them in the age group over 80. Among those in their seventies, there are six women licensed for every ten men who are. Among those in their sixties, the ratio is seven to ten, and, among those in their fifties eight women drivers for every ten men have licenses. The ratio is rapidly approaching unity, and among senior citizens of future decades the present pattern of few women drivers will no longer hold. This can be attributed to changing social expectations for the two sexes during the past several decades. Projections based on current patterns of sex differences among the elderly would

28. Gillan and Wachs, "Lifestyles and Transportation Needs."

likely lead to gross errors. Since later generations of men and women were much more likely to become drivers, the elderly of the future are also more likely to be drivers than are the elderly of today. It is now common that an elderly woman becomes immobilized in physical as well as emotional terms by the death of a husband who was the household's only driver. In the future it can be expected that elderly women will be licensed to drive in much greater numbers and that older women will be less critically dependent upon their husbands for mobility.

Related to lower rates of car ownership and license possession is the common finding that the elderly make fewer vehicular trips than younger people make. Data from the Los Angeles Regional Transportation Study (LARTS) showed, for example, that on days for which trip logs were kept, 37 percent of the elderly respondents made no trips, while only 21 percent of the non-elderly respondents had not traveled.[29] It is reasonable to conclude that part of this decline in travel is related to income, since low-income people invariably travel less than those having higher income. In addition, if lifestyles of the elderly include less reliance on driving and a greater likelihood of residence in older central-city locations, some important definitional concepts may cause underestimation of travel. Because many urban transportation studies define "trips" in terms of vehicle movements, pedestrian movements are not included in counts of trips made. Elderly persons living in dense, inner-city communities may be able to shop, visit, and obtain essential services by walking. Many retirement communities are specifically designed to minimize the need for vehicular traffic. Surveys of such communities would presumably show relatively little vehicular travel. It would seem erroneous to conclude that low trip rates necessarily imply unmet travel needs. It would be doubly incorrect to assume that low rates of *vehicular* trips imply unmet needs, especially in denser communities where walking can satisfy a large proportion of a

29. Ibid.

person's needs. Yet frequencies of vehicular trips alone are consistently cited in discussing the transportation needs of the elderly. It is certain that many older persons have substantial travel requirements that are not met and that their quality of life suffers because of these unmet needs. But much of the evidence widely cited to illustrate these unmet travel needs is at best incomplete and at worst extremely misleading.

It was stated earlier that location and residential density are as likely to be a function of lifestyles brought into old age as of aging. It is similarly true that travel patterns and mobility are explainable in terms of variations in lifestyle as well as generalizations about the impact of aging on mobility. The conclusion is that it is not possible to predict future transportation requirements of the elderly without developing a deeper understanding of variations in lifestyles among the elderly of the future.

The Concept of Lifestyle

The concept of lifestyle is a potentially powerful explanatory tool when considering residential location and travel patterns among the elderly. In this research, lifestyle will mean particular combinations of socioeconomic and demographic variables that represent situations in which persons live. A particular combination of income, family status, educational attainment, residential density, and similar variables differentiates the patterns of living of those who share them from those who are represented by other ranges of the same variables. In the elderly population, we might find one lifestyle group of single persons living alone in high density, low income, and ethnically diverse areas, in relatively poor health. This lifestyle group would have very different travel needs and behavior than one consisting largely of husband-and-wife families in good health, living independently on moderate to high incomes in ethnically homogeneous areas. Still others among the elderly might live in family settings on moderate to upper incomes in homes which they own in suburban areas.

It is likely that members of a lifestyle group live in close proximity to other members of the same group and that lifestyle patterns can, therefore, be used to distinguish between residential communities. Thus, for example, in Los Angeles the first of the above lifestyle groups might be found concentrated in the community of Venice, the second in the area of Beverly Hills, and the last in the western San Fernando Valley.

Lifestyle is intended to measure simultaneously environmental constraints and personal choices given those constraints. It provides an opportunity to explain and predict human behavior in relation to combinations of choices, chances, and constraints. This research is based on the premise that a manageable number of lifestyle groups can be identified and that travel behavior varies with membership in these groups. Furthermore, it is hypothesized that locational patterns established by lifestyle groups are stable over time. If this hypothesis is valid, travel patterns of today's elderly were partly determined many years ago when their basic lifestyle patterns were established. Similarly, it should be possible to anticipate future locational and travel patterns of the elderly by observing the patterns of younger population groups at the present time.

The term lifestyle has received limited attention in describing the diversity of urban life. Perloff suggests that it may be used to characterize how groups in society live.[30] For him the core elements in individual and family lifestyles are the patterns that center on how an individual family or peer group functions from one time period to the next (day to day, week to week, etc.) using the culture or subculture as the context within which these sequences of activities occur. He cites five major interdependent factors which influence lifestyle: 1. who the family members are and what their backgrounds are, 2. what they do, 3. how they do what they do, 4. with whom they carry out their activities, and 5. where they carry out their activities.

30. Harvey S. Perloff, "Lifestyles and Environment—The Future Planning Game," *Planning* (June 1973), p. 3.

Greer defines lifestyle primarily in terms of locational choice and the degree and nature of participation in the social structure: "Lifestyle refers to the way of life chosen by the population—whether the family-committed life of the suburbs, or the life of the working couple in the apartment house areas of the city."[31] Ethnicity, ethnic identity, and social rank are perceived by Greer as lifestyle modifiers.

Michelson, beginning from an individualistic, egocentric view of people and their environments, discusses lifestyle in terms of role emphasis. Although city dwellers may play a number of roles as they participate in various groups, all roles are not equally meaningful: "Lifestyle, then, is a composite of those aspects of the roles a person strongly emphasizes. It refers *not* to styles of dress or furnishings, but rather to styles of *living*." Two elements are cited as being essential to lifestyle: 1. a set of behaviors which must be performed to satisfy a role with other persons being appropriately present or absent and 2. a sphere of life (such as political control, economic supply, participation, etc.) which is stressed.[32] According to Bengston lifestyle is defined as "the observable organization of an individual's activities in terms of his use of time, his investment of energy, and his choice of interpersonal objects." He endorses the concept's usefulness as a bridge between the personal and social systems and in analyzing what occurs over the life cycle.[33] Similarly, in a study of the city as an environment for the aged, Carp isolates three lifestyle dimensions: use of time, of space, and of the social network. Evaluation of these dimensions includes the extent of, the autonomy of, and the satisfaction with these uses.[34]

31. Scott Greer, *The Emerging City: Myth and Reality* (New York: Free Press, 1962), pp. 31–32.

32. William Michelson, *Man and His Urban Environment: A Sociological Perspective* (Reading, Mass.: Addison Wesley, 1970), p. 63.

33. Vern L. Bengston, *The Social Psychology of Aging* (Indianapolis: Bobbs-Merrill, 1973) pp. 36–37.

34. Frances Carp, "Lifestyle and Location Within San Antonio," mimeographed (Berkeley, Ca., 1970).

It is apparent from these definitions that each author defines lifestyle for his or her particular purposes within a specific context. While the definitions are not contradictory, neither is any intended to be inclusive. Each is, in broadest terms, related to the individual's interaction with all aspects of his or her environment. A particular lifestyle may be viewed as giving rise to interacting locational preferences, activity patterns, and travel demands.

Although lifestyle can include a rich combination of sociological and perceptual variables, it is not practical to conduct research at the metropolitan level employing subjective variables such as perception. For this reason, lifestyle will be measured in terms of socioeconomic and demographic variables obtained from the census or from commonly available administrative records. Included among these variables are measures of ethnicity, social living arrangements, housing characteristics, economic resources, educational attainment, health status, and automobile ownership and drivership. Each of these has been found important in differentiating and understanding styles of living in old age. These elements, singly and in concert, impact the elderly population differentially, making lifestyle a combination of imposition and choice. In terms of transportation, they affect motility (the desire to be mobile) and mobility. The use of such variables, however, is predicated on the belief that they are consistent with more complex measures which might emerge from attitudinal and behavioral studies. These data are taken only as indicators of lifestyles that are more complex and richer than as represented by the variables alone.

The Role of Lifestyle in the Study of Locational and Travel Behavior of the Elderly

Many elderly persons today live in older central-city communities characterized by low rates of automobile ownership and vehicular travel, relatively good public transportation service, high densities of residents and services, and low incomes. While many old people live under conditions far different from these, such concentrations are common. It is probable, however, that transportation planners have misinterpreted these patterns. They reason that people become poorer as they age and that residential choices are narrowed as old people become unable to drive. Those elderly dependent upon local transportation are seen as people forced to live in older, high density neighborhoods where they can rely on public transit in the absence of automobiles which they can no longer afford or are no longer able to drive. This perception leads to the conclusion that the elderly inevitably *become* dependent upon public transit as they age and that the elderly of the future may also be expected to become dependent. If, however, today's elderly grew up in an era of walking and public transit, they may have developed lifestyles which are not dependent upon automobiles. If they do not drive, it may be because many of them never drove. If home ownership is an important correlate of location, it may be that the elderly grew old with their inner-city communities, rather than moving to those communities as they grew older. If they reside in areas with dense transit service, it may be because transit service was established before the era of the automobile. This may also help to explain why many never learned to drive. Thus, such persons may be characterized by a lifestyle which differs from that of younger Americans. If this characterization is correct, it would be reasonable to say that not all elderly people became dependent upon public transit as they aged; it may also be true that some never became dependent upon the automobile when they were younger. Their transit dependence does not only represent a need which must be met; it represents a lifestyle which must be understood in its entirety.

If lifestyle is an acceptable complement to the common view of transportation planners, and if today's elderly did not necessarily all become more transit dependent as they aged, there are important implications for considering the lifestyles of the future elderly.

Methods of forecasting residential patterns and demand

for transportation services among the elderly should be reexamined. Relationships between locations or trip patterns and age are often established empirically, but it is assumed that these relationships (whatever they are) will also characterize the population of 1990 or 2000. An alternative approach is required in which relationships are explored between today's elderly and their lifestyles when they were a younger population, and in which relationships are sought between today's middle-aged population and the elderly of the next two decades. It is possible to anticipate future lifestyles of the young-old and to estimate the numbers, locations, and mobility needs of the old-old of the future since these groups are already alive and their life patterns already established. Methods and approaches now employed to estimate travel requirements of the elderly are inadequate, however, for the accomplishment of these tasks. It is the objective of this study to explore new methods which incorporate the basic concept of lifestyles.

Chapter 2
Lifestyles of the Current Elderly of Los Angeles County

*T*his chapter contains the results of empirical analyses conducted in order to identify and interpret several lifestyle groups within the elderly population of Los Angeles. In later chapters the ability of these lifestyle groups to distinguish travel patterns and needs will be tested and the stability of the groups over time will be investigated. Finally, forecasts of the elderly and their travel patterns will be presented for each lifestyle group. The definition of lifestyle groups within the elderly population thus forms the core of the methodology used in the analysis of current and changing transportation patterns of the elderly.

Research Technique for Defining Lifestyle Groups

The technique used in the definition of lifestyle groups among the senior citizens of Los Angeles County is one which has been used increasingly by social scientists in recent years to reduce large sets of data to manageable and interpretable patterns. The technique has been referred to by many authors as "factorial ecology" and involves several tasks which are outlined in this section.

The primary data source was the 1970 files of the U.S. Bureau of the Census. Detailed data on specific age groups describing automobile ownership, income, house-

hold composition, and employment were not available
from regular census tabulations. These data were obtained
as a special tabulation directly from the Bureau of the Census. Data describing the health status of the elderly, including morbidity and mortality rates and mental health
case admissions, were obtained from the Los Angeles
County Department of Health Services. The census and
health data were merged to form comprehensive files of
data describing the elderly population of Los Angeles
County.

Although the health data were collected in 1970, they
were recorded according to 1960 census tracts. It was,
therefore, necessary to aggregate all data to a "correspondence zone" level. A correspondence zone, hereafter referred to as a zone, is defined to be an aggregate of 1960
and 1970 census tracts which share a common physical
area. Data for approximately 1,600 tracts in 1970 and 1,300
tracts in 1960 were aggregated to form 1,159 zones. These
zones constituted the basic units of analysis used in the
definition of lifestyle groups and all succeeding tasks in
this study. Together these zones covered all of Los Angeles
County, the study area which is sketched in Figure 1.

The Identification of Lifestyle Dimensions

For each of the 1,159 analysis zones, values were obtained for each of fifty-one variables representing the
socioeconomic and demographic characteristics of the
population over age 65. These data constituted the basic
building blocks for the measurement of lifestyle. The
fifty-one variables are listed in Table 5 and describe such
population characteristics as age, household composition, health, automobile ownership, home ownership,
and income.

The variables selected to describe the elements of lifestyle were reduced to lifestyle dimensions by the application of R-principal components factor analysis with
Varimax rotation.[1] This process produced factors or di-

1. A complete description of the mathematical technique of factor
analysis is beyond the scope of this book. Readers who are unfamiliar

mensions which accounted for the major variations within the age group. Each factor was a composite of the original variables entered into the factor analysis and could, therefore, itself be considered a variable. The correlation coefficient between a factor and a variable is referred to as factor loading. By examining the factor loadings, it was possible to describe each factor, or dimension, in terms of the variables with which it was most closely associated.

Because of the sensitivity of factor analysis to the form in which the variables are expressed, it was necessary to control for the effects which differences in the absolute sizes of the elderly populations of the zones could have on the results. Variables were, therefore, expressed as relative frequencies (percentages). For example, the number of elderly females in a zone was expressed as the percentage of the elderly in the zone who were female. In addition, all unnecessary redundancy was removed from the set of variables; those which could be expressed as a combination of other variables were not included. For example, elderly households were classified into four categories according to household income, but only three categories were represented in the variable set. The fourth was excluded because it could be expressed as the difference between 100 percent and the sum of the other three variables.

It is customary to retain only the most important factors for rotation. In this study the appropriate number of factors was determined by examining the eigenvalues of the unrotated factors and the interpretability of the rotated factors. The procedure involved the following steps. Initially, all factors with eigenvalues greater than 1.0 were rotated. These factors were examined to determine how well they could be interpreted in the context of this study. If a factor was incapable of being interpreted, the unrotated factor with the smallest eigenvalue was eliminated

---

with factor analysis are referred to: R.J. Rummel, "Understanding Factor Analysis," *Journal of Conflict Resolution*, Vol. 11 (December 1967), pp. 444–80. A more detailed treatment by the same author is: R.J. Rummel, *Applied Factor Analysis* (Evanston, Ill.: Northwestern University Press, 1970).

Table 5. List of Variables Used in the Definition
of Lifestyle Groups Among Age Group 65+

Variable Number	Abbreviation	Variable Definition*
1	AUTOFO	Percentage of the housing units occupied by age group "husband-wife" and "other" families with 0 autos available
2	AUTOF2	Percentage of the housing units occupied by age group "husband-wife" and "other" families with 2 or more autos available
3	AUTOPO	Percentage of the housing units occupied by age group "primary individual" families with 0 autos available
4	AUTOP2	Percentage of the housing units occupied by age group "primary individual" families with 2 or more autos available
5	B1949	Percentage of occupied units, with the head of household in the age group, built in 1949 or earlier
6	B6064	Percentage of occupied units, with the head of household in the age group, built from 1960 to 1964
7	B6570	Percentage of occupied units, with the head of household in the age group, built from 1965 to 1970
8	CNEGRO	Percentage of the age group that is negro
9	CSPAN	Percentage of the age group that is Spanish American
10	CWHITE	Percentage of the age group that is white
11	DENPOP	Density, in persons per gross acre, of persons in the age group
12	EDLT5	Percentage of the age group having completed less than 5 years of education
13	ED912	Percentage of the age group having completed 9 to 12 years of education
14	EDCOLL	Percentage of the age group having completed 1 or more years of college education
15	EMPL52	Percentage of the age group employed 50 to 52 weeks in 1969
16	FEMALE	Percentage of the age group that is female
17	HUSWFE	Percentage of households, with the head of household in the age group, classifed as "husband-wife" households
18	ILT3K	Percentage of occupied units, with the head of household in the age group, having a household income of less than $3,000
19	I7K15K	Percentage of occupied units, with the head of household in the age group, having a household income of from $7,000 to $15,000
20	IGT15K	Percentage of occupied units, with the head of household in the age group, having a household income of $15,000 or more
21	MARRY	Percentage of the age group that is married
22	MENTAL	Annual visitation rate among the age group, per 100 persons, at Los Angeles County Mental Health facilities
23	MOBLE	Percentage of the age group occupying mobile homes or trailer units
24	MORBID	Annual morbidity rate of communicable diseases among the age group, per 100 persons, reported at Los Angeles County Health facilities
25	MORTAL	Annual mortality rate in the age group, per 100 persons
26	NEGROC	Percentage of the negro population in the age group
27	NOTEMP	Percentage of the age group not employed in 1969
28	O1949	Percentage of occupied units, with the head of household in the age group, occupied by head before 1949
29	O6064	Percentage of occupied units, with the head of household in the age group, occupied by head from 1960 to 1964

Variable Number	Abbreviation	Variable Definition
30	06570	Percentage of occupied units, with the head of household in the age group, occupied by head from 1965 to 1970
31	OCCBC	Percentage of the age group members of the labor force classified as blue collar workers
32	OCCSER	Percentage of the age group members of the labor force classified as service workers
33	OCCWC	Percentage of the age group members of the labor force classified as white collar workers
34	OWNOCC	Percentage of occupied units, with the head of household in the age group, owner occupied
35	POP	Percentage of the total population in the age group
36	PRMIND	Percentage of households, with the head of household in the age group, classifed as "primary individual" households
37	RTLT60	Percentage of renter occupied housing units, with the head of household in the age group, rented at a monthly contract of less than $60
38	RT6099	Percentage of renter occupied housing units, with the head of household in the age group, rented at a monthly contract of from $60 to $99
39	RTGT150	Percentage of renter occupied housing units, with the head of household in the age group, rented at a monthly contract of $150 or more
40	SPANC	Percentage of the Spanish American population in the age group
41	UNITS1	Percentage of renter occupied housing units, with the head of household in the age group, in 1 unit structures
42	UNITS3	Percentage of renter occupied housing units, with the head of household in the age group, in 3 or more unit structures
43	VLLT15	Percentage of owner occupied housing units, with the head of household in the age group, valued at $15,000 or less
44	VL1520	Percentage of owner occupied housing units, with the head of household in the age group, valued at $15,000 to $19,000
45	VLGT25	Percentage of owner occupied housing units, with the head of household in the age group, valued at $25,000 or more
46	WHITEC	Percentage of the white population in the age group
47	BENFIT	Percentage of persons in the age group receiving social security or railroad retirement payments
48	FAMILY	Percentage of persons in the age group residing in homes for the aged or other dependent situations
49	POOR	Percentage of persons in the age group classifed as being below the poverty level
50	RELATV	Percentage of families with family members in the age group in residence (other than the head of household or his wife)
51	WWIVET	Percentage of persons in the age group classified as World War I veterans

*The variables utilized were derived from two sources. All available age-specific data on the elderly (65 years of age and older) were retrieved from the Second and Fourth Count Census Tapes publicly distributed by the U.S. Bureau of the Census. Supplementary age-specific data on employment, income, automobile-ownership, etc., were obtained directly from the Bureau of the Census as a special tabulation.

Terms such as "husband-wife families," "Spanish-surnamed," "labor force," etc., are nomenclature established by the Bureau of the Census. Definitions may be found in: U.S. Department of Commerce, Bureau of the Census, *1970 Census Users' Guide* (Washington, D.C.: U.S. Government Printing Office, 1970).

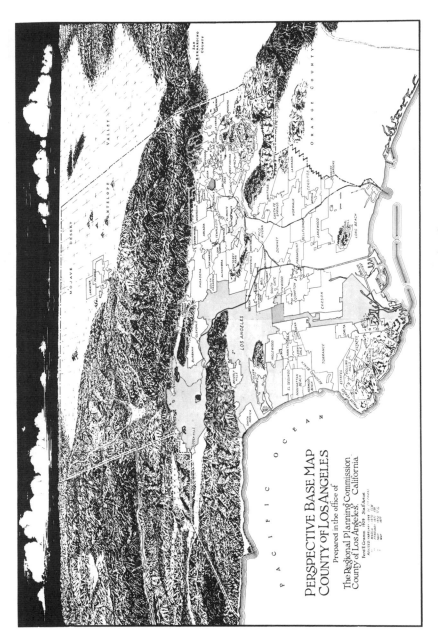

Figure 1. The Study Area: Los Angeles County

and the remaining factors were rotated and examined for improvement. These steps were repeated until it was determined that all factors were interpretable.

Factor scores were then computed which assigned to each zone a value, or position, on each of the lifestyle dimensions. Scores were mapped so that the spatial manifestation of each lifestyle dimension could be studied. Each dimension was described and interpreted in terms of the original lifestyle elements with which it was most closely associated and the spatial distribution of factor scores.

The Identification of Lifestyle Areas

Areas in Los Angeles County were next identified in which the elderly were relatively homogeneous with respect to lifestyle dimensions or factors. Each area identified a subgroup of the elderly which was unique in terms of its characteristic lifestyle. This was accomplished by grouping zones with similar values of lifestyle dimensions through the application of a technique known as "cluster analysis."[2]

Before cluster analysis could be applied, it was first necessary to define the similarity between a pair of zones in mathematical terms. In this study similarity was measured by Euclidean distance. If p factor scores were associated with a zone, then the zone could be considered to occupy a unique point in a p-dimensional Euclidean space. The distance between two zones, x and y, could then be defined by the familiar formula for computing Euclidean distance:

$$dxy = \sqrt{\sum_{i=1}^{P} (x_i - y_i)^2}$$

2. As was the case with factor analysis, a complete mathematical development of the techniques of cluster analysis is beyond the scope of this book. Readers who are unfamiliar with cluster analysis might wish to review: Michael R. Andersberg, *Cluster Analysis for Applications* (New York: Academic Press, 1973).

where x_i and y_i are the factor scores for the ith lifestyle dimension for zones x and y, respectively.

The clustering of zones was accomplished through the application of a computer routine based on a variation of the K-Means procedure developed by MacQueen.[3] As applied in this study, the procedure involved the following sequence of steps:

1. The desired number of clusters, k, was chosen. From among the zones to be clustered, k "seed points" were chosen at random to define the initial configuration of clusters.

2. Each zone was assigned to the cluster with the nearest seed point in the p-dimensional Euclidian space.

3. The initial seed point of each cluster was then replaced by the cluster centroid. The cluster centroid is the point in the p-dimensional space defined by the mean values of the factor scores of the zones in the cluster.

4. Step two was then repeated, followed by step three, and the process of repeating these steps was continued until no zones changed cluster membership at step two.

The number of clusters in the final solution was determined by examining solutions with from five to twenty clusters and choosing the solution in which the clusters were most easily identified and interpreted. Each cluster was interpreted as an area within the county in which the residents of the age group tended to share common lifestyles.

Lifestyles of the Current Elderly

Results of Factor Analysis

The fifty-one variables listed in Table 5 were subjected to principal components factor analysis in order to extract a parsimonious number of orthogonal (independent) di-

3. J. B. MacQueen, "Some Methods for Classification and Analysis of Multivariate Observations," *Proceedings of the Fifth Berkeley Symposium on Mathematical Statistics and Probability* 1 (1967), pp. 281–97; also see G. H. Ball and D. J. Hall, "A Clustering Technique for Summarizing Multivariate Data," *Behavioral Science* 12 (1967), pp. 153–55.

mensions which form the basis of lifestyle calculations. The application of principal components analysis resulted in the extraction of twelve factors with eigenvalues greater than 1.0. The iterative procedure of rotating successively fewer factors was then followed, and it was determined that each of the factors in the seven factor solution was logically interpretable. Although five factors with eigenvalues greater than 1.0 were dropped, the seven factors still accounted for 57.0 percent of the variance in the original data matrix. Table 6 summarizes the results of the factor analysis by showing the variables which were most strongly associated with each of the seven resulting factors. By examining the factor loadings shown in this table, it was possible to interpret and label each of the resultant dimensions. It was found that the factors described bundles of variables which paralleled many conditions of the elderly frequently described in the social science literature. A brief description of each factor, or lifestyle dimension, follows:

Lifestyle Dimension I: Density/Centrality. The first dimension was strongly associated with variables describing social living arrangements, economic resources, and automobile ownership and appeared to be an index of population density and proximity to services, including public transportation. Elderly residents of zones having high positive scores on this dimension tended to live alone in densely populated areas of the county, have low income, and reside in older apartments. The rate of automobile ownership among these residents was relatively low.

Lifestyle Dimension II: Financial Security. Several variables which reflected wealth, occupational status, and income were correlated with this dimension. In portions of the county with positive factor scores, the elderly tended to live in expensive houses and apartments on moderate to high incomes, with apartment living a common physical living arrangement. A large proportion of the elderly residents owned automobiles and had college educations, and those who worked generally occupied white-collar positions.

Table 6. Factor Loadings of at Least .250 for 65+ Age Group —1970 Analysis

No.*	Abbreviation	Density/Centrality I	Financial Security II	Isolation III	Long-Term Residence IV	Service Employment V	Spanish American VI	Poor Health VII
36	PRMIND	.827		.292				
17	HUSWFE	-.822						
34	OWNOCC	-.812			.276			
35	POP	.757	.295					
11	DENPOP	.738						
46	WHITEC	.653			.263	.315	-.293	
5	B1949	.547			.629			
42	UNITS3	.527	.373		-.292			
1	AUTOFO	.524					.322	
18	ILT3K	.512	-.526	.330			.251	
19	I7K15K	-.512	.427					
3	AUTOPO	.509	-.260	.390				
48	FAMILY	-.467		.264				.421
49	POOR	.437	-.369				.397	
2	AUTOF2	-.362	.307	-.546				
40	SPANC	.357				.260		
30	06570	.357			-.660			
38	RT6099	.349	-.533	.274	.256			
41	UNITS1	-.336	-.281		.271			
50	RELATV	.321	.307		.265			.474
28	01949	-.290			.794			
45	VLGT25		.820					
33	OCCWC		.739			-.307	-.384	
14	EDCOLL		.719				-.299	
39	RTGT150		.679					
44	VL1520		-.628					
31	OCCBG		-.607				.344	
43	VLLT15		-.486			.376	.342	
20	IGT15K		.434	-.723				
15	EMPL52		.425					
32	OCCSER		-.381			.699		
27	NOTEMP		-.298	.689				
13	ED912		.280				-.627	
12	EDLT5		-.280				.749	
16	FEMALE			.705			-.349	
4	AUTOP2			-.667				
47	BENFIT			.592				
7	B6570				-.605			
6	B6064				-.661			
29	06064				-.417			
8	CNEGRO					.891		
10	CWHITE					-.865		
26	NEGROC					.293		
9	CSPAN						.783	
37	RTLT60						.428	
51	WWIVET							.749
25	MORTAL							.695
21	MARRY							.634
24	MORBID							.418
23	MOBLE							
22	MENTAL							
% Variation explained by factor		13.34	11.60	7.45	6.54	6.37	6.82	4.89

* Variable numbers correspond with those used in Table 5.

Lifestyle Dimension III: Isolation. Like the density/centrality and financial security dimensions, the third dimension was closely associated with income variables. Descriptors of employment status, automobile ownership, and the sex composition of the elderly population were also correlated with this factor. Many of the senior residents of the zones with positive scores were socially isolated and immobile. They were characterized by low automobile ownership, employment levels, and incomes. A relatively large proportion of the households received social security or railroad retirement benefits as the principal source of income. Elderly females far outnumbered males of retirement age, suggesting that a relatively high percentage of the elderly females were widows.

Lifestyle Dimension IV: Long-Term Residence. The fourth factor was almost exclusively related to physical living arrangements, including variables descriptive of the age of housing and the year of initial occupancy. Zones with positive scores on this factor were among the most stable residential areas of the county. Many elderly residents moved into their homes before 1950, and a large proportion occupied single-family dwellings.

Lifestyle Dimension V: Race and Occupation. The fifth dimension reflected the ethnic composition of the elderly population and the occupations of those who worked. Black elderly and persons with service-related occupations tended to live in zones with positive factor scores. Zones having high scores on this dimension had relatively few white persons among their elderly populations, yet the elderly whites living in these areas constituted the vast majority of the white people living in these zones. The values of the homes in these areas were relatively low, supporting the fact that service employment is associated with low income.

Lifestyle Dimension VI: Spanish-American Ethnicity. The Spanish-American dimension was also associated with variables descriptive of ethnicity and occupational status and was strongly related to measures of educational attainment of the elderly. Positive scores identified areas in which both the Anglo- and Spanish-American cultures were represented. Elderly persons with Spanish-American background, low levels of formal education, and blue-collar occupations were concentrated in these areas. Home values, rents, and the level of automobile ownership were relatively low, and a significant proportion of the elderly families was classified as living in poverty.

Lifestyle Dimension VII: Poor Health. The seventh dimension was an index of the health status of the elderly and was closely related to mortality and morbidity rates. In addition, variables describing the proportion of the elderly population which participated in World War I and that which lived in homes for the aged and dependent were correlated with this dimension. These variables also appeared to be indirectly related to health. High morbidity and mortality rates, relatively high proportions of married elderly persons, and significant numbers of seniors living in homes for the aged distinguished the zones with positive scores. Because females tend to be healthier than males after retirement age is reached, the elderly characterized by poor health may have included a relatively large proportion of males. A much higher proportion of elderly males are married than females (72 percent versus 36 percent in the United States in 1970). As a result, this dimension also appeared to be strongly related to marital status.

Results of Cluster Analysis

The seven lifestyle dimensions represented the major sources of variation in the original set of fifty-one variables, and each dimension represented an important characteristic which distinguished the elderly populations of the zones in Los Angeles County from one another. Cluster analysis was then applied to the matrix of factor scores in order to identify homogeneous lifestyle groups among the elderly. After solutions with from five to twenty clusters were examined, the seven cluster solution was chosen because of the high degree of geographic contiguity among the zones within the clusters, and because the areas represented by the clusters could be easily identified and described.

The factor and cluster analysis revealed strong relationships between the dimensions of lifestyle and the elderly subpopulations of the county. Examination of mean factor scores associated with the various lifestyle areas indicated a strong correspondence between dimensions of lifestyle and the characteristics of lifestyle areas. Each lifestyle dimension figured significantly in the definition of at least one area. Also, in most cases, one dimension was especially prominent in the area definitions.

Brief descriptions of each lifestyle group are provided in the following paragraphs because these findings form the basis for many of the variations in forecast travel demands presented in later chapters. These descriptions are drawn from detailed census data which were aggregated to the cluster level to provide socioeconomic and demographic profiles of the lifestyle groups. Computer-drawn maps of the clusters were also produced so that residential locations of the lifestyle groups could be identified.

Lifestyle Group 1: The Central-City Dwellers. The first lifestyle group represented about 26 percent of the county's 610,700 elderly persons and included many people who resided in and near its major urban centers (see Figure 2). This lifestyle group was unique in terms of rates of home and automobile ownership, the percentage of single-person households, the average income, and the age of the dwellings. In the county nearly 50 percent of the residences occupied by elderly households were owned by their occupants. Only about 26 percent of the central-city dwellers owned their homes, however. Almost 47 percent of the elderly households in this group had moved into their residences after 1965, a percentage considerably higher than the county average of about 36 percent. Most of the units were quite old, however; more than 69 percent were built prior to 1950. Almost 47 percent of the households were composed of single persons, compared to the county average of 34 percent. In addition, about 71 percent of the people living alone did not own a car. It would therefore be expected that dependence on friends and relatives who drive and on public transportation is especially

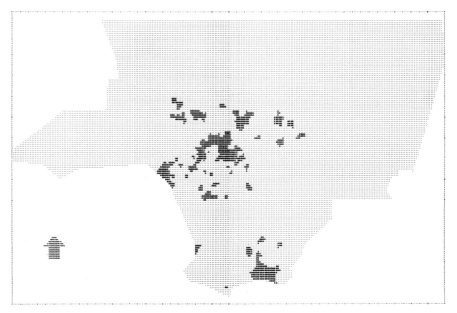

Figure 2. The Central-City Lifestyle Area

high in this lifestyle area. It is probable that the low level of automobile ownership was related to the inability of many residents to afford cars (almost half of the households reported incomes of less than $3,000 per year). In summary, this group lived at high densities, in older homes, and consisted of many persons living alone, on lower incomes, and having low rates of automobile ownership.

Lifestyle Group 2: The Financially Secure. The second lifestyle area included the most affluent portion of the elderly population (see Figure 3). About 14 percent of the county's elderly were members of this group. Typically, members of the financially secure group earned high incomes, lived in expensive homes and apartments, and had high school or college educations. Many of the residents had lived in their homes for a long period of time and had grown old with their neighborhoods and communities. About 60 percent of the housing units occupied by members of this group were owner-occupied, and more than 70 percent of the homes were valued over $25,000. Among

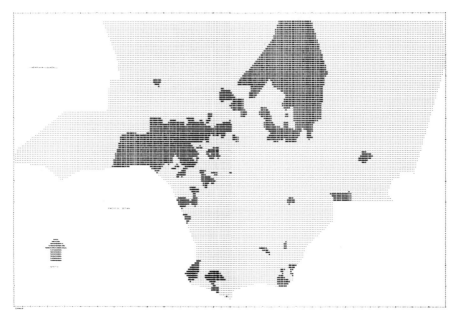

Figure 3. The Financially Secure Lifestyle Area

those who rented, about 40 percent paid $150 or more per month. This percentage was substantially higher than the county figure of 12 percent. About one-quarter of the elderly had lived in their homes for twenty years or more, and approximately the same proportion had moved into their residences after 1965. Education and employment levels were also quite high. More than 32 percent of the group were college-educated, compared to a county-wide figure of about 17 percent of the elderly. Forty-five percent of the residents continued to work past retirement age in some capacity, primarily in white-collar occupations.

Lifestyle Group 3: The Institutionalized. The third lifestyle area was unique in that it consisted of only 14 census tracts (see Figure 4). A large positive mean value on the poor health dimension indicated that this area was the location of seniors who frequently experienced health problems and visited county medical facilities. An examination of census data on a zone-by-zone basis revealed that this lifestyle group included less than 1 percent of the county's

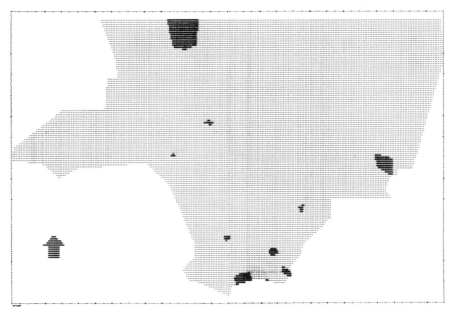

Figure 4. The Institutionalized Lifestyle Area

elderly population and that a large proportion resided in health care centers, such as hospitals, convalescent homes, or other group quarters for the aged.

Lifestyle Group 4: The New Suburbanites. The new suburbanites lived in the most recently populated areas of the county and represented 12 percent of its elderly population (see Figure 5). They had sufficient economic resources to maintain homes in low density areas, and many probably had little need for the public services available in more urbanized areas. About 48 percent of the elderly households moved into their residences in 1965 or later, while the county-wide percentage was less than 37 percent. Family living was common; approximately 90 percent of the elderly lived with spouses or relatives. As would be expected in suburban areas, the level of home ownership was high. About six out of ten units occupied by members of this subgroup were privately owned. Those who rented tended to choose large apartment complexes. About 24 percent of the units occupied by seniors were located in

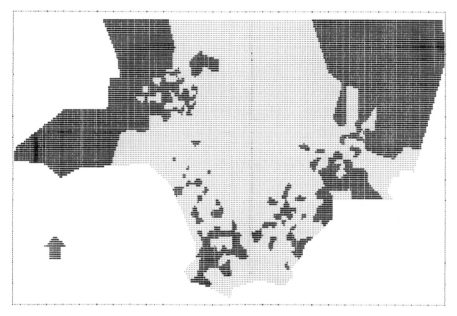

Figure 5. The New Suburban Lifestyle Area

structures with three or more units, a percentage slightly higher than the county-wide figure of 17 percent.

Lifestyle Group 5: The Black Community. The fifth lifestyle area was the principal location of the black elderly population (see Figure 6), having high scores on the race and occupation dimension. Of the 42,579 members of the group, over two-thirds were black. These persons accounted for more than three-quarters of the black elderly population of the county, although this lifestyle group constituted only 7 percent of the elderly population in the county. Of those who worked, most were employed in service occupations, although some were employed in blue-collar positions.

The average member of the group lived on an extremely low income. Over one-half of the elderly households reported incomes of $3,000 or less. Although the level of home ownership was relatively high, the average home had a low market value. Less than 10 percent of the units owned by elderly persons were valued over $25,000, and

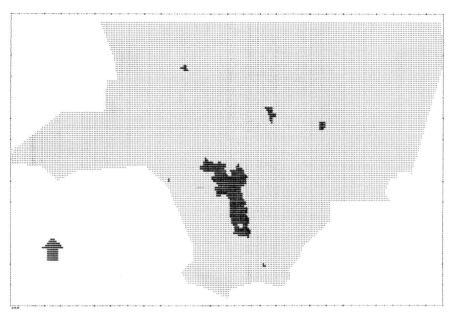

Figure 6. The Black Lifestyle Area

40 percent had values of less than $15,000. The rents paid by the elderly residents were also low. Less than 1 percent of the units rented by seniors had monthly rents greater than $150, while the percentage for the county's elderly population was more than 11 percent.

Lifestyle Group 6: The Spanish-American Community. This lifestyle group was distinguished by a high proportion of persons of Spanish-American background. Over one-half of the group members had Spanish surnames, and more than 30 percent of the elderly with Spanish surnames in the county were residents of this lifestyle area (see Figure 7). Low levels of education were common among the elderly residents; 40 percent of the group had received less than six years of formal education. Employment in blue-collar occupations was common, and the number of seniors employed in blue-collar jobs was more than twice the number of those in service occupations. Housing in this lifestyle area was relatively old. About 82 percent of the group lived in dwellings

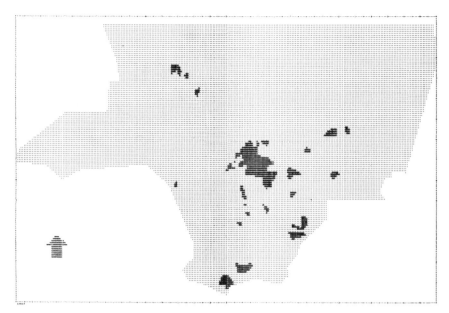

Figure 7. The Spanish-American Lifestyle Area

constructed earlier than 1950, and about one in every three elderly households had moved into their homes before 1950.

Lifestyle Group 7: The Early Suburbanites. The early suburbanites lived in the areas of Los Angeles which were on the urban fringe in the 1940s and 1950s but which have more recently become densely populated (see Figure 8). The average member of the group lived in a moderately valued structure which he or she owned. The level of home ownership was higher in this lifestyle group than in any of the other six groups; more than 63 percent of the elderly households owned homes. Most houses fell into the $15,000 to $20,000 range, and only a small proportion had values greater than $25,000. The minority which did not own homes paid relatively low rents. Less than 5 percent of the rented units in this area (compared to 12 percent for the county as a whole) had monthly rental rates greater than $150. Because of the group's large size, it was evident that the residents were relatively diverse. Nearly

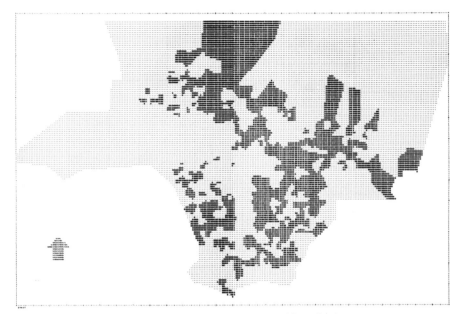

Figure 8. The Early Suburban Lifestyle Area

35 percent of the elderly population of the county lived in this lifestyle area, although only 8 percent of the total population in the area was elderly.

Observations and Conclusions

While it is likely that specific lifestyle groupings would differ if the technique were to be applied to data from other metropolitan areas, this analysis has demonstrated that the elderly population is heterogeneous in its settlement patterns, financial status, participation in the labor force, and tendency to move with advancing age. In Los Angeles the analysis showed that, while many did conform to the stereotypical view of the elderly as central-city dwellers, many others had recently moved to areas of low density at the periphery of the county. A major finding was the large elderly population which resided at very low densities in the new suburban areas of the county. About 13 percent of the elderly population resided in this lifestyle area. Others continued to reside in familiar neighborhoods where they had lived for many years. Many of these long-term residents were home owners. In the case of the financially secure, they were owners of relatively expensive homes.

Financial security was an important aspect in the heterogeneity of this population. While most elderly were characterized by lower incomes, several areas were distinguished by higher incomes and a lack of the restraints frequently accompanying advancing age. In most cases, this relative affluence was accompanied by higher educational attainment and continued participation in the labor force, especially in white-collar jobs.

Ethnicity was also an important factor in the lifestyle of the elderly. Many of the black and Spanish-American elderly were found concentrated, perhaps not by choice, in particular areas of the county. Language and poor educational attainment may be special barriers to members of the Spanish-American elderly population. Working beyond the traditional retirement years, often in blue-collar or service occupations, seemed common among both groups.

Although these findings demonstrate that the elderly population includes people of many different situations and backgrounds, they only suggest that the transportation needs of these subpopulations might also differ. Chapter 3 will examine the extent to which lifestyle and travel are systematically related. Similarly, the identification of lifestyle groups in the 1970 census does little to establish the temporal stability of these groups. In Chapter 5 we will return to the task of analyzing the stability of lifestyles and their use in the forecasting of future demographic and travel patterns.

Chapter 3
Relationships Between Lifestyle and Travel Behavior of the Elderly

*T*he results presented in the last chapter showed that the elderly are a diverse group in terms of their socioeconomic characteristics, demography, and location. Because travel demands are affected by these variables, the results also suggested that travel patterns of the elderly vary considerably across lifestyle areas. Chapter 3 studies these variations in travel behavior to determine their relationships with the lifestyle patterns of the elderly. Composed of two major sections, this chapter first describes the research approach and the primary source of data for this task, the home-interview survey of the 1967 Los Angeles Regional Transportation Study. The second section describes the travel patterns of the elderly residents of each lifestyle area and presents the results of analysis of variance and difference-of-means tests for the presence of statistically significant differences in the patterns.

Research Technique for Studying
Relationships Between Lifestyle and Travel

Travel Data and the Selection of Travel Variables

The Los Angeles Regional Transportation Study (LARTS), conducted in 1967 by the California Division of Highways, in part consisted of a home-interview questionnaire administered to a 1 percent sample of the households in a five-county area including Los Angeles County. Approximately 68,000 persons in Los Angeles County were interviewed, including 5,768 elderly persons who represented about 8.5 percent of the sample.[1] Data describing these persons and their travel behavior constituted the data base for this research.

Only trips made on weekdays were considered in this investigation. It is customary in transportation studies to analyze weekday and weekend trips separately because significantly different travel patterns characterize these two portions of the week. The LARTS survey asked those respondents keeping a log of their trips on Friday also to record their Saturday trips; those recording Monday trips also kept data on their Sunday travel.[2] Persons reporting weekend travel, therefore, constituted only about two-fifths of the total sample. The size of the weekend sample and the number of reported weekend trips were considered too small to yield reliable results in this study.

The mode of travel and the purpose of the trip were recorded for every vehicular trip made on the day of the survey. Eight travel modes were included: automobile driver, automobile passenger, taxi driver, taxi passenger, truck driver, pickup truck driver, truck or pickup truck passenger, and public bus passenger. Walking and motorcycle trips were counted in the survey only if they were made for the first trip to work on the survey day. Because only this small subsample of all walking and motorcycle trips was included in the LARTS data base, these modes could not be included in the analysis reported upon here. From among the remaining trips, Table 7 indicates that the automobile driver, automobile passenger, and public bus passenger modes accounted for the great majority of trips made by the elderly. Less than 3 percent of the vehicular trips were made by the other five travel modes, and, consequently, only the three principal modes were considered. In addition, trips were classified into four

1. Los Angeles Regional Transportation Study, *LARTS Base Year Report.* (Los Angeles: State of California, Division of Highways, District 07, December 1971).
2. Ibid.

Table 7. Distribution of Vehicular Trips Reported by
the Elderly by Travel Mode and Trip Purpose

Travel Mode	Percent of Total Trips	Number of Trips
Auto Driver	61.5	5,237
Auto Passenger	28.2	2,405
Taxi Driver	0.0	0
Truck Driver	0.1	11
Pickup Truck Driver	1.9	162
Truck or Pickup Passenger	0.1	12
Taxi Passenger	0.8	69
Public Bus Passenger	7.4	629
	100.0	8,525
Trip Purpose		
Personal Business	44.9	3,830
Leisure	18.3	1,557
Work	12.1	1,033
Shopping	24.7	2,105
	100.0	8,525

broad categories according to purpose: personal business, leisure, work, and shopping. These categories were exhaustive in that each trip was considered to fall into only one of the classes of trip purpose. Each of the four purposes was well represented in the trips reported by the elderly, as shown in Table 7.

From the LARTS data, a set of seventeen variables was constructed describing whether each elderly person had a driver's license, his choices of travel modes, and the purposes of his vehicular trips. The variables describing trips were expressed both as absolute frequencies and as percentages of the total number of trips made. In order to reduce this set to a manageable size and to reduce redundancy, a variable selection procedure was developed. Pearson product-moment correlation coefficients were calculated for each pair of variables. For the purposes of this study, it was considered that if a correlation coefficient exceeded .8 in absolute value, the two variables were accounting for the same aspect of travel behavior. Consequently, if a coefficient exceeded .8 or fell below -.8, one of the variables was eliminated. After Pearson product-moment correlation coefficients were computed for each pair of variables, nine of the seventeen variables were retained. Two of these were dummy variables indicating whether a person possessed a valid driver's license and whether at least one vehicular trip was reported on the day of the survey. Three variables consisted of totals of the number of trips made by the automobile driver, automobile passenger, and bus passenger modes. The remaining four variables were totals of the number of trips made for the four purposes identified above. The correlation coefficients for all pairs of these nine variables are shown in Table 8. The set of nine travel variables was employed to identify differences in aggregate travel patterns between lifestyle areas.

Table 8. Travel Variable Correlation Coefficients

	Driver's License (yes=1, no=0) 1	Vehicular Travel (yes=1, no=0) 2	Number of Auto Driver Trips 3	Number of Auto Passenger Trips 4	Number of Public Bus Passenger Trips 55	Number of Personal Business Trips 6	Number of Trips for for Leisure 7	Number of Work Trips 8	Number of Shopping Trips 9
1. Driver's License (yes=1, no=0)		.03	.08	-.04	-.06	.03	.03	.03	.02
2. Vehicular Travel (yes=1, no=0)			.53	.42	.23	.62	.38	.24	.50
3. Number of Auto Driver Trips				-.14	-.10	.56	.55	.29	.39
4. Number of Auto Passenger Trips					.04	.33	.29	-.02	.27
5. Number of Public Bus Passenger Trips						.12	-.02	.03	.06
6. Number of Personal Business Trips							.32	-.02	.11
7. Number of Trips for Leisure								-.04	.24
8. Number of Work Trips									.50
9. Number of Shopping Trips									

*Differences in Travel Behavior of the
Elderly Between Lifestyle Areas*

LARTS travel data were analyzed to describe the aggregate travel behavior of the elderly residents of each lifestyle area and to test statistically for differences in travel patterns of the elderly between lifestyle areas. Each elderly person in the LARTS survey was assigned to the lifestyle area which included his place of residence. The elderly persons residing in a single lifestyle area constituted a sample of a "lifestyle group."

The identification of differences in travel behavior between the lifestyle groups was accomplished in two steps. First, the statistical technique of analysis of variance was applied for each travel variable to test for overall differences between the lifestyle groups. An F statistic was computed to measure the ratio of the variance between lifestyle groups to the variance within groups. If overall differences existed, then the variance between groups would greatly exceed the variance within groups, and the value of F would be large. The differences for each variable were considered to be significant if the value of F exceeded the value required to insure statistical significance at the .01 level. Second, after the variables on which overall differences existed had been identified, tests for the presence of significant pairwise differences between the groups were conducted. Difference-of-means tests (t-tests) were applied for each pair of lifestyle groups on each of the travel variables for which overall differences between the groups were found. Differences were considered significant if the t statistic indicated statistical significance at the .01 level. From the results, it was possible to identify the travel characteristics which distinguished each lifestyle group and to identify the major differences in aggregate travel behavior between lifestyle areas.

Variations in Travel Behavior with
Differences in Lifestyle: Research Results

The analysis of the LARTS survey data showed that the travel patterns of the elderly varied widely across Los

Angeles County and that the lifestyle areas could be statistically distinguished from one another on the basis of the travel behavior of the elderly residents within these areas. Through the application of analysis of variance on each of the travel variables, statistically significant overall differences between the lifestyle areas were found on eight of the nine travel variables. Difference-of-means tests were then performed for each pair of lifestyle areas on each of the travel variables in order to determine the characteristic travel behaviors which most distinguished the areas. The travel patterns of the Spanish-American community were not significantly different from those of the black community, and the early suburban and new suburban lifestyle areas were similar to each other. Statistically significant differences were found, however, for all other pairs of lifestyle areas on at least two travel variables.

Elderly residents of the institutionalized lifestyle areas were not considered in these analyses because of the small amount of data available describing their travel patterns. Table 9 shows that twenty-three persons in the LARTS survey maintained residences in this area, while at least 300 elderly persons resided in each of the other six lifestyle areas. This sample size was considered to be too small to give a reliable description of the travel patterns of the elderly residents. As described in Chapter 2, only fourteen of the 1,159 zones in the county comprised this lifestyle area, and many of these consisted entirely of medical facilities or other institutions. Because the elderly population was extremely small, an insignificant amount of

Table 9. Distribution of the LARTS Sample Across Lifestyle Areas

Lifestyle Area	Sample Size	Percent of the Sample
Spanish American Community	308	5.3
New Suburbanites	706	12.2
Black Community	387	6.7
Central City Dwellers	1,528	26.5
Early Suburbanites	2,080	36.1
Financially Secure	736	12.8
Institutionalized	23	0.4
	5,768	100.0

information on elderly travel patterns was lost by not considering this area.

Overall Differences in Travel of the
Elderly Between Lifestyle Areas

Statistically significant overall differences between the lifestyle areas were found on eight of the nine travel variables. The means of the travel variables in each lifestyle area, along with a number of other statistics describing elderly travel patterns, are shown in Table 10. The mean values of the dummy variables are equivalent to percent-

Table 10. Travel Variable Means for the Lifestyle Areas and the County

Travel Variable	Spanish American Community	New Suburbanites	Black Community	Central-City Dwellers	Early Suburbanites	Financially Secure	County	F
Percent with Drivers' Licenses	23	48	33	35	46	59	42	39.2*
Percent Reporting Vehicular Travel	31	48	34	41	47	56	45	19.2*
Number of Auto Driver Trips	.40	1.04	.56	.66	1.02	1.38	.91	23.9*
Number of Auto Passenger Trips	.23	.43	.21	.35	.49	.52	.42	8.6*
Number of Public Bus Passenger Trips	.19	.04	.16	.21	.05	.09	.11	26.1*
Number of Personal Business Trips	.44	.62	.53	.59	.70	.92	.66	12.1*
Number of Trips for Leisure	.09	.30	.13	.23	.29	.43	.27	12.0*
Number of Work Trips	.13	.23	.16	.13	.19	.23	.18	2.4
Number of Shopping Trips	.21	.39	.16	.31	.43	.46	.36	13.0*
Descriptive Statistics								
Total Trips	.87	1.54	.98	1.26	1.61	2.04	1.47	
Percent of Auto Driver Trips	44.8	66.9	57.1	51.6	63.4	67.6	61.5	
Percent of Auto Passenger Trips	26.3	27.9	21.4	27.8	30.4	25.5	28.2	
Percent of Public Bus Passenger Trips	21.8	2.6	16.3	16.7	3.1	4.4	7.4	
Percent of Personal Business Trips	50.6	40.3	54.1	46.8	43.5	45.1	44.9	
Percent of Trips for Leisure	10.3	19.4	13.3	18.3	18.0	21.1	18.3	
Percent of Work Trips	14.9	14.9	16.3	10.3	11.8	11.3	12.1	
Percent of Shopping Trips	24.1	25.3	16.3	24.6	26.7	22.5	24.7	

* Statistically significant at the .01 level.

ages, and they are labeled accordingly in this table. For example, the mean value of the dummy variable representing those elderly residents having drivers' licenses in the Spanish-American lifestyle area was .23, indicating that 23 percent of the elderly residents possessed drivers' licenses. Also shown in the table are the values of the F statistic of analysis of variance which were calculated for the travel variables. The value of F measured the strength of the overall differences between lifestyle areas on the travel variable. The values of F were compared to tabled values to test for the statistical significance of the differences between lifestyle areas.

The largest values of F corresponded to the three variables describing those who drove automobiles, those who rode buses, and those who possessed drivers' licenses, indicating that the overall differences between areas were strongest on these three travel variables. This confirmed the importance of these three variables established in the cross-classification analyses and again suggested that the availability of an automobile, the ability to drive, and the proximity of the residence to public transportation services are key factors which influence and are the product of elderly lifestyles.

The lifestyle areas were not significantly different from one another in terms of the number of trips made for work purposes. The average number of trips made to work did not vary as significantly across the lifestyle areas as did the rates for trips with other purposes. Table 10 shows that the mean numbers of trips made to work varied only slightly, from low values of .13 trips per person in the Spanish-American community and central-city lifestyle area to high values of .23 trips per person in the new suburban and financially secure areas. The lack of variation was certainly due, in part, to the fact that very few trips were made for this purpose. Relatively uniform employment rates across the lifestyle areas may have also explained the lack of variation. The new suburban lifestyle area, characterized by a relatively high proportion of elderly who were employed, was the only area that was unique in terms of employment rates. The average number of trips made to work was relatively high in this area (.23 trips per person versus a county average of .18), but it was not high enough to cause the overall differences between areas to be statistically significant.

After establishing that overall differences were significant on eight of the travel variables, difference-of-means tests were conducted to determine the significance of pairwise differences between areas. The results of these tests are included below, along with a description of the travel behavior of the elderly residents of each area.

Travel Patterns of the Elderly in the Central-City Community

Although it is commonly assumed that the central-city areas house the most immobile segment of the elderly population, the LARTS data showed that this is not the case in Los Angeles. While the average number of vehicular trips reported by members of this lifestyle group was below the average for the county's elderly, it was much higher than the rates for the black and Spanish-American communities. The central-city group had the highest rate of bus travel and a relatively large number of trips as automobile driver and passenger. The average number of trips reported by the members of this group on the survey day was 1.26 or about 85 percent of the county average. Forty percent reported at least one trip, only four percentage points lower than the county-wide figure and seven and nine percentage points higher than for the black and Spanish-American communities, respectively. The rate of driving was much lower than the county-wide rate, reflecting the low level of automobile ownership among the residents. However, the average number of automobile passenger trips was .35, only slightly lower than the county average of .42. Bus ridership was nearly double the county average of .11 trips per person per day. Rates for the four trip purposes were all somewhat lower than the county rates.

Table 11 gives the results of the difference-of-means

Table 11. Summary of the Difference-of-Means Analyses for the Central-City Lifestyle Area

Travel Variable	Lifestyle Area Mean	County Mean	Significantly Different Means Lifestyle Area				
			Span. American Community	New Suburbanites	Black Community	Early Suburbanites	Financially Secure
Percent with Drivers' Licenses (yes=1, no=0)	35	42	23	48		46	59
Percent Reporting Vehicular Travel (yes=1, no=0)	41	45	31	48		47	56
Number of Auto Driver Trips	.66	.91	.40	1.04		1.02	1.38
Number of Auto Passenger Trips	.35	.42			.21	.49	.52
Number of Public Bus Passenger Trips	.21	.11		.04		.05	.09
Number of Personal Business Trips	.59	.66				.70	.92
Number of Trips for Leisure	.23	.27	.09				.43
Number of Shopping Trips	.31	.36			.16	.43	.46

tests for the central-city elderly. The first two columns include the mean values of the travel variables for the central-city lifestyle area and for the entire elderly population of the county. The next five columns give the mean values of the travel variables for the other five lifestyle areas which were determined to be significantly different from the central-city lifestyle area.

The travel patterns of the elderly residents of this lifestyle area were significantly different (on at least two travel variables) from those of the senior residents of each other area. Differences were found primarily in the proportion of persons possessing a driver's license, those reporting at least one vehicular trip, and the average number of trips driven in automobiles. The central-city means were significantly higher than those of the Spanish-American community on these three indicators of mobility but lower than the values for the early suburbanites, new suburbanites, and financially secure lifestyle areas. While the central-city and black areas were very similar in terms of their mean values on the travel variables, significantly more automobile passenger and shopping trips were made by the elderly residents of the central-city areas.

Travel Patterns of the Elderly in the Financially Secure Lifestyle Area

The average number of daily trips reported by members of this lifestyle group was 2.04, over one-third higher than the county-wide rate and the highest among the lifestyle groups. The proportion of licensed drivers (59 percent) and the proportion which reported at least one vehicular trip (56 percent) were much larger than the corresponding proportions for the elderly of the county. The average number of trips to work was relatively high, and the frequencies of traveling for other purposes were much greater than in any other lifestyle area. The daily number of personal business trips per person was .92. This was approximately as high as the average rate of trips for the Spanish-American and black community groups for all trip purposes combined and significantly higher than the county average of .66 trips per person. Automobile passenger trips also were made more frequently in this area than in any other lifestyle area.

As Table 12 shows, because of the extreme mean values on many of the travel variables, this area was statistically distinguishable from each of the other areas on at least four of the nine travel variables. The mean number of trips made by an automobile driver and for personal business were significantly lower in each of the other five lifestyle areas. This was also the case with the proportions of elderly possessing drivers' licenses and the proportions having made at least one vehicular trip on the day of the survey. It is clear that the financially secure elderly have the greatest mobility.

**Table 12. Summary of the Difference-of-Means Analyses
for the Financially Secure Lifestyle Area**

Travel Variable	Lifestyle Area Mean	County Mean	Significantly Different Means Lifestyle Area				
			Span. American Community	New Suburbanites	Black Community	Central City Dwellers	Early Suburbanites
Percent with Drivers' Licenses (yes=1, no=0)	59	42	23	48	33	35	46
Percent Reporting Vehicular Travel (yes=1, no=0)	56	45	31	48	34	41	47
Number of Auto Driver Trips	1.38	.91	.40	1.04	.56	.66	1.02
Number of Auto Passenger Trips	.52	.42	.23		.21	.35	
Number of Public Bus Passenger Trips	.09	.11	.19			.21	
Number of Personal Business Trips	.92	.66	.44	.62	.53	.59	.70
Number of Trips for Leisure	.43	.27	.09		.13	.23	.29
Number of Shopping Trips	.46	.36	.21		.16	.31	

Travel Patterns of the Elderly in the New Suburban Lifestyle Area

Elderly residents of the newer suburban areas of Los Angeles traveled slightly more and tended to rely on the automobile to a greater degree than did elderly residents of other areas. The small number riding public buses was undoubtedly related to the fact that public transportation was not available in a large part of this area. If these persons are able to maintain their homes in the suburbs, the availability of public transportation may become increasingly important as they get older and lose their driving skills.

Each elderly person in this area made an average of 1.54 daily trips, only slightly higher than the county-wide average of 1.47 trips per elderly person. While the rate

of driving automobiles was 1.04 trips per person—
substantially higher than the county rate of .91—the average number of bus trips was only .04. This was the lowest
level of bus ridership among the six lifestyle areas. Nearly
50 percent of the people possessed drivers' licenses—
slightly higher than the county-wide proportion. The rate
of vehicular trips for work purposes was relatively high
at .23 trips per person, although this was still close to
the county average of .18. On all other travel variables, the
mean values for this lifestyle area were indistinguishable
from the mean values for the county.

The travel patterns of the elderly in the new suburban
lifestyle area were most strongly distinguished by the
proportion of residents with drivers' licenses, the proportion who reported at least one vehicular trip on the survey
day, and the average number of trips made as automobile
drivers. The mean values of these variables were all significantly different from the values of four of the other five
lifestyle areas (see Table 13). These differences showed
that the residents of the new suburban area were more
mobile and traveled more frequently than did residents of
the Spanish-American, black, and central-city lifestyle
areas. They also made significantly fewer trips than the
elderly of the financially secure lifestyle area. The elderly
of the central city did not, however, make substantially
fewer auto passenger trips nor were their rates of making
trips for the four trip purposes distinguishable from those
of the residents of the new suburban area. No significant differences in the mean values of the travel variables
were found between the new suburbanites and the early
suburbanites.

Travel Patterns of the Elderly in the
Black Community

While more mobile and apparently less dependent on
public transportation than residents of the Spanish-
American community, elderly residents of the black community traveled by vehicle much less frequently than did
the average elderly person in the county. This was indi-

Table 13. Summary of the Difference-of-Means Analyses for the New Suburban Lifestyle Area

Travel Variable	Lifestyle Area Mean	County Mean	Significantly Different Means Lifestyle Area				
			Span. American Community	Black Community	Central City Community	Early Suburbanites	Financially Secure
Percent with Drivers' Licenses (yes=1, no=0)	48	42	23	33	35		59
Percent Reporting Vehicular Travel (yes=1, no=0)	48	45	31	34	41		56
Number of Auto Driver Trips	1.04	.91	.40	.56	.66		1.38
Number of Auto Passenger Trips	.43	.42	.23	.21			
Number of Public Bus Passenger Trips	.04	.11	.19	.16	.21		
Number of Personal Business Trips	.62	.66					.92
Number of Trips for Leisure	.30	.27	.09	.13			.43
Number of Shopping Trips	.39	.36	.21	.16			

cated by especially low numbers of automobile trips as a driver or passenger. The rate of riding buses was relatively high, with bus trips constituting a sizeable proportion of the reported trips. This suggests that many black elderly persons in Los Angeles rely to a great extent on public transportation.

The average number of trips reported by residents of this area was only .98, which was about two-thirds of the county-wide average. A low rate of automobile driving accounted for much of this difference, with the area mean of .56 trips per person significantly lower than the rate of .91 for the county. Only 33 percent of the elderly possessed drivers' licenses, and about two-thirds of the elderly residents did not report a trip. The average daily number of trips made as automobile passengers was especially low (only .21), suggesting that opportunities for sharing rides in this area were scarce. While the frequencies of traveling for the purpose of personal business and work were nearly as high as the county-wide figures, rates for leisure and shopping trips were only about half as high as county averages.

Table 14 shows that the travel variable means of the black and Spanish-American lifestyle areas were quite similar, and the differences were not statistically significant. Systematic differences were found, however, between the black community and the early suburban, new suburban, and financially secure lifestyle areas. Significantly fewer elderly residents of the black community possessed drivers' licenses, and fewer residents reported a trip than in the three other areas. The rate of making trips in automobiles as a driver or passenger was low, as were

Table 14. Summary of the Difference-of-Means Analyses for the Black Lifestyle Area

Travel Variable	Lifestyle Area Mean	County Mean	Span. American Community	New Suburbanites	Central=City Dwellers	Early Suburbanites	Financially Secure
Percent with Drivers' Licenses (yes=1, no=0)	33	42		48		46	59
Percent Reporting Vehicular Travel (yes=1, no=0)	34	45		48		47	56
Number of Auto Driver Trips	.56	.91		1.04		1.02	1.38
Number of Auto Passenger Trips	.21	.42		.43	.35	.49	.52
Number of Public Bus Passenger Trips	.16	.11		.04		.05	
Number of Personal Business Trips	.53	.66				.70	.92
Number of Trips for Leisure	.13	.27		.30		.29	.43
Number of Shopping Trips	.16	.36		.39	.31	.43	.46

the mean numbers of trips for the purposes of leisure and shopping. The travel patterns of the residents of the central city were significantly different from those of the black community only in terms of the average numbers of automobile passenger and shopping trips, which were higher in the central-city area.

Travel Patterns of the Elderly in the
Spanish-American Community

Elderly members of the Spanish-American community reported, on the average, fewer vehicular trips than did elderly residents of any other lifestyle area. A low rate of automobile travel and a relatively high rate of bus travel were prominent in their travel patterns. The average number of trips made for leisure purposes was also low, reflecting both the overall low number of trips and the possibility that many seniors of Spanish-American background were not able to engage in activities outside the home due to language or educational barriers.

Only 23 percent of the group possessed drivers' licenses, compared with 42 percent for the county's elderly, and the number of trips made as drivers was less than half of the county rate. The number of trips made as an automobile passenger and for the four trip purposes previously mentioned was also low, although the average number of trips related to work was nearly as high as the average for the county's elderly population. Bus trips accounted for nearly 22 percent of the reported trips, and the daily rate of .19 bus trips per person was almost twice the rate throughout the county.

Table 15 gives the results of the difference-of-means analyses for the Spanish-American community. The travel patterns of elderly residents in this lifestyle area could be consistently distinguished from those of the elderly residents in the new suburban, early suburban, and financially secure lifestyle areas. The elderly of those areas were, on the average, significantly more mobile and less dependent on public transportation. Differences were especially evident in the proportion of elderly residents who possessed drivers' licenses, the number of trips per

**Table 15. Summary of the Difference-of-Means Analyses
for the Spanish-American Community**

Travel Variable	Lifestyle Area Mean	County Mean	Significantly Different Means Lifestyle Area				
			New Suburbanites	Black Community	Central City Dwellers	Early Suburbanites	Financially Secure
Percent with Drivers' Licenses (yes=1, no=0)	23	42	48		35	46	59
Percent Reporting Vehicular Travel (yes=1, no=0)	31	45	48		41	47	56
Number of Auto Driver Trips	.40	.91	1.04		.66	1.02	1.38
Number of Auto Passenger Trips	.23	.42	.43			.49	.52
Number of Public Bus Passenger Trips	.19	.11	.04			.05	
Number of Personal Business Trips	.44	.66				.70	.92
Number of Trips for Leisure	.09	.27	.30		.23	.29	.43
Number of Shopping Trips	.21	.36	.39			.43	.46

person made as an automobile driver, and the number of trips made for leisure and shopping purposes. The elderly of the Spanish-American community also differed from the central-city dwellers on four of the nine travel variables. The central-city dwellers more often possessed drivers' licenses, more often reported at least one trip on the travel day, and made significantly more automobile trips as a driver, as well as trips for leisure. It is also significant to note that the Spanish-American community could not be distinguished from the black community with respect to any of the nine travel variables.

*Travel Patterns of the Elderly in the
Early Suburban Lifestyle Area*

The high number of automobiles and the low dependence on public transportation usually associated with suburban living were reflected in the travel patterns of the elderly residents of this area. Trips were made more frequently by automobile—as driver or passenger—and less frequently by bus in this area than in the county as a whole. Because over one-third of the county's elderly resided in this area—and because this group was diverse in terms of a number of lifestyle dimensions—there was more variation in individual travel patterns among the early suburbanites than there was among the members of any other lifestyle area.

The average number of vehicular trips per person for this area was 1.6, somewhat higher than the county average of 1.47. Relatively high numbers of trips were made for personal business and shopping purposes. The average number of work-related trips per person was .19, only slightly above the county average. Also slightly higher than the county figures was the proportion of elderly residents who possessed drivers' licenses and who reported one or more vehicular trips on the survey day.

The travel patterns of the elderly in this area were nearly identical to those of the new suburban lifestyle area (see Table 16). While the travel variable means for both of these areas were very similar to the county means, they were in many cases significantly different from those of the other four lifestyle areas. In the Spanish-American community, black community, and central-city areas, the elderly tended to travel less frequently. The proportions of elderly who possessed drivers' licenses, who reported at least one trip, and who made automobile trips as a driver or passenger were significantly lower in each of these areas, while the mean numbers of bus trips were significantly larger. The residents of the financially secure lifestyle area were significantly more mobile, especially in terms of the average number of automobile trips driven and trips made for personal and leisure purposes.

Summary and Conclusions

This chapter demonstrated that there is a significant association between the lifestyle patterns of the elderly and their travel behavior. The results showed that the lifestyle

Table 16. Summary of the Difference-of-Means Analyses for the Early Suburban Lifestyle Area

Travel Variable	Lifestyle Area Mean	County Mean	Span. American Community	New Suburbanites	Black Community	Central City Dwellers	Financially Secure
Percent with Drivers' Licenses (yes=1, no=0)	46	42	23		33	35	59
Percent Reporting Vehicular Travel (yes=1, no=0)	47	45	31		34	41	56
Number of Auto Driver Trips	1.02	.91	.40		.56	.66	1.38
Number of Auto Passenger Trips	.49	.42	.23		.21	.35	
Number of Public Bus Passenger Trips	.05	.11	.19		.16	.21	
Number of Personal Business Trips	.70	.66	.44		.53	.59	.92
Number of Trips for Leisure	.29	.27	.09		.13		.43
Number of Shopping Trips	.43	.36	.21		.16	.31	

(Columns 3–7 fall under the heading "Significantly Different Means — Lifestyle Area")

areas could be consistently distinguished from one another on the basis of the travel behavior of the elderly residents within the area. It was shown that travel patterns varied significantly across subgroups of the elderly population and that the elderly's needs and demands for transportation are associated with specific spatial locations within the county. These findings are extremely important because they are necessary for the development of transportation service policies which must differ according to location within a metropolitan area.

Another major finding was that elderly residents of the central-city areas made more vehicular trips than did elderly residents of two other lifestyle areas. Central-city residents are often assumed to be the least mobile of the elderly population. Residents of the black and Spanish-

American lifestyle areas, however, traveled by vehicle less frequently than did elderly residents of the other five areas, including the central-city lifestyle area. As might be expected, relatively high numbers of trips were made in the new suburban and early suburban lifestyle areas. The financially secure were unquestionably the most mobile elderly in the county.

It was found that lifestyle patterns among the elderly were most distinguished by those who made automobile trips, those who rode public buses, and those who possessed drivers' licenses. These were the travel variables most strongly related to the lifestyle dimensions, and the lifestyle areas could be consistently differentiated from one another with respect to the three variables. The ability to drive, the availability of an automobile, and the accessibility of public transportation are, therefore, key aspects of lifestyle. They reflect the lifestyle choices which have been made by the elderly and, at the same time, they are factors which can influence and limit the activity of those in retirement.

A final major finding of this analysis was that there were significant differences in travel patterns between central-city and suburban elderly. The use of public transportation was especially high among those in inner-city areas, while the automobile was the predominant mode of travel among the suburban elderly. Much of this difference can perhaps be attributed to the high levels of public transportation services in central-city areas. Perhaps more important is the fact that residents of suburban areas chose a lifestyle in which living at low densities in single-family homes was a key element, one in which there was little need for public transportation. The next chapter investigates the relationship between existing transit service levels and lifestyle.

Chapter 4
Current Transportation
Services for the Elderly

*T*hus far it has been established that the elderly include members of a wide variety of lifestyle groups
and that the travel patterns of senior citizens vary considerably, depending upon differences in their lifestyles.
These findings were arrived at, however, without detailed
consideration of the variety and quality of transportation
service available to each lifestyle group. There are at least
two reasons for including an analysis of the supply of
service in a study of lifestyles and transportation needs of
the elderly. First, and most important, is the concern that if
lifestyles and travel patterns vary dramatically among
senior citizens, transportation policymakers should tailor
services to the unique living patterns and travel needs of
these older people. If available service does not vary across
lifestyle areas in appropriate recognition of this uniqueness, then policymakers might do well to study the transportation services that are available and make suggestions
for improvements to match services to need in a more efficient way. Second, it should also be observed that manifest travel behavior is the result of interaction between the
need to travel and existing opportunities to travel. The
economist would say that observed travel behavior is the
result of an equilibrium between travel demand and supply. Thus, travel patterns—the subject of Chapter 3—

cannot be fully understood without studying the supply of services available to travelers. It may be, for example, that members of one lifestyle group traveled a great deal more by bus than did members of another primarily because they had much better bus service available.

Selection of Sample Communities

Sample communities from each lifestyle area were selected for detailed analysis of transportation services currently available to the elderly in Los Angeles County. Information provided by the City of Los Angeles and the Southern California Association of Governments (SCAG) was utilized for the examination of bus and taxi service, and a telephone survey was conducted to gather information about specialized transportation services operated by social service agencies or municipal governments.

In order to examine the range of transportation services currently available to the elderly, a representative sample of communities within each lifestyle area was selected for detailed study. It was believed that a carefully selected sample would adequately reflect the range of transportation services and that a complete and costly inventory for Los Angeles County would not be necessary. The major criterion for selecting a community was the distance of its census tracts from the centroid of its lifestyle area. The centroid for each lifestyle area was determined as part of the cluster analysis described in Chapter 2. It was a composite measure for each lifestyle area, based on the seven descriptive factors presented in that chapter. A small distance from the centroid of a particular cluster indicated that the tract was similar to the averages for that lifestyle area or was "typical" of that lifestyle. Where possible, communities close to the cluster centroids were chosen in such a way that they also led to a broad geographic distribution of sample communities throughout the county.

Although an attempt was made to achieve consistency in the geographical units of analysis, there was so much variation in the geographical units utilized by governmental agencies in the provision of services that it was not possible to have identical study areas for the three major forms of transportation examined in this chapter. To facilitate the use of existing data on transportation services, the original sample areas were expanded from clusters of census tracts to somewhat larger areas used by SCAG in its *Short Range Transit Plan*.[1] The boundaries of these areas were drawn along city limits for smaller cities and around otherwise identifiable communities. SCAG used these regions for an analysis of bus service. In addition, it was found that taxi and specialized transportation services used administrative boundaries which coincided with city limits rather than with census tract boundaries. Thus the larger SCAG regions proved more useful than did census tracts in analyzing transportation services. Figure 9 is a map of the SCAG regions in Los Angeles County selected for analysis in this part of the study, showing the lifestyle areas to which each selected community belonged. The institutionalized lifestyle area was not included because of its small size (fourteen census tracts) and the special character of the travel needs of its elderly. Because of variations in size of the lifestyle areas and their differing geographical distributions, more communities were selected in some of the lifestyle areas than in others.

Identification of Transportation Services

After the sample communities were identified, a complete list of agencies providing transportation services to the elderly in each of these areas was compiled. Information on bus and taxi service was provided by SCAG and the Los Angeles Board of Public Utilities and Transportation (BPUT). Information on special public and private transportation services was obtained through a telephone survey of paratransit providers and social service agencies. An initial list of approximately 250 potential providers of transportation services for the elderly was developed, based on a list of social service agencies and specialized

1. Southern California Association of Governments, *Short Range Transit Plan*, Vol. 2 (Los Angeles: Southern California Association of Governments, 1977), p. A–6.

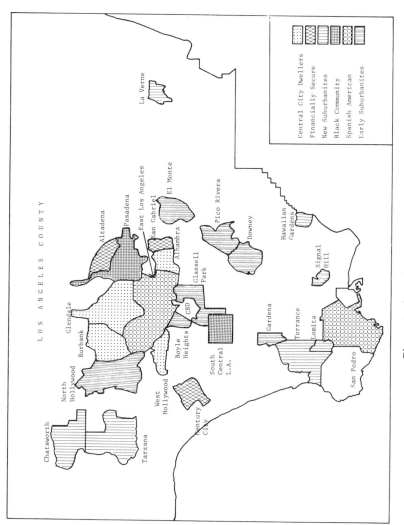

Figure 9. Sample Communities

transit programs which had been compiled earlier by SCAG. This list was checked against agencies receiving funding support through the Los Angeles Area Agency on Aging and supplemented with suggestions from the agencies contacted during the survey.

Because the survey was conducted by telephone, it was decided that the questionnaire had to be short to ensure participation by those contacted, yet it had to elicit information on several key points. These points included: service areas; proportions of passengers who were elderly; numbers of passengers served; trip purposes served; number, type, and accessibility of vehicles; days and hours of operation; cost to passengers; modes of service; advertising methods; length of time in service; budget sources; and whether drivers were salaried or volunteers. It would have been desirable to obtain more details about each operation. Many of the agencies contacted did not keep complete records, however, and some of the private carriers were reluctant to participate in the survey at all. They were especially reluctant to divulge financial information.

Bus Service

The *Short Range Transit Plan* prepared by SCAG[2] identified a number of different transit companies providing bus service in various parts of the county. These included the Southern California Rapid Transit District (SCRTD) and eight municipal bus companies of various sizes operating in different parts of the county. Buses are the public transit service most commonly used by the elderly. They are more generally available than are specialized transportation services, they are not restricted to certain categories of eligible passengers, and they are less expensive than taxis. Bus companies have generally responded to the special needs of the elderly in one or more of the following ways: reduced fares, development of special routes or schedules, and incorporation of special design

2. Ibid., Figure 3, System Map Except SCRTD.

features for the handicapped.[3] SCRTD has ordered 200 new buses which are accessible to the handicapped, and they have instituted a reduced fare of ten cents per ride for senior citizens at all times of the day, on nearly all scheduled routes. Seniors must pay half fare for special park-and-ride or express service. In addition, all of the municipal bus companies have instituted reduced fares of ten cents per ride for senior citizens. Some operators have issued special passes to the elderly and others rely on medicare cards for identification purposes. Each municipal bus operator and SCRTD is required periodically to submit a Short Range Transit Plan to SCAG. These plans include sections on special provisions for the elderly and the handicapped.

The *Short Range Transit Plan* included an analysis of the level of bus service for the selected communities based on measures of intensity of bus service (bus miles per week per square mile), the coverage of the community (route miles per square mile), and bus miles operated per week per capita. In addition, SCAG developed standards of minimally acceptable service based on population density, automobile ownership, and intensity of bus service—a combination of variables designed to reflect a community's need for transit service. The standard appeared to be influenced predominantly by existing levels of bus service and surrogate measures of transit dependency, such as automobile ownership, rather than by a rigorous analysis of need. Therefore, the standard may not be sufficiently demanding as a minimum service level. Two additional measures of service—bus miles operated per elderly person and bus miles of service per carless household—were included in the following discussion of bus service for the elderly, because they were judged to be more accurate indicators of dependency upon public transportation by the elderly.

3. National Cooperative Highway Research Program, *Transportation Requirements for the Handicapped, Elderly, and Economically Disadvantaged* (Washington, D.C.: Transportation Research Board, 1976), p. 22.

Table 17 presents these five measures for each sample community, in addition to averages for the sample communities in each lifestyle area. The level of service can be seen to vary considerably from community to community. Service levels were generally highest in the black and central-city lifestyle areas on all measures, except bus miles per week per carless dwelling unit. The Spanish-American lifestyle area was served by fewer bus miles per week per capita and attained a lower percentage of the SCAG standard, but it had slightly more bus miles per week per capita for the elderly population. Moderate service levels existed in the early suburban and financially secure lifestyle areas. The lowest level of service, overall, was found in the new suburban area, yet bus miles per week per capita for the elderly was the highest there, probably because of a thinly distributed elderly population in these communities.

In general, the ranking, on the basis of service level, was

Table 17. Bus Service Levels by Lifestyle Areas

Lifestyle Area and Communities	Bus Miles Per Week Per Square Mile	Bus Miles Per Week Per Capita Total Population	Bus Miles Per Week Per Capita Elderly Population	Bus Miles Per Week Per Carless Dwelling Unit	SCAG Standard Bus Miles Per Week Per Square Mile	Percent of SCAG Standard Existing
Central City Dwellers						
Alhambra	2275	.28	1.70	4.78	1000	228
Burbank	1754	.28	2.59	6.94	730	240
Glendale	924	.12	.75	1.96	957	97
West Hollywood	7566	.55	2.63	3.36	1800	420
Average	3130	.31	1.92	4.26	1122	246
Financially Secure						
Altadean	825	.21	1.82	7.25	470	176
Century City	2701	.21	1.74	2.22	1670	162
San Gabriel	1756	.24	1.85	6.44	870	202
Average	1760	.22	1.80	5.30	1003	180
New Suburbanites						
Chatsworth	1633	.31	8.34	45.35	600	272
Hawaiian Gardens	700	.06	1.53	3.26	1540	45
LaVerne	365	.16	1.00	3.92	200	183
Lomita	873	.08	.71	2.16	1400	62
Tarzana	1563	.28	9.90	20.35	600	261
Torrance	1249	.15	3.77	10.57	1130	111
Average	1064	.17	4.21	14.27	911	156
Black Community						
Pasadena	1781	.34	2.03	4.44	600	297
South Central Los Angeles	3720	.27	3.46	2.57	1800	207
Average	2750	.31	2.75	3.51	800	252
Spanish American						
Boyle Heights	4485	.35	4.07	1.95	1670	269
East Los Angeles	3197	.30	.72	3.63	1265	253
San Pedro	1279	.19	2.23	3.35	870	147
Average	2987	.28	2.34	2.98	1268	223
Early Suburbanites						
Downey	1099	.16	2.52	8.50	870	126
El Monte	1613	.22	2.99	5.33	870	185
Gardena	1954	.23	2.89	8.62	1130	173
Glassel Park	4485	.35	4.07	1.95	1670	269
North Hollywood	1426	.21	2.23	6.10	870	164
Pico Rivera	1018	.14	2.60	7.76	870	117
Signal Hill	1160	.28	1.92	5.68	470	247
Average	1822	.23	2.75	6.23	964	183

reversed when the measure of bus miles per week per carless dwelling unit was used. The highest average value appeared in the new suburban area and the lowest in the Spanish-American community. Thus, those areas with the most bus miles per capita had the fewest bus miles per dwelling unit without automobiles. A low score on this service measure could result from two different situations: few bus miles operated or a large number of carless households. The elderly living in the most central areas tend to have fewer automobiles than those living in the suburbs. For example, 62 percent of the Spanish-American elderly, 59 percent of the central-city dwellers, and 49 percent of the black community owned no automobiles. Conversely, only 28 percent of the financially secure, 33 percent of the new suburbanites, and 39 percent of the early suburbanites owned no automobiles. The elderly of the Spanish-American, black, and central-city lifestyles thus tended to score lower on the measure of bus miles per week per carless household. This tends to confirm the common view that there is greater dependence upon public transit in the more central parts of the urban area, even though bus service was less dense in areas having a more suburban character.

Although the average figures for bus service by lifestyle area were easily interpretable and consistent with expectations, there were several communities within each group which differed greatly from the average for that lifestyle area. This was especially apparent in the new suburban lifestyle area. Here Hawaiian Gardens had the lowest level of bus miles per week per capita in the entire sample (0.06), while Chatsworth, also in this cluster, had one of the highest levels of bus miles per week per capita (0.31). Although the differences were the most pronounced among the new suburban communities, there was a great deal of variation within each of the lifestyle areas, except within the financially secure area. Glendale and West Hollywood, both in the central-city lifestyle area, had levels of bus miles per week per capita of .12 and .55, respectively. Boyle Heights and San Pedro, both in the Spanish-

American area, had levels of bus miles per week per capita of .35 and .19 respectively. Several neighborhoods representing different clusters were found to have very similar levels of service in terms of bus miles per capita. For example, Burbank, a central-city community, Signal Hill, an early suburban community, and Tarzana, a new suburban community, exhibited similar levels of per capita bus mileage. This is due, in part, to the nature of bus service planning and provision as will be discussed more fully later.

To test whether the differences in service levels in the various lifestyle areas were statistically significant, an analysis of variance was conducted; F tests were performed for the bus miles per capita and for the bus miles per carless household measures. The results of these tests showed no significant differences in service levels between areas at the .05 level of significance, indicating that there was as much variation within the clusters as between them. In addition, difference-of-means t-tests were performed for bus miles per capita and for bus miles per carless household to determine whether there were significant differences in service levels between any two of the lifestyle areas. Again, there were no significant differences found between the groups on the basis of these measures.

The fact that there were no significant differences in bus service among the groups is especially important in light of the finding, detailed in Chapter 3, that travel behavior varied significantly with lifestyle area. Specifically, it was found that public bus ridership was strongly related to lifestyle. There were no significant differences in service among the lifestyle areas, but significant differences in the travel behavior of the elderly did exist among the areas. It appeared, therefore, that bus service levels were not matched to the distinct travel needs of the elderly of the various lifestyles.

Because the bus companies plan their routes and schedules to accommodate the entire population and passengers during peak hours in particular, it is not unexpected that levels of service did not differ significantly among the various elderly lifestyle areas. SCRTD estimated that approximately 16 percent of their riders were over 62 years of age, based on counts on board vehicles and sale of monthly passes to seniors.[4] Estimates of elderly passengers for municipal bus operators ranged from 4 percent of total ridership in Gardena to 26 percent of total ridership in Long Beach. These estimates do not differentiate between riders during peak and off-peak hours, and seniors may comprise a much larger proportion of off-peak riders.

Taxi Service

Taxis represent an important alternative form of transportation for the elderly. They provide highly personalized, door-to-door, demand-responsive service, which is especially important for those communities poorly served by bus. Taxis are, however, considerably more expensive than are buses.

It is unfortunate that lack of information precluded development of a measure of intensity or quality of taxi service comparable to those measures developed for bus service. Information was available for the City of Los Angeles with respect to several service characteristics, including answering time for telephone calls, response time to requests for service, and the percent of "no shows" in response to requests for service. Franchises for taxi operations are regulated by BPUT.[5] Because franchise fees are

4. This information was provided by Steve Parry, Planning Department, Southern California Rapid Transit District, 425 S. Main Street, Los Angeles, California 90013.

5. Yellow Cab Company, the largest taxi company in Los Angeles and the exclusive operator in some areas of the city, declared bankruptcy and ceased operation on November 30, 1976, as this study was being conducted. Since that time, the city has been involved in reestablishing service in those areas formerly covered by Yellow Cab. Franchises have been offered to a number of taxi operators, and Yellow Cab's assets have been purchased by another taxi company. Based on discussions with the staff of BPUT, it was assumed that service at least comparable to that provided by Yellow Cab will be reestablished. Therefore the results of previous tests conducted by the BPUT have been used for comparative purposes.

based in part on performance, the city has an on-going testing process to assess service levels for those taxi companies which they franchise. The franchise fee paid by each taxi company is based on a percentage of gross receipts; the percentage is determined by a base rate plus penalty increments assessed when a taxi operator fails to meet service standards adopted in 1969 by BPUT.

The geographical areas utilized by BPUT in evaluating service levels were considerably larger than those used by SCAG, thus prohibiting analyses of differences between sample communities. Figure 10 is a map showing the franchise areas established by the Board. Table 18 includes information on telephone answering time from surveys conducted by the BPUT staff. The standards require that 90 percent of all telephone calls must be answered within forty-five seconds. Although all taxi companies met the standard, there were differences in the distribution of their answering time. For example, San Pedro Cab (serving area F) and Yellow Cab (serving areas A, B, C, C-1, C-2, and D) answered over 70 percent of their telephone calls within six seconds. On the other hand, Red and White (serving area C-2) and Valley Checker Cab (serving area A) answered only about 50 percent of their calls within the same time interval.

A much more important measure of service—response to orders—is illustrated in Table 19. This table includes information on response time and the percent of "no shows" for each taxi company franchised to operate within the City of Los Angeles.[6] The BPUT standards require that 75 percent of all calls in area A must be responded to within fifteen minutes, 80 percent of all calls in areas B, C, and D must be responded to within fifteen

6. As part of the survey procedure the BPUT staff selects test sites from records of calls received by all taxi companies franchised to operate in a particular area. An individual taxi company is then tested on sites within their franchise area from which they actually received calls, and sites within the area from which no calls were received. In that way the BPUT staff can test for service to all potential clients of a taxi operator, not only those currently utilizing the service.

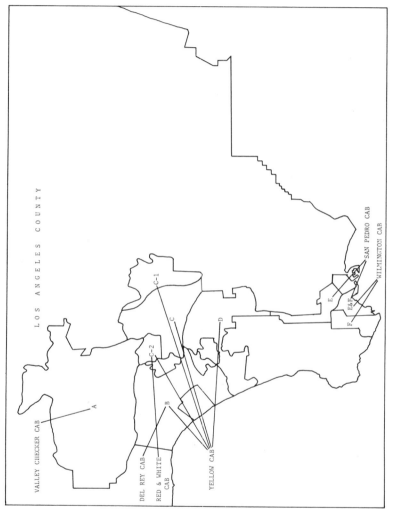

Figure 10. Taxi Franchise Areas: City of Los Angeles

Table 18. Telephone Answering Time of Taxi Operators

Company	Cumulative Percent of Calls Answered (Time in Seconds)								Number of Sites Tested
	6	18	30	42	45	48	60	60+	
Yellow Cab	70.1	86.3	93.3	97.7	98.1	98.4	99.2	100.0	388
Red & White	46.0	81.6	90.8	96.6	97.2	97.7	98.8	100.0	87
Valley Checker	50.0	90.0	96.7	98.3	98.3	98.3	100.0		60
Del Rey Trans.	51.9	82.1	94.3	98.1	98.6	99.1	99.1	100.0	106
San Pedro	73.8	95.2	100.0						42
Wilmington	62.8	97.7	97.7	100.0					43

Source: Public Utilities and Transportation, Staff Report, E1, E18, December 30, 1976.

Table 19. Telephone Order Response Time by Taxi Operators

Company	Service Area	Cumulative Percent of Test Calls Cab Response Time in Minutes							Percent No Shows	Number of Tests
		5	10	15	20	25	30	30+		
Yellow Cab	B,C,D	30.2	63.7	79.4	84.8	87.4	88.1	88.4	12	388
Red & White	C-2	28.7	64.4	75.9	82.8	88.5	90.8	93.1	7	87
Del Rey	B	26.4	61.3	81.1	85.9	90.6			9	106
Valley Checker	A	18.2	47.3	69.1	81.8	87.3	89.1		11	55
San Pedro	F	61.9	87.5	90.5	95.2				5	42
Wilmington	E	65.1	86.0	97.7	100.0				0	43

Source: Public Utilities and Transportation, Staff Report, E1, E18, December 30, 1976.

minutes, and 85 percent of all calls in areas E and F must be responded to within the same time interval.

Considerable variation among reported response and "no show" rates for the different taxi companies was observed. Yellow Cab (serving areas B, C, C-1, C-2, and D) was slightly below the performance standard, sending a cab to 79.4 percent of their calls within fifteen minutes. In area B, however, Yellow Cab operated substantially below standard with only 69.1 percent of their calls resulting in service within fifteen minutes. In addition, complete failure to respond occurred in 22 percent of the test calls. Red and White Cab (serving area C-2) performed below the standard, responding to only 75.9 percent of their calls within fifteen minutes and failing to respond to 7 percent of the test orders. In contrast, San Pedro and Wilmington taxi companies performed above the standards of 85 percent for areas E and F, responding to 90.5 and 97.7 percent of their calls, respectively, within the fifteen-minute standard. In addition, they displayed the lowest "no show" rates, 5 percent and 0 percent, respectively.

The standards adopted and utilized by BPUT are a direct measure of the quality of taxi service existing in a particular franchised area (as compared to indirect measures of service, such as bus miles per square mile or per capita used in the preceding section). In general, it appeared that service was best in areas E and F, which include sample communities from the Spanish-American and black lifestyle areas. Service was average in areas C, C-1, C-2, and D. Area C includes sample communities from the central-city, and financially secure lifestyle areas, area C-1 includes communities from the Spanish-American and early suburban lifestyle areas, area C-2 did not include any sample communities, and area D included sample communities from the Spanish-American and the black lifestyle areas. Service was worst in areas A and B. Area A includes sample communities from the early suburban, new suburban, and central-city lifestyle areas, and area B includes a sample community from the financially secure lifestyle area. It thus appeared that, in terms of taxi operators' responses to requests for service, the Spanish-American and black communities enjoyed the best service, the new suburban and early suburban life-styles experienced the worst service, and the central-city dwellers and financially secure lifestyle areas had moderate service levels.

These findings may be reinforced by the fact that the tests conducted by BPUT do not include testing of walk-up service. Since standards have not been adopted for walk-up service, and since it is not used in determining the franchise fee, there has been no testing of this aspect of taxi service. It might be reasonable to assume that the majority of the elderly telephone for service rather than walking to a taxi station and that they are less affected by the level of walk-up service than by the level of other taxi services. According to the staff of BPUT: ". . . approximately 38 percent of the taxicab business in Los Angeles originates from walk-up locations. This walk-up demand represents about 44 percent of Yellow Cab's business and about 2 percent of Valley Checker Cab's business. Most other companies operate between 1 and 20 percent walk-up business."[7] Walk-up requests for service are much more common in the business and shopping centers than in the suburban residential areas, and, as a consequence, walk-up taxi stations are more prevalent in these areas. It is probable, therefore, that the Spanish-American, black, and central-city lifestyle areas enjoy additional service due to the greater availability of walk-up taxi service.

Variations in prices of service were also examined. Prices for an average three-mile trip, without delays, were computed for each of the sample communities based on the fee structure reported by the taxi operator(s) providing service in that community. Table 20 includes, for each sample community, the taxi company providing service and the price of an average three-mile trip.

The price for a hypothetical three-mile trip was found to vary considerably, from a high of $3.55 in Downey, which

7. City of Los Angeles, Board of Public Utilities and Transportation, *Staff Report* (January 29, 1974).

Table 20. Illustrative Taxi Fares

Community/LSA	Taxi Company	Average Cost for Three Mile Trip
Central-City Dwellers		
Alhambra	San Gabriel Yellow Cab	2.60
Burbank	Red Top-American Eagle	3.20
Glendale	Montrose Cab, Red Top-American Eagle	3.03
West Hollywood	Yellow Cab	3.20
	Average	$3.01
Financially Secure		
Altadena	Red Top-American Eagle	3.20
Century City	Yellow Cab, Red Top-Del Rey	2.75
San Gabriel	Yellow Cab of San Gabriel, San Gabriel Yellow Cab	2.65
	Average	$2.87
New Suburbanites		
Chatsworth	Valley Cab	2.70
Hawaiian Gardens	Diamond Cab	3.20
LaVerne	Paul's Yellow Cab	3.10
Lomita	Yellow Cab of the South Bay	3.20
Tarzana	Valley Cab	2.70
Torrance	Yellow Cab of the South Bay	3.20
	Average	$3.02
Black Community		
Pasadena	Red Top-American Eagle	3.20
South Central Los Angeles	Yellow Cab	3.20
	Average	$3.20
Spanish American		
Boyle Heights	Yellow Cab	3.20
East Los Angeles	Yellow Cab	3.20
San Pedro	San Pedro Cab	3.20
	Average	$3.20
Early Suburbanites		
Downey	Southeast Checker Cab	3.55
El Monte	Yellow Cab of San Gabriel Valley	2.70
Gardena	Yellow Cab of the South Bay	3.20
Glassel Park	Yellow Cab	3.20
North Hollywood	Valley Cab	2.70
Pico Rivera	Cooks Yellow Cab, Stella's Cab	2.70
Signal Hill	Diamond Cab	3.20
	Average	$3.04

is part of the early suburban lifestyle area, to a low of $2.60 in Alhambra, a central-city community. In general, prices were lowest in the financially secure area (an average of $2.87) and highest in the black and Spanish-American lifestyle areas (averages of $3.20). It appeared that the cost of the trip was inversely related to the income of the lifestyle area. The financially secure, composed of highly educated elderly who received high incomes in white collar jobs and who lived in homes or apartments with high values, paid the lowest overall fare for taxi service. In contrast, the black community, composed of elderly with low incomes, residing in homes or apartments with low values, paid the highest fares. Differences in prices within as well as between lifestyle areas were also evident; thus the differences in rates were not statistically significant when tested using analysis of variance.

In general, it appeared that, while taxi service levels were higher in the black and the Spanish-American lifestyle areas, the fares were also higher. While service levels appeared lower in the new suburban and early suburban lifestyle areas, the prices were also slightly lower. Overall, differences in service level among lifestyle areas did not appear to be statistically significant.

Specialized Transportation Services

During the past several years there has been a tremendous increase in the number of specialized transportation programs designed to serve those elderly whose needs are not adequately met by private transportation, public transit, or taxis. The Institute of Public Administration estimated that there were approximately 1,000 special transportation projects serving the elderly and handicapped in the United States in 1974 and that the number had grown to over 3,000 by 1976.[8] These transportation systems are characterized by highly personalized, door-to-door service. Although some agencies do provide transportation for work trips, the major purposes served are to provide access to social services, medical care, shopping, and recreation.

These programs can be funded from a variety of local, state, and federal sources, in addition to private donations. In January 1976, Region IV of the Department of Health, Education, and Welfare released an inventory of federal sources of funding for establishing transportation services or payment for clients' transportation.[9] While the

8. Joseph S. Revis, *Transportation for Older Americans—1976: Progress, Prospects, and Potentials* (Washington, D.C.: Institute for Public Administration, 1976).

9. U.S. Department of Health, Education, and Welfare, *Transportation Authorities in Federal Human Services Programs* (March 1, 1976).

inventory included all sources of funds and was not limited to those sources restricted to elderly or handicapped clients, over sixty different programs which could provide funding for special transportation programs were identified.

The proliferation of specialized providers of transportation service under a variety of funding sources has led to a serious problem of coordination among individual services. According to a report prepared by the Institute of Public Administration in 1976, there were five major barriers to coordination of transportation programs. The most common problems related to funding and included lack of continuity, restrictions on the agency's use of funds, insufficient funding, or the inability to raise required local matching funds. A second problem area included operating difficulties: for example, conflicts with franchised operators such as taxis, scheduling conflicts, and insurance complications. Another barrier consisted of restrictions in client eligibility and incompatibility, arising because certain funding sources were restricted to use by a particular client group, thus prohibiting different types of passengers from sharing rides. Planning and organizational issues constituted a fourth obstacle, and the fifth involved conflicting state and federal guidelines and difficulties in interpreting these at the local level.

In order to assess the level and variety of specialized services available to the elderly in Los Angeles County— and to determine whether these coordination problems are serious in Los Angeles—providers were surveyed by telephone. Approximately 250 potential providers of transportation were identified and contacted. Of these, forty-nine agencies directly provided transportation for the elderly in one or more of the selected sample communities. Eight of the forty-nine agencies served the entire county and the remaining forty-one served smaller areas, providing almost 630,000 trips for the elderly during the previous year. Programs ranged from a volunteer organization with one car carrying thirty elderly passengers per year, to a full-time transportation system operating eight vans and two buses which provided transportation for

118,000 passengers per year, 50 percent of whom were elderly. Some agencies carried passengers for a single trip purpose, such as for medical care or nutrition programs, while others were multipurpose carriers. Although passengers were not charged for most trips, one consistent exception was for medical trips, the charge for which was usually included as part of the patient's medical bill. All organizations provided door-to-door travel, and only two operated on fixed routes. Eighteen of the programs had at least one vehicle that was accessible to wheelchair passengers. The various organizations had different arrangements for responding. Almost all required reservations at least one day in advance, although several indicated a willingness to respond to emergency calls. Only one or two of the projects had the capability to act as dial-a-ride systems, responding to calls within fifteen minutes to one hour of the request.

Twenty-four of the programs received funds under either Title III or Title VII of the Older Americans Act; some relied solely on these funds plus the 10 percent local match required under this program. Others generated larger local matches than required or combined their financing under the Older Americans Act with other Federal programs or with private donations of equipment, money, and time. Some companies were financed entirely through fares, either collected per ride or attached to medical bills.

There was little coordination in the provision of service either among specialized service operators or between those operators and bus or taxi operators. Service areas of the agencies typically overlapped, with some providing transportation for only a single purpose and others providing service to only one group of clients. Such arrangements appeared to place undue hardship on many passengers. For example, a particular individual might in one day need to visit a medical clinic, do some shopping, stop at the bank, and visit a senior citizens' center or a nutrition site. In order to complete all of these trips, the passenger might have been required to utilize the services of three or more different providers, each of which served only trips originating or ending at the person's home! For each service, the passenger would have been required to make reservations anywhere from one day to two weeks in advance.

Table 21 summarizes all public transportation services available to the elderly in the sample communities. There were numerous organizations providing transportation for the elderly in the black, Spanish-American, and early suburban areas, while few agencies provided service in the new suburban communities. The probable reason for this distribution of service is the common assumption that the elderly residing in the black, Spanish-American, and early suburban areas have a greater need for services. Central-city dwellers, however, experienced a surprisingly low level of specialized service. Members of the central-city, black, and Spanish-American lifestyle areas make the fewest trips. They have less access to private automobiles and thus place greater reliance on public modes of transportation.

Because the agencies varied so widely in terms of the number of trips served, a comparison was attempted between the number of elderly passengers served and the elderly population of the service area. The available data were very limited, and this problem was compounded by the fact that some projects provided transportation to only a portion of a SCAG region. It therefore may be misleading to compare the number of trips served to the elderly population for the entire SCAG region. Other agencies served several SCAG regions encompassing several of the lifestyle areas defined in this study, making it impossible to divide the total number of trips into those provided in one SCAG region or another. In spite of these problems, the estimates presented in Table 22 are useful to illustrate not only the substantial differences in levels of service in the different lifestyle areas, but the overall low level of specialized service. While early suburbanites made the largest number of trips employing specialized service, they made only 5.42 trips per capita per year. It should be

Table 21. Summary of Transportation Services Available to the Elderly

LSA/Community	Total Population	Elderly Population	Trips Per Day	Carless Dwelling Units	Bus Miles Per Week Per Square Mile	Bus Miles Per Week Per Capita Total Population	Bus Miles Per Week Per Capita Elderly Population	Percent of SCAG Standard	Bus Miles Per Week Per Carless Dwelling Unit	Taxi Cost Three Mile Trip	Number of Specialized Transportation Operators	Number of Trips Served
Central-City Dwellers												
Alhambra	62,172	10,174		3,626	2,275	.28	1.70	228	4.78	2.60	1	5,400
Burbank	84,605	9,277		3,462	1,754	.28	2.59	240	6.94	3.20	1	33,600
Glendale	131,307	21,574		8,301	924	.12	.75	97	1.96	3.20	1	9,000
West Hollywood	108,249	22,654		17,680	7,566	.55	2.63	420	3.36	3.20	1	1,800
AVERAGE			7.05		3,130	.31	1.92	246	4.26	3.01		
Financially Secure												
Altadena	42,338	4,958		1,246	825	.21	1.82	470	7.25	3.20	2	31,000
Century City	173,586	20,810		16,290	2,701	.21	1.74	162	2.22	2.75	2	6,800
San Gabriel	30,015	4,033		1,121	1,756	.24	1.85	202	6.44	2.65	1	5,400
AVERAGE			8.11		1,760	.22	1.80	180	5.30	2.87		
New Suburbanites												
Chatsworth	89,124	3,322		611	1,633	.31	8.34	272	45.35	2.70	0	0
Hawaiian Gardens	10,362	435		204	700	.06	1.53	45	3.26	3.20	0	0
La Verne	10,682	1,705		427	365	.16	1.00	183	3.92	3.10	1	2,400
Lomita	19,694	2,207		727	873	.08	.71	62	2.16	3.20	2	1,030
Tarzana	105,182	3,024		1,471	1,563	.28	9.90	261	20.35	2.70	1	13,880
Torrance	135,632	3,286		1,885	1,249	.15	3.77	111	10.57	3.20	1	1,000
AVERAGE			6.38		1,064	.17	4.21	156	14.27	3.02		
Black Community												
Pasadena	112,956	19,199		8,773	1,781	.34	2.03	297	4.44	3.20	3	78,550
South Central Los Angeles	143,694	11,408		15,349	3,720	.27	3.46	207	2.57	3.20	7	82,700
AVERAGE			5.04		2,750	.31	2.75	252	3.51	3.20		
Spanish American												
Boyle Heights	219,349	18,958		39,480	4,485	.35	4.07	269	1.95	3.20	5	98,500
East Los Angeles	423,937	51,572		37,412	3,199	.30	.72	253	3.63	3.20	4	41,880
San Pedro	110,228	9,233		6,147	1,279	.19	2.23	147	3.35	3.20	3	13,030
AVERAGE			5.00		2,987	.28	2.34	223	2.98	3.20		
Early Suburbanites												
Downey	88,503	5,564		1,650	1,099	.16	2.52	126	8.50	3.55	2	72,200
El Monte	69,031	5,038		2,830	1,613	.22	2.99	185	5.33	2.70	2	75,080
Gardena	42,966	3,374		1,131	1,954	.23	2.89	173	8.62	3.20	5	61,500
Glassel Park	219,349	18,958		39,480	4,485	.35	4.07	269	1.95	3.20	5	98,500
North Hollywood	165,975	15,677		5,744	1,626	.21	2.23	164	6.10	2.70	3	39,800
Pico Rivera	76,190	1,549		1,340	1,018	.14	2.60	117	7.76	2.70	1	59,000
Signal Hill	5,273	774		262	1,160	.28	1.92	247	5.68	3.20	0	0
AVERAGE			7.42		1,822	.23	2.75	183	6.23	3.04		

**Table 22. Estimated Specialized Transportation Service Trips
Served by Lifestyle Area**

Lifestyle Area	Elderly Population	Trips Served	Trips Per Capita
Central City Dwellers	63,679	49,800	0.78
Financially Secure	29,670	43,200	1.46
New Suburbanites	15,979	17,310	1.08
Black Community	30,607	161,250	5.27
Spanish American	79,763	153,410	1.92
Early Suburbanites	53,376	289,080	5.42

noted that these figures represent measures of utilization
and may not adequately represent need. More effective
measures for evaluation of specialized services might include trips served in relation to the elderly who did not
own cars, who had low incomes or who were disabled.

Although these figures are rough estimates only, they
indicate striking differences among the lifestyle areas. The
early suburbanites made 5.42 trips per capita, almost
seven times the rate for the central-city dwellers. The black
community utilized these services about as often as the
early suburbanites (5.27 trips per capita); Spanish-
Americans made considerably fewer trips (1.92), followed
by the financially secure (1.46), the new suburbanites
(1.08), and central city dwellers (.78).

Because specialized services are created in response to
the perceived special needs of particular populations, it is
not surprising that levels of service are not uniform
throughout the county. The fact that most of these agencies are fairly new and may not have reached all eligible
passengers also contributes to a disparity in service levels.
Service levels, however, did not appear to meet needs.
Spanish-American and central-city dwellers made relatively low use of specialized service (1.92 and .78 trips per
capita per year, respectively) and at the same time relied
heavily on public transit. Members of the Spanish-
American lifestyle group made 21 percent of their trips by
public transit, while central-city dwellers made 13 percent.
Early suburbanites made only 2.4 percent of their trips by
public transit, yet their estimated rate of specialized trips
per capita was over seven times as high as that of central-
city dwellers.

Summary and Conclusions

The investigation revealed that there is great variation in the quantity and quality of transportation service currently available to the elderly in the sample communities representing the different lifestyle areas. Levels of bus service, measured in terms of bus miles per square mile, bus miles per capita, and bus miles per dwelling unit without cars, were found to be highest overall in the black community and the central-city area and lowest in the financially secure and new suburban areas; the early suburban and Spanish-American lifestyle areas had moderate levels of service. Taxi service, measured in terms of price and response to requests for service, was found to be best in the Spanish-American and black communities. These lifestyle areas also experienced uniformly high taxi prices, however. The financially secure and new suburban lifestyle areas experienced lower levels of service, but it was available at lower cost. Moderate levels of service, at moderate prices, existed in the early suburban and central-city lifestyle areas.

As with bus and taxi service, the black community also enjoyed a high level of specialized service, measured by trips served per capita for the elderly population. Members of the Spanish-American lifestyle area, however, made comparatively little use of specialized systems. The early suburbanites utilized specialized service more often than did any other lifestyle area. Low usage was found in the financially secure and new suburban lifestyle areas, with the lowest found in the central-city lifestyle area.

Although there were variations in levels of service provided among lifestyle areas, there was often more variation within than between them. Statistical tests indicated that there were no significant differences in levels of service provided by lifestyle area. This is especially important in light of the finding in Chapter 3 that significant differences in travel patterns existed between lifestyle areas. It thus appears that there is no current effort to match transportation service with the different needs of the elderly in each lifestyle area. Members of the Spanish-American community, for example, had very low incomes and very few owned automobiles or possessed drivers' licenses. Yet they were served by fewer bus miles per week of transit service than most others, and, while taxi service there was of high quality, the average cost was high—a certain barrier to this low-income group. Specialized transit services can, to some extent, provide a lower-cost substitute for the door-to-door service provided by taxis. It is interesting to note, therefore, that Spanish-Americans made far less use of specialized transit service than did members of early suburban communities, even though the latter have much higher access to automobiles, somewhat lower taxi fares, and better bus service in general.

It is significant that the diverse transportation needs among the elderly of various lifestyles is not mirrored by the range of currently available services. The final chapter of this book will address this theme again, and will suggest better policy options to match service with lifestyles. Before making these policy recommendations, however, the next several chapters will examine the probable stability of lifestyles and travel patterns among the elderly over time and forecast the elderly population and number of trips they will make in Los Angeles through the turn of the twenty-first century.

Chapter 5
The Changing Social Setting of the Elderly

A t the beginning of this book it was argued that the elderly are changing rapidly and that their transportation needs in the year 2000 might be even more diverse than they are in the 1970s. While the analysis conducted in the last three chapters has established the diverse living patterns and wide range of travel patterns among the elderly, the process of social change impacting the elderly over time has received little attention. In order to set the scene for specific forecasts of the living patterns and travel needs of the elderly of the future it is necessary first to analyze the process by which demographic and social changes have been occurring over time among the elderly and among currently middle-aged people—the elderly of the next two decades.

When studying problems and trends among the elderly, social scientists frequently infer that situations observed at one time were the result of social processes which operated continuously over time. For example, the observation that senior citizens resided at higher densities than did younger persons in a single census year often gives rise to the conclusion that elderly persons tend to give up their homes and move to locations of higher density as they age and their children move away. The observation that fewer elderly persons possess drivers' licenses than do younger groups is similarly interpreted to mean that many give up driving as they age because of physical infirmities or fear of driving. While such observations are frequently made as part of the "conventional wisdom" about aging, it is clearly inappropriate to reach such conclusions about aging—a time dependent process—on the basis of observations taken at only one or two periods in time. Indeed, alternate explanations for such phenomena are equally plausible. The elderly might today be found living in neighborhoods of higher densities than younger groups without having moved to these neighborhoods as they aged. Instead, those who are now elderly might have acquired houses many years ago when all residential neighborhoods were characterized by higher densities than are common in today's suburban areas. These persons might have remained in their homes and grown old with their neighborhoods. The higher densities might, then, represent choices made many years ago rather than reflecting the effects of aging. Similarly, many of our senior citizens may have grown up before the automobile was as popular as it is today and, consequently, might never have learned to drive. Expectations are often formulated for the elderly of the future on the basis of potentially erroneous assumptions. Elderly groups of the future are expected to give up suburban residences and move to inner-city locations. Similarly, all persons are expected to give up driving as they age. If the alternate explanations of patterns among today's elderly offered above are as plausible as the more common explanations, it might be equally expected that the next generation of senior citizens will reside in areas of lower density and will include many more drivers. The elderly of the future might reflect life-style choices made in the 1940s and 1950s, just as today's elderly reflect choices made in the 1920s and 1930s.

In order to understand better the processes which result in the observed social and demographic patterns among the elderly, it is necessary to conduct longitudinal analyses of those who are now elderly. Three tasks were performed in order to explore the stability of social relationships and lifestyles among the elderly over time. The first part of the longitudinal analysis was an examination of the residential locations of the elderly in Los Angeles County from 1940 through 1970. This analysis was intended to discover the extent to which the elderly have been concentrating or dispersing within the metropolitan area and to place a comparison of the elderly with the middle-aged into proper evolutionary perspective. Next, the process of factor and cluster analysis already performed on data describing the elderly from the 1970 census was repeated using information describing those who were middle-aged. This analysis was done in order to determine whether lifestyles and locational patterns of the middle-aged population were similar to those found among the elderly. Similarities would indicate stability over time in the lifestyles of the elderly and would imply that plans to accommodate the diverse travel patterns of today's elderly would remain valid over time. The final task was an analysis of certain social and economic conditions over time, which might have impacted the current locational patterns of the elderly and which might continue to influence their locational trends and lifestyles during the remainder of this century. In combination, these tasks were intended to yield greater understanding of the factors which will determine the social settings in which the elderly will be living in the future. Together, they provide a foundation for the forecasts of elderly population, locational patterns, and travel which will be presented in the next two chapters.

Analytical Framework for the Longitudinal Analysis

Because the analysis which follows involves the study of a variety of populations in several census years, it is useful at this point to introduce a few terms which will allow more systematic discussion and consistent terminology throughout this chapter.

A *cohort* is composed of individuals who were born within the same time interval. An *age group* is composed of individuals within some age range. Those who populate an age group at a given time are members of the same cohort. At a later time, however, a younger cohort occupies the age group. Whereas age-group analysis emphasizes successive groups of similar age, cohort analysis focuses on a single group over successive time periods. Figure 11 provides an illustration of the relationship among cohorts, age groups, and periods of time. The figure shows, for example, that those individuals aged 25 to 34 in the 1940 census were members of a single cohort (cohort 6 in the figure) which appeared in the 1950 census as those aged 35 to 44. The same cohort can be traced diagonally across the figure and appears in the most recent census as those aged 55 to 64. In the earlier chapters of this study, analysis focused exclusively upon those who were 65 years of age and older in the 1970 census. Exclusive attention has thus been given to cohorts 4 and 5 in the single time period of 1970. In this chapter, these cohorts will be traced back through 1940, when they were much younger. Cohorts 6 and 7 will also be studied; these include persons who were 45 to 64 years old in 1970 and who will be entering old age between now and the turn of the century. The final task will include an analysis of all cells in the matrix.

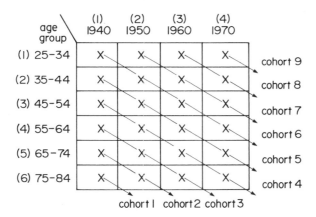

Figure 11. Illustration of Longitudinal Study

History of the Elderly's Residential Location

In order to arrive at an understanding of the current locational patterns of the elderly, densities per acre of those aged 65 to 74 in each of the last four census years were mapped using the SYMAP computer program. To enable comparison of locational trends between cohorts, similar maps were prepared for the cohorts aged 65 to 74 and 75 to 84 in 1970, at ten-year intervals in the aging process. A map was thus prepared for each cell in Figure 12, which is marked with an "X."

Locations on the maps (see Figures 13 through 28) were expressed in terms of two coordinates: one measured vertically from the top map border, the second measured horizontally from the left border. Grid coordinates were

Year Age Group	1940	1950	1960	1970
35-44				
45-54				
55-64				
65-74	X →	→ X →	→ X →	→ X
75-84				

Age Group Analysis

Year Age Group	1940	1950	1960	1970	
35-44	X ↘				
45-54	X ↘	↘ X ↘			
55-64		↘ X ↘	↘ X ↘		
65-74			↘ X ↘	↘ X	Cohort 5
75-84				↘ X	Cohort 4

Cohort Analysis

Figure 12. Age Groups and Cohorts Used in Historical Study of Population Density

assigned to each tract centroid and to boundary points to form outline maps. Values of the variables to be mapped were then assigned to each tract centroid. The computer package combined this information in order to assign each character location on the output map the value of the data point nearest to it. Separate base maps were prepared from census tract maps for 1940, 1950, 1960, and 1970. In the maps presented here, an equal number of tracts was represented by each value symbol. The darkest character thus means that the nearest tract falls within the highest quintile on the variable mapped.

The practice of proximal mapping creates some difficulties which should be taken into consideration when interpreting the maps. Census tracts are established by the Bureau of the Census to contain certain numbers of inhabitants; geographical size of tracts varies considerably. The northern sections of the map and the western peninsula are sparsely inhabited making the tract sizes extremely large. Tract centroids are, therefore, widely separated. If one area has a high value on some variable, a disproportionate area of the county may appear to have that value. As a general rule, the maps are more accurate toward the center, because tract centroids are more densely distributed there.

Cohort 4, the older of the two cohorts, included those aged 75 to 84 years in 1970. The densities per acre at which cohort members resided are shown in Figures 13, 14, 15, and 16 for 1940, 1950, 1960, and 1970, respectively. In 1940, when the cohort was entering middle age, the concentrations of highest density were in the central-city and Long Beach areas, as well as areas peripheral to them. The major portion of the county was only thinly inhabited by members of the 75-84 age group. In 1950 this basic pattern intensified, as more cohort members settled around the core areas in late middle age. By 1960, however, the trend had reversed. A pronounced dispersal pattern evolved as the cohort aged. An inner suburban ring of elderly residents became evident and the Wilshire corridor developed rapidly. Even more striking was an emerging migration to

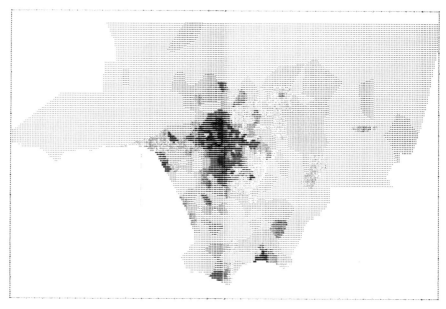

Figure 13. Cohort 4 (Aged 45–54)
Population Density, 1940

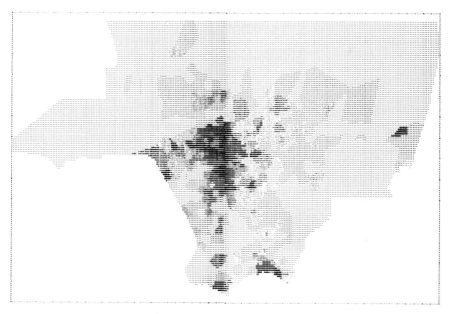

Figure 14. Cohort 4 (Aged 55–64)
Population Density, 1950

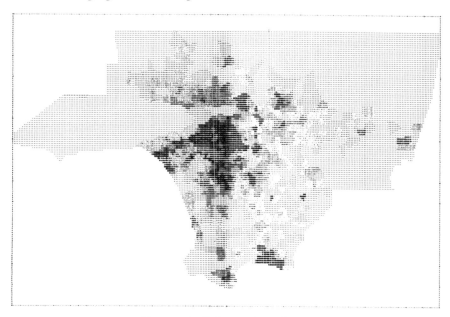

Figure 15. Cohort 4 (Aged 65–74)
Population Density, 1960

Figure 16. Cohort 4 (Aged 75–84)
Population Density, 1970

the suburbs, notably the San Fernando Valley. While densities in the central-city area had decreased, all three 1940 core areas were still densely inhabited by the cohort when it had reached advanced age.

Density maps for the younger group (cohort 5) for the four census years are shown in Figures 17 through 20. The same general trends are observable; an initial concentration around three major settlement areas was followed by wide dispersal as the cohort aged.

It should be noted that, although very similar trends characterized both cohorts, they were occupying different age groups in a given census year. A comparison of the two map series by year, regardless of age group, showed nearly identical areas of concentration. Density maps of the total population were, therefore, prepared as a basis for comparison. These maps are shown in Figures 21 through 24 for 1940 through 1970. A comparable dispersal pattern was evident, but the areas in which new concentrations appeared were different from those of either elderly cohort. The most obvious example is the definitely lower values of density found in the Wilshire corridor and San Fernando Valley for the general population by 1970. The most likely explanation for this divergence in settlement patterns is that, in about 1960, older cohorts purchased suburban homes in greater numbers than did their successors in subsequent years.

Similar maps (Figures 25 through 28) were examined for the age group 65 to 74 for each of the four census years. This map series shows quite clearly that over time the elderly population, like the total population, has been decentralizing within the metropolitan area. It is apparent that this is due, in part, to decentralization within each cohort over time, in addition to the fact that each cohort entering retirement age is more decentralized than the one which preceded it.

In combination, study of the map series gives rise to a few very important generalizations. In the last forty years, there has been a clear and consistent overall trend toward suburbanization in Los Angeles County. Early elderly con-

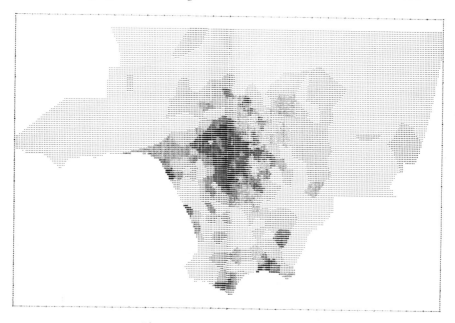

Figure 17. Cohort 5 (Aged 35–44)
Population Density, 1940

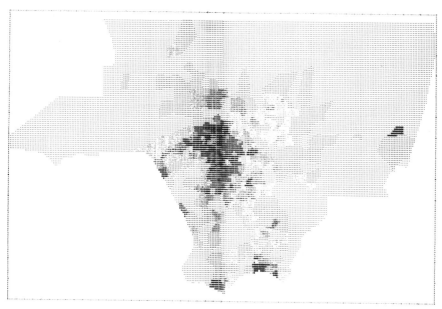

Figure 18. Cohort 5 (Aged 45–54)
Population Density, 1950

Figure 19. Cohort 5 (Aged 55–64)
Population Density, 1960

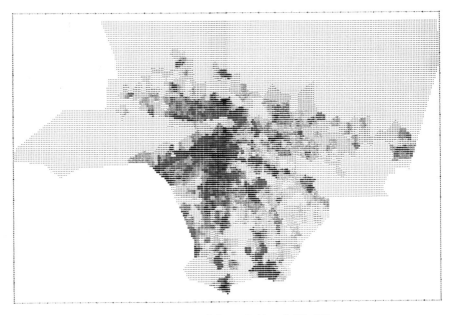

Figure 20. Cohort 5 (Aged 65–74)
Population Density, 1970

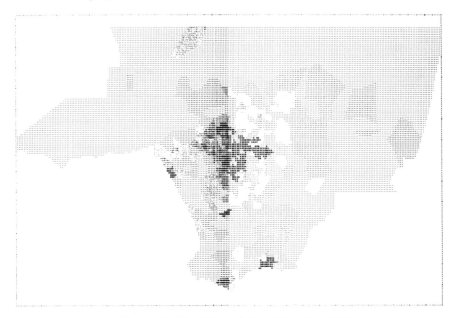

Figure 21. Total Population Density, 1940

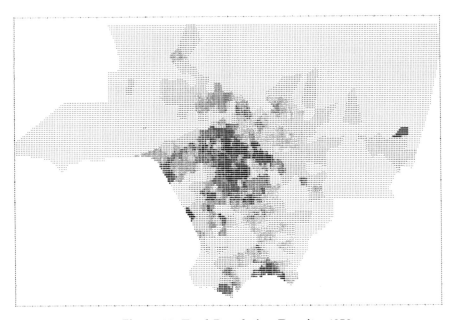

Figure 22. Total Population Density, 1950

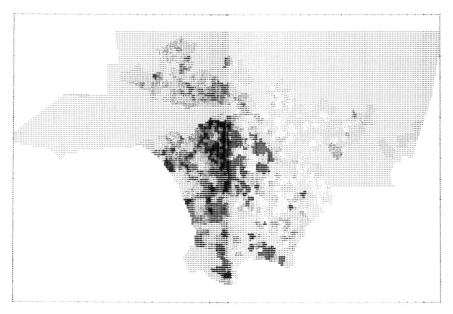

Figure 23. Total Population Density, 1960

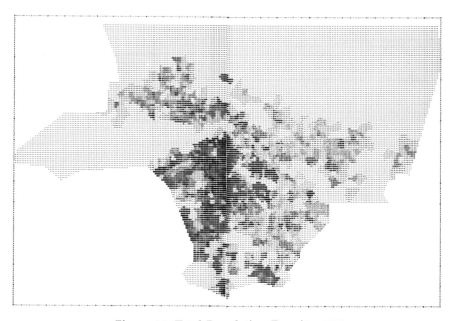

Figure 24. Total Population Density, 1970

Figure 25. Age Group 65–74
Population Density, 1940

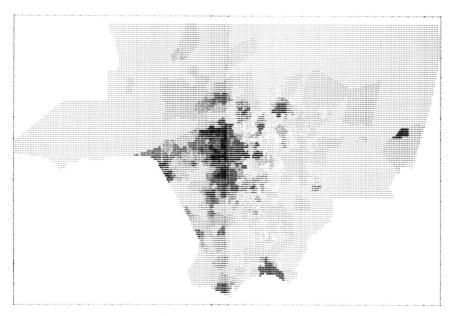

Figure 26. Age Group 65–74
Population Density, 1950

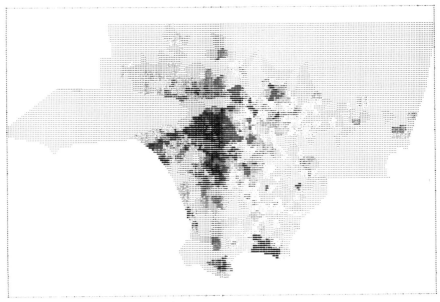

Figure 27. Age Group 65–74
Population Density, 1960

Figure 28. Age Group 65–74
Population Density, 1970

centrations were found in three urban core areas—the central cities of Los Angeles, Long Beach, and Santa Monica. Since 1960 there has been a marked trend toward decentralization among the elderly. Although there has been a similar trend among the general population, the specific areas where the elderly are concentrated differ somewhat from those of the overall population. Of particular interest in this respect is the settlement pattern in the San Fernando Valley.

Dimensions and Areas of Lifestyle of the Middle-Aged Population

The preceding analysis of residential density patterns among the elderly over time was conducted at an aggregate level. While it has been shown that the elderly include many different lifestyle groups, the differences among these groups in location and density were not analyzed in the preceding section of this chapter. If the seven lifestyles were to serve as a useful foundation for forecasting the residential and travel patterns of the elderly in the future, it was necessary to estimate the relative stability of these lifestyles over time. For this reason, the analysis described in Chapter 2 was repeated on another set of data, which consisted of the characteristics of the population presently considered middle-aged (ages 45 to 64). Lifestyle patterns of the middle-aged were then compared with those of the elderly.

Results of Factor Analysis

This study, like that of the elderly population, utilized 1970 census and compatible administrative data to identify and describe dimensions and locate spatial patterns of lifestyle. Forty-six variables in common with the data on the elderly population were factored. Following the procedure used in the factor analysis of the elderly population, seven factors having eigenvalues of 1.0 or greater were selected for orthogonal rotation and description. These factors, prior to rotation, explained 67.7 percent of the variation.

Table 23 shows the results of the factor analysis of

socioeconomic and demographic variables describing the
middle-aged population, aged 45 through 64. The variable
names are mnemonics which are identical to those used
in the analysis of the elderly population in Chapter 2, and
complete definitions of the variables are given in Table 5.
Only the first forty-six of the variables included in Table 5
were used in the case of the middle-aged population. The
other five variables which had been used for the elderly
were not relevant to the middle-aged population, because
they dealt with proportions of the population who were
veterans of World War I, who were receiving social security benefits, and similar information.

Table 23 shows the factor loadings which were at least
.250 and is identical in format to Table 6, which showed
the results of the factor analysis of data describing the
elderly. Between the two age groups, structure, but not
order, of factors was considerably similar. Spatial patterns
on most factors, especially those reflecting socioeconomics, service employment, and density/centrality
were also found to be similar to those of the elderly
population.

Descriptions of the dimensions follow in a comparative
format, with similarities and differences between the two
age groups forming the major focus.

Lifestyle Dimension I: Financial Security.   Factor I of the
middle-aged population contained most variables normally associated with socioeconomics and was strongly
similar to the financial-security factor of the older age
group. This dimension consisted of variables related to the
elements of lifestyle: educational attainment, occupational
status, physical living arrangements, income, ethnicity,
and automobile ownership. Areas in which this dimension
of lifestyle was prominent were those in which educational attainment and full-time employment in white-
collar occupations were high. Incomes, housing values,
and monthly rental rates were moderate to high. Housing
tended to be in recently built structures containing multiple dwelling units.

Lifestyle Dimension II: Density/Centrality.   This dimen-

Table 23. Factor Loadings of at Least .250 for the 45–64 Age Group—1970 Analysis

No.*	Abbreviation	Financial Security — I	Density/ Centrality — II	Unemployment — III	Long-term Residence — IV	Good Health — V	Service Employment — VI	Spanish American — VII
14	EDCOLL	.908						
31	OCCBC	-.896						
33	OCCWC	.888					-.278	
45	VLGT25	.848						
20	IGT15K	.753	-.507					
44	VL1520	-.735						
35	POP	.695			.406			.276
39	RTGT150	.676	-.277					
46	WHITEC	.664			.395			.291
38	RT6099	-.579	.324				.354	
43	VLLT15	-.577		.417			.378	
12	EDLT5	-.524		.593				
2	AUTOF2	.506	-.670	-.251				
32	OCCSER	-.441	.261				.707	
19	17K15K	.424		-.627				
42	UNITS3	.410	.679	-.252				
18	ILT3K	-.392	.547	.457			.359	
3	AUTOPO	-.387	.572	.407				
15	EMPL52	.382		-.546				
41	UNITS1	-.380	-.673					
40	SPANC	.352			.392			
1	AUTOFO	-.336	.578	.454				
27	NOTEMP	-.284		.626				.325
10	CWHITE	.272					-.880	
7	B6570	.265			-.659			
26	NEGROC	.250		.426			.251	
36	PRMIND		.879					
34	OWNOCC		-.827					
17	HUSWFE		-.817				-.258	
30	06570		.768		-.320			
28	01949		-.687		.541			
11	DENPOP		.607		.311	.266		
5	B1949		.431	.367	.548			
25	MORTAL		.404			-.345		
21	MARRY		-.388			-.285		.750
4	AUTOP2		-.337			-.470		
29	06064		.323		-.261	.266		
22	MENTAL		.321			-.731		
13	ED912			-.780				
37	RTLT60			.602				
6	B6064				-.723			
23	MOBLE				-.298			
24	MORBID					-.703		
16	FEMALE					.575		
8	CNEGRO						.910	
9	CSPAN							.769
% Variation explained by factor		19.37	15.49	9.22	6.29	5.12	7.72	4.07

* Variable numbers correspond with those used in Tables 5 and 6.

sion reflected the following elements of lifestyle: income, physical living arrangements, automobile ownership, educational attainment, and ethnicity. It was characterized by older units with multiple dwellings which had low rents and were in areas with high density surrounding the larger business districts of the county. Low levels of income, a high occurrence of individuals living alone, and employment in service occupations were also characteristic of the dimension. The death rate and visitation rate to mental health facilities were relatively high. There was a marked similarity between the factor loadings and spatial distribution of factor scores and the density/centrality factor of the elderly. As with the older group, this dimension of lifestyle suggested that its members lived where they did because of poor finances and mobility, usually in dense inner-city areas consisting of older and less expensive apartments. Also consistently present in both factors were the elements of social and physical living arrangements and automobile ownership, suggesting circumstances and ranges of options similar to those of the elderly.

Lifestyle Dimension III: Unemployment.   The third factor for the middle-aged group had no counterpart in the elderly factoring. It consisted of variables reflective of the physical living arrangements, educational attainment, automobile ownership, income, occupational status, and ethnic elements of lifestyle. Areas having high scores on this factor were characterized by high unemployment and low educational attainment. It is not surprising that unemployment appeared uniquely among the middle-aged, since current work patterns are less a determinant of lifestyle among senior citizens in America.

Lifestyle Dimension IV: Long-Term Residence.   This factor was descriptive of populations which tended to be ethnically mixed and which had resided for many years in their present location. These areas tended to be rather densely settled and were populated by many in this middle-aged group. In terms of both variables loading on this factor and geographic distribution of the factor scores, this dimension was quite similar to the long-term residence dimension which had emerged in the analysis of the elderly population.

Lifestyle Dimension V: Good Health. This dimension of lifestyle focused upon health variables but also contained variables reflecting density and social living arrangements, automobile ownership, and physical living arrangements. Areas having high scores on this factor were those having low rates of morbidity, mortality, and visitation to mental health facilities. Denser, newer communities in which the middle-aged population resided in family settings rather than alone had higher loadings on this factor. It appeared that this factor was the "mirror image" of the poor health factor among the elderly population, containing several similar variables but with their signs reversed.

Lifestyle Dimension VI: Service Employment. Factor VI consisted of occupational status, ethnicity, physical and social living arrangements, and income. The pattern of this factor was heavily influenced by ethnicity and occupation and suggested a common dimension of lifestyle in which employment in service occupations, resulting in low income levels and attendant housing with low rental and low value, was common. Strong similarities were found between this lifestyle dimension and the service-employment factor of the older age group.

Lifestyle Dimension VII: Spanish-American Ethnicity. The final factor describing the middle-aged group related to the ethnic and social living arrangements of the group and their employment status. High scores on this dimension were characteristic of areas which had a large Spanish-American population, a large proportion of which was middle-aged. Most of the middle-aged in areas having high scores of this factor were married, and unemployment among them tended to be high. While this factor was similar in some respects to the Spanish-American ethnicity factor among the elderly, it also overlapped with several other factors among the elderly.

Results of Cluster Analysis

Lifestyle areas of the middle-aged, consisting of tracts having substantially similar characteristics, were identified using the K-Means clustering procedure in the same manner that areas of the elderly population were identified. The results of the two clustering problems were compared by matching mean factor scores of the middle-aged areas to those of the elderly areas. Since not all factors, and hence not all factor scores, had counterparts in the two factoring problems, this matching procedure was less straightforward than that used in comparing factors. The highest mean factor scores on paired factors were matched and the other associated scores examined for similarity. This procedure continued until all clusters having counterparts were matched. The remaining clusters without counterparts were then compared on the basis of the best match of mean factor scores.

The results of the clustering showed great similarity between the lifestyle areas of the middle-aged population and the elderly. There was, in fact, even greater similarity in the results of the clustering procedure than there had been in the results of the factor analysis. Computer drawn maps were produced showing the locations of the middle-aged lifestyle groups, just as those included in Chapter 2 showed the locations of the elderly lifestyle groups. With the following descriptions of the middle-aged lifestyle groups, however, maps are presented which facilitate the comparison of the lifestyle groupings among the two age groups. These maps are a composite of the results of the clustering for the two age groups and show, for each lifestyle, areas of the county which contained the members of one, the other, or both age groups.

Lifestyle Group 1: The Central-City Dwellers. The central-city lifestyle group was located primarily in the urban centers of Los Angeles, Long Beach, Santa Monica, and the eastern portion of the San Fernando Valley. This area had an average density of about seven persons per gross acre, or about twice the county average. The group was predominantly white and contained 18.5 percent of the total population of the county. About one and a quarter million persons, of whom 325,000 were between the ages of 45 and 64, resided in this area. Ninety percent of the total population and 95 percent of the middle-aged population of the area were white. Sixty-eight percent of the units occupied by the cohort were rented, compared to about 38 percent county-wide. About one in five middle-aged households—also over twice the county average—resided in apartments. Sixty percent of the middle-aged, or about 120,000 persons, had moved to their present residences within the last five years. Only 6.5 percent had resided at the same location for over twenty years. Older structures were common locations for the residences of the middle-aged, with over one-third having been built prior to 1940. As Figure 29 shows, correspondence for this lifestyle existed between these two age groups in the Wilshire corridor, Santa Monica, Long Beach, Pasadena, and Los Angeles central business districts. However, many areas were unique to a particular cohort. The middle-aged were

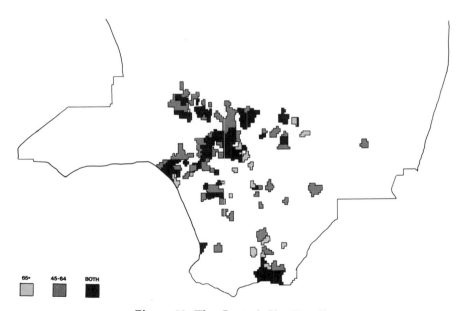

Figure 29. The Central-City Dwellers

more dispersed, especially in the San Fernando and San Gabriel Valleys, in Culver City, and in the southeast county areas. These comparisons and data suggested a similarity of circumstances and locations among the two age groups. Both groups had only recently moved to their present locations and both had made similar housing choices. Also, both groups had high percentages of persons who resided alone and were without cars. Spatially, however, the middle-aged persons characterized by this lifestyle pattern tended to be more dispersed.

Lifestyle Group 2: The Financially Secure. The relatively affluent middle-aged were generally found in an area extending across the north central portion of the county adjacent to the Santa Monica and San Gabriel mountains. This area is shown in Figure 30. Tracts included in this group scored high on the financial security dimension and negatively on the density/centrality dimension. This pattern of scores was associated with areas in which homes of high value, high monthly rents, high educational attainment, and employment in white-collar occupations were

Figure 30. The Financially Secure

common. High rates of car ownership were also common in these areas. About 10 percent of the county population—690,000 persons—resided in this lifestyle area. Ninety-five percent of the total population of this area and about 98 percent of its middle-aged were white. Three persons in ten in this group were middle-aged. Home ownership among the middle-aged was high, with about three-quarters of all residences being privately owned. On a county-wide basis, by comparison, about one-half of all residences occupied by the middle-aged were owned. Ninety percent—nearly double the county average—of the privately owned homes were valued greater than $25,000. Among those middle-aged who rented, high monthly rents were common, with over one-half paying more than $150 per month. County-wide, only about one in five middle-aged renters paid such rents. This middle-aged group also had a high level of educational attainment. About one-half had obtained a college education, and about six of every ten reported being in white-collar occupations. Spatially, as demonstrated in Figure 30, these lifestyle groups of the elderly and middle-aged populations showed considerable correspondence, especially in the areas south of the Santa Monica and San Gabriel mountains, Palos Verdes Peninsula, and Marina del Rey areas. There were few dispersed areas unique to either group. Rather, there were areas unique to age groups at or near the periphery of the major shared areas. This pattern suggested that these age groups were distinguished from other lifestyle groups on the basis of income and socioeconomic status rather than age.

Lifestyle Group 3: The Institutionalized.   Lifestyle group 3 of the middle-aged, like group 3 of the elderly population, was unique. It was composed of fourteen scattered tracts containing state mental hospitals, Veterans Administration facilities, and other institutions. Less than 5,000 persons, of whom 1,800 were middle-aged, resided in this lifestyle area. Subareas which made up this scattered lifestyle are indicated in Figure 31. Like the elderly, the middle-aged had high incidences of poor health. Further,

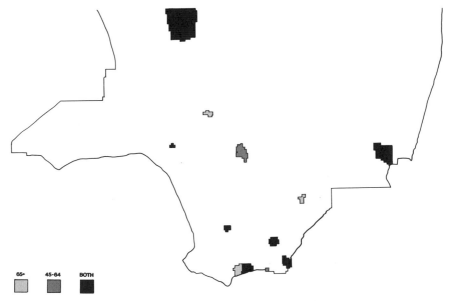

Figure 31. The Institutionalized

the middle-aged were characterized more strongly by
the lifestyle dimensions of density/centrality, Spanish-
American, and long-term residency. Spatially, a high
degree of correspondence was observed, but with two not-
able differences. First, there was a large subarea unique
to the middle-aged near the central city of Los Angeles.
Second, the Sepulveda and Sawtelle Veterans' facilities in
the San Fernando Valley and West Los Angeles areas were
unique to the elderly population. These data were suggestive of lifestyles and requirements largely provided for by
prosthetic environments. No significant differences
germane to this study were observed between the two age
groups for this lifestyle.

Lifestyle Group 4: The New Suburbanites. One-quarter
million middle-aged persons resided in this lifestyle area,
and comprised about 18 percent of the total population.
Ninety-six percent of the middle-aged in this group were
white. As can be seen in Figure 32, the census tracts comprising the new suburban lifestyle group were located
primarily at the periphery of the Los Angeles metropolitan

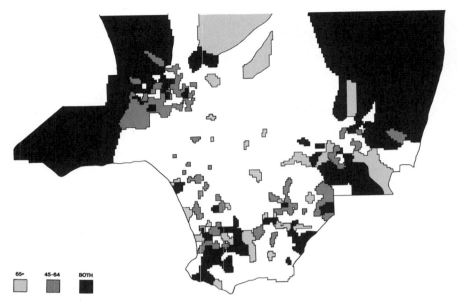

Figure 32. The New Suburbanites

area. On the average, the area was not very densely populated. Large areas spatially overlapped the lifestyles of
both age groups, as shown in Figure 32. Overlapping was
especially pronounced in the eastern and western pe-
ripheries of the county and in the Palos Verdes Peninsula
area. Areas unique to the middle-aged were found in the
San Fernando Valley, while some unique to the elderly
were found in the eastern portions of the county in the
Pomona area. The data showed significant similarity between the elderly and middle-aged populations inhabiting
these areas. Both were occupying relatively new homes
which most of them owned. It was common for members
of both groups to own more than one car and most lived in
family settings rather than alone. Both cohorts had recently moved into this area and had made similar housing
choices.

Lifestyle Group 5: The Black Community. This lifestyle
group, most of which was located between the central
cities of Los Angeles and Long Beach, was, on the average, the most densely populated of all areas identified.

Area 5 was where the majority of the county's black middle-aged resided, and many were in service occupations. This area is illustrated in Figure 33. The 680,000 people residing in this area represented 10 percent of the total population of the county. Seventeen percent of the population in the area were between the ages of 45 and 64 years. About 80 percent of the area's total population and about 75 percent of the middle-aged were black. Approximately 75 percent of the county's total black population and about 80 percent of the black middle-aged population resided in this area. About one in every four middle-aged persons in this area—over twice the county average—was employed in a service occupation. A third of the cohort population, however, was unemployed. This lifestyle area corresponded spatially with the elderly population almost in total, as shown in Figure 33. Minor concentrations unique to the middle-aged were found in the Long Beach, Santa Monica, and Pomona areas, while the elderly cohort was found uniquely only at the northern edge of the major concentration in the south-central portion of Los Angeles. These data suggested a living pattern in which segregation by race but not by age characterized the black population of the county. They further suggested that the two cohorts shared similar circumstances other than ethnicity, with service occupations being the most common one. The minor concentrations of black middle-aged in areas other than the south-central part of Los Angeles may have been suggestive of some, but very limited, outward mobility.

Lifestyle Group 6: The Spanish-American Community. Lifestyle group 6 was located primarily in East Los Angeles and in the eastern portions of the county. This area, shown in Figure 34, had an average density only slightly below the county average. One-half million persons resided in this area, of which 16 percent were between the ages of 45 and 64 in 1970. County-wide, this age group represented one-fifth of the total population. Over one-half of this cohort and two-thirds of the general popu-

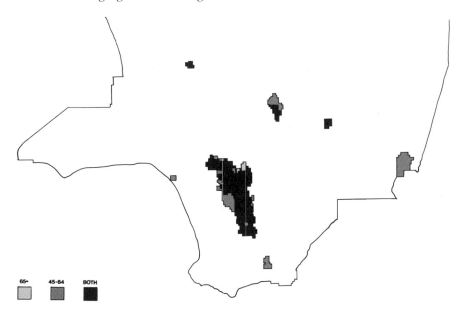

Figure 33. The Black Community

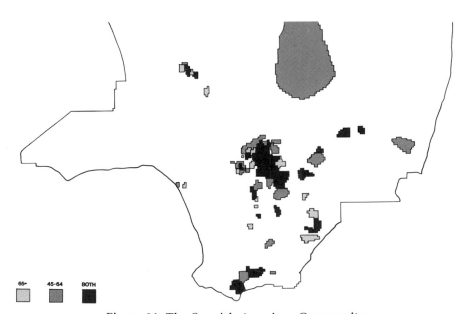

Figure 34. The Spanish-American Community

lation were Spanish-American. In both comparisons, this area greatly exceeded the county averages. Approximately 45 percent of the middle-aged population in this area held blue collar occupations, and 37 percent reported being unemployed. Only about 28 percent of this cohort reported being unemployed. About one in six persons had received five or less years of formal education. This percentage was approximately five times the county average. Comparisons of the spatial distributions, as shown in Figure 34, revealed that these two age groups largely shared the same space, with the largest concentration of both found in the East Los Angeles area. Smaller concentrations, in which both age groups resided, were found in the San Pedro, San Fernando (City), and San Gabriel Valley areas. Comparisons suggested that, while the Spanish-American dimension of lifestyle was an important facet of both cohorts, the middle-aged experienced other circumstances which significantly modified this basic dimension. Financial insecurity and unemployment, especially, were significant modifiers. Long-term residency seemed less influential in the middle-aged lifestyle pattern. This was perhaps reflective of more outward mobility from the large concentrated area in the community of East Los Angeles. Small concentrations of the middle-aged lifestyle area in the eastern and northern portions of the county tended to support this interpretation.

Lifestyle Group 7: The Early Suburbanites.   This group lay in an arc between the central urban-activity centers of Los Angeles, Santa Monica, Long Beach, and Pasadena and the new low-density areas at the periphery of the county. It contained 498,000 middle-aged residents, making it the largest single subpopulation of the cohort. The area was dense (nine persons per gross acre) and almost exclusively white. Figure 35 shows this lifestyle area. Family settings predominated, with only one in ten middle-aged persons living alone. Privately owned homes were the characteristic physical living arrangement, and this was the case with seventy percent of all middle-aged households. These

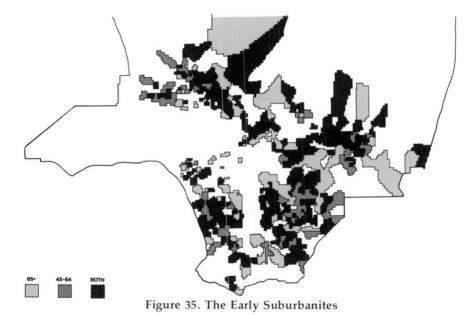

65+   45-64   BOTH

Figure 35. The Early Suburbanites

structures were older, with many having been built prior
to 1940. About 15 percent of all middle-aged households
resided in these older structures, and about 11 percent of
these households had located there prior to 1950. Income
in this area tended to be about average for the county.
About one in five of the middle-aged had achieved a college education, which was also about average for the
county. Spatially (see Figure 35), the areas which were
mutual to both age groups, and unique to each, appeared
to be about equal in size and distribution within the
"middle-city" area where this lifestyle group was dominant. This group represented, in many respects, the
"average middle-aged Angeleno." Mean factor scores
were frequently at or near county averages. The middle-
aged of this area did not appear to differ significantly from
the elderly population. The way of life, at least from the
data available, appeared to be one of relative stability. It
may be said of this lifestyle area, as of its counterpart in
the elderly population, that residents matured with their
neighborhoods.

Observations and Conclusions

The foregoing comparisons have revealed that the middle-aged and elderly populations, in most cases, had patterns which were more similar between than within age groups. This implied circumstances and options available to these groups which were independent of age. Some patterns, such as those associated with financial security, home ownership, educational attainment, and occupational status, were especially strong and persistent across age groups.

Ethnicity, as in the case of the elderly population, was an important determinant of lifestyle among the middle-aged. There appeared, however, to be more ethnic mixing and spatial dispersal in the middle-aged group than in the elderly one. These patterns may have indicated a lessening of segregation and increased opportunities for the middle-aged.

One additional dimension—unemployment—must be added to the important determinants of lifestyle in middle age. This factor was associated with four of the seven lifestyle areas identified. It could not be determined from the available data whether this dimension reflected changes in the requirements of the labor market to which the middle-aged were adjusting poorly, or whether it was the result of the recessionary period which existed at the time of the 1970 census.

There was a strong correspondence of lifestyle areas, both in terms of characteristics and spatial distribution. Comparisons of the lifestyle dimensions and areas of the two age groups identified many areas of similarity and, therefore, substantiated the hypothesis that the heterogeneity of both populations was largely independent of age. These data and analyses could not, however, identify the specific trends associated with each age group. They also could not reveal the role which historic events and the aging process may play, singly or in concert, in the observed similarities and differences. The remaining section of this chapter will describe these influences of lifestyle.

Differentiation of Cohort, Aging, and Period Effects

The third task of the longitudinal analysis was designed to differentiate between the effects of aging, historical period, and cohort membership on locational choice. A *period effect* is present if, as a variable changes over time, the change uniformly affects all age groups and cohorts. For example, if mass production of the automobile results in many new drivers of all ages in a particular year, a period effect has occurred. An *aging effect* is present when the value of a variable is found to be a function of age, regardless of which cohort occupies a given age group in a time period. For example, if possession of a driver's license declines at age 65 regardless of the year of birth, there is an aging effect. A *cohort effect* is present if the value of a variable differs systematically between cohorts over time after aging effects have been considered. For example, it may be that more women drivers are consistently found in one cohort than in another through time. It is also possible that interactions between period, aging, and cohort effects may be evident, thereby presenting a particular challenge for the analyst.

The generalizations presented at the beginning of this chapter, which stated that elderly persons move to areas of higher density as they age and that they give up driving as they age, incorporated assumptions that housing density and driving patterns are influenced primarily by aging effects. The counter proposals, that many of today's elderly have long lived at higher densities and that many never learned to drive, incorporated assumptions that cohort effects more strongly influence residential densities and driving.

Researchers have recently begun to demonstrate the utility of longitudinal analysis in identifying the influence of period, aging, and cohort effects on behavior. Several authors have conceptually differentiated between those presently of retirement age and the next generation of elderly. Their works identify characteristics which are changing and suggest implications for future demand for public services.

Cain identified differences while describing "historic hinge" or "watershed" occurring around 1900 which set earlier and later cohorts on different developmental paths. Cohorts show differences in education, family structure, occupational choice, and political activity. He notes that changes in immigration, unionization, technological innovation, and urbanization affect these cohorts.[1] In a later study Cain added improved health status and suburbanization as forces creating distinctions.[2] Neugarten noted the same differences as Cain noted in describing the "new-old" and added improved purchasing power and affluence as distinguishing characteristics.[3] Ryder also related the cohort concept to social change and to generational differences. He noted that period effects such as war, depression, revolution, urbanization, and technological innovation are important determinants of cohort differences. These events transform people and the transformations are persistent. Ryder concluded, "as a minimum, the cohort is a structural category with the same kind of analytical utility as a variable such as social class." (p. 847). He recognized, however, that aging alters cohort differences: "in later years, the cohort identify is blurred. Age becomes progressively less precise as an index of a person's social characteristics . . . adjacent cohorts tend to permeate each other as the pattern of life chances works itself out."[4]

With longitudinal data sets, alternative hypotheses in-

1. Leonard Cain, "Age Status and Generational Phenomena: The New Old People in Contemporary America," *The Gerontologist* 7 (1967), pp. 83–92.

2. Leonard Cain, "Planning for the Elderly in the Future," in *Planning and the Urban Elderly: Today and Tomorrow*, Summary of a Two-Day Workshop (Los Angeles: University of Southern California, April 1971).

3. Bernice L. Neugarten, "Age Groups in American Society and the Rise of the New Old," in F.R. Eisele, ed., *Political Consequences of Aging, Annals of the American Association of Political and Social Sciences* 415 (1974), pp. 187–98.

4. N.B. Ryder, "The Cohort as a Concept in the Study of Social Change," *American Sociological Review* 30 (1965), pp. 843–61.

volving the presence of cohort, aging, and period effects can be tested. A particular challenge may face the analyst when combinations of these three effects are present, but even in such cases it is possible to separate the relative contributions of each effect from the others. Here, a graphical method is presented for visually displaying the relative magnitudes of the three effects in a particular variable, and a multiple regression technique is also described for more precisely testing for each effect. The graphical and regression techniques are applied to the longitudinal analysis of several census variables describing the current elderly population of Los Angeles County in order to determine the relative influence of each of the three types of effects.

Graphical Display of Period Effects,
Aging Effects, and Cohort Effects

The work of Baltes has been cited as seminal in the development of an empirical approach to the analysis of period, cohort, and aging effects in longitudinal data sets.[5] The graphical presentation of longitudinal data, which facilitates the visual display of the three effects, is drawn largely from his work and is illustrated in Figure 36. On a set of orthogonal axes, the ordinate (Y) represents the value of some socioeconomic or demographic variable under investigation. The abscissa (X) identifies age groups of successively increasing age as distance increases from the origin. In spaces defined by these two axes separate curves, hereafter called "cohort profiles," are drawn for each cohort under study. Because each cohort of a population occupies a particular age group in a different year, it is also useful to indicate, in this space, the year corresponding to a particular data point. In Figure 36, the years are shown in parentheses (40 = the year 1940, 50 = 1950, etc.),

5. P.R. Baltes, "Longitudinal and Cross-Sectional Sequences in the Study of Age and Generation Effects," *Human Development* 2 (1968), pp. 145–71.

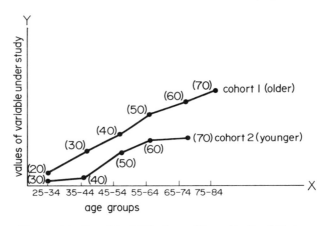

Figure 36. Graphical Display of Longitudinal Data

and two cohorts are shown for purposes of illustration. Cohort 1 was aged 75–84 in the 1970 census, and consequently was aged 65–74 in the 1960 census. This cohort can be followed back to ages 25–34 in the census of 1920. Cohort 2 is ten years younger, having been aged 65–74 in the 1970 census. Notice that cohort 2 occupies each age group ten years later than does cohort 1.

Figure 37 illustrates the manner in which plots of variables in such a simple space may be used to display the relative effects of cohort, aging, and period effects. The years have been omitted from Figure 37, and only three or four age groups are shown in order to keep the illustration as simple as possible. Panel (a) demonstrates a cohort effect. Vertical distances between the cohort profiles show consistent cohort differences in the values of Y which persist over age groups A_1 to A_3. Panel (b) illustrates an aging effect: cohorts display increasing values of Y with age, but all have the same value of Y for each age group. Panel (c) shows a combination of age and cohort effects. Each cohort has unique values of Y, but the cohorts change in similar fashion as they age. Panel (d) demonstrates the joint presence of cohort and period effects. The vertical separation of the curves shows evidence of a cohort effect,

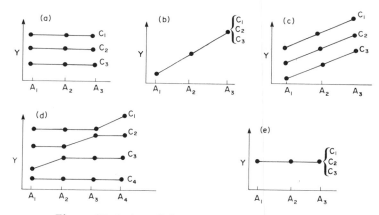

Figure 37. Aging, Cohort, Period, and Combined Effects Shown Graphically

as in panel (a), and an aging effect is absent because the curves are generally horizontal. But note that in a particular year (when each cohort occupied a different age group) there was a significant shift in the values of Y. Finally, panel (e) demonstrates the absence of any of the three effects, since there is no change or difference in Y with time, and the cohorts all have the same value of Y.

To summarize, in interpreting the graphic representations, the following relationships can be associated with each effect:

(a) *Parallelism of cohort profiles.* Profiles observed to change slope at the same time period, in the same direction, and in approximately the same amount, represent a period effect. A period effect is one in which all cohorts and age groups experience similar changes over time.

(b) *Vertical separation of cohort profiles.* In the graphic presentations, cohorts are plotted for years when they occupied particular age groups. Vertical separations at similar ages, therefore, are associated with cohort differences.

(c) *Overall slope of cohort profiles.* A systematic increase or decrease in values of Y by all cohorts with advancing age represents an aging effect in that all cohorts responded in a similar manner as they aged.

Regression Technique for Identifying the Effects

A mathematical technique was developed by Mason *et al.* to identify and to test for the significance of cohort, aging, and period effects in a set of longitudinal data.[6] The procedure utilizes a multiple regression technique to regress values of a dependent variable against dichotomous (dummy) independent variables representing the presence or absence of age, period, and cohort components. These independent variables are derived from the construction of a matrix, the cells of which contain the elements of age, period, and cohort expressed in the equation:

$$Y = \mu + \beta + \gamma + \delta + e$$

where Y = the dependent variable, μ = the grand mean of the dependent variable, β = the age component of the cell, γ = the period component of the cell, δ = the cohort component of the cell, e = error term.

In the matrix of Figure 11, age groups (rows) are numbered $1 \ldots n$ from the top down, periods (columns) are numbered $1 \ldots m$ from left to right, and cohorts (diagonals) are numbered $1 \ldots k$ from the lower left to the upper right. The matrix is shown for the case in which $n = 6$ and $m = 4$. Independent variables represent the mean, age group, period, and cohort components of each cell. Cell 1 (upper left corner) in Figure 11, for example, contains components of the mean—age group 1, period 1, and cohort 6— and is expressed: $\mu + \beta_1 + \gamma_1 + \delta_6$. Cell 2, immediately to the right of cell 1, contains components of the mean—age group 1, period 2, and cohort 7—and is thus coded $\mu + \beta_1 + \gamma_2 + \delta_7$.

Such mathematical expressions may be transformed into dichotomous variables for each independent variable of age, cohort, and period, with 1 representing the presence of the variable in the cell. Cells 1 and 2 from the previous example would thus be coded as follows, with

6. K. O. Mason *et al.*, "Some Methodological Issues in Cohort Analysis of Archival Data," *American Sociological Review* 38 (1973), pp. 242–58.

entries of 1 indicating components which are present in a cell:

	μ	β_1	β_2	β_3	β_4	β_5	β_6	γ_1	γ_2	γ_3	γ_4	δ_1	δ_2	δ_3	δ_4	δ_5	δ_6	δ_7	δ_8	δ_9
Cell 1	1	1	0	0	0	0	0	1	0	0	0	0	0	0	0	0	0	1	0	0
Cell 2	1	1	0	0	0	0	0	1	0	0	0	0	0	0	0	0	0	0	1	0

As discussed by Mason *et al.*, this regression equation is estimable only if two age groups, cohorts, or periods are assumed to be equal. In practice this is accomplished by leaving the dummy variables corresponding to the pair out of the equation. Unless this is done, there are more variables than data points, and the equation is inestimable. While the selection of any of these combinations is sufficient constraint on the regression to make the equation estimable, the selection of several constraints, such as assuming two age and two cohort groups to be equal, results in a more distinct identification of the period, cohort, and aging effects. According to the authors, however, selection of multiple constraints should be made on theoretical grounds.

Data Analysis for Los Angeles County

The graphical and regression methods were applied to selected variables describing the population of Los Angeles County. Census data from 1940, 1950, 1960, and 1970 provided the data base, and in each census period the data were aggregated from tract-level information as reported in those years. Although census tracts changed from year to year during this period, for aggregate analysis of this type it was possible to derive average values of each variable of interest by weighting variable values for each tract by the population of the tract. For any census year (t) the value of any one of the six variables for a particular cohort (c) was determined as follows:

$$\overline{X}_{ct} = \sum_{i=1}^{n} \frac{P_{cit}(X_{it})}{\left(\sum_{i=1}^{n} P_{cit}\right)}$$

where $\overline{X}_{ct}$ = mean cohort value of variable X at time t, P_{cit} = cohort population in census tract i at time t, X_{it} = value of variable X for census tract i at time t, n = number of census tracts in study area.

The values of such population-weighted variables were deemed adequate to estimate the magnitudes of cohort, aging, and period effects at the county-wide or aggregate level. The technique would be equally valid, however, if applied to data at a more disaggregate level.

Figure 11 indicates that for each census year between 1940 and 1970 values were computed for six age groups, the youngest including persons aged 25 to 34 and the oldest including persons aged 75 to 84. If a cohort is considered to be a population group born during a particular ten-year period, the four census periods and the six age groups give rise to the possibility of studying the nine cohorts shown in Figure 11. The diagonal lines in the figure follow each cohort through time, and indicate that for the purposes of this study, some cohorts existed in as few as one census period, while others could be traced through all four census periods.

The reader will recall that the regressions are estimable only if two age groups, cohorts, or periods are assumed to be equal. For this study, alternate models were tested in which it was assumed that three combinations of age groups, cohorts, and periods were equal. The model resulting in the highest percentage of variation explained was considered the best predictor of the effects. Each model tested is summarized in Table 24. The constraints chosen reflect the following rationale:

(1) The younger age groups (25 to 34 and 35 to 44 years of age) were considered relatively homogeneous in that they were involved in the processes of establishing homes and rearing children. As a result, these age groups could be assumed to be equal in the regression. On the other hand, later age groups were more likely to manifest changes in patterns which were related to residential choice due to death, migration, and children growing up and leaving the family home. Also this study was focused

Table 24. Assumptions of Equality Made to Produce Estimable Regressions

		Model (1)	Model (2)	Model (3)
Age Groups	1	X	X	X
	2	X		X
	3			
	4			
	5			
	6			
Periods	1	X	X	X
	2	X	X	
	3			
	4			
Cohorts	1			
	2			
	3			
	4			
	5			
	6			
	7			
	8		X	X
	9	X	X	X

upon trends in later stages of the life cycle. For these reasons, age groups one and two were assumed equal in the models in varying combinations with cohorts and periods.

(2) Earlier periods (1940 and 1950) were times of growth in Los Angeles County. They were considered likely to demonstrate greater similarity than any other two periods and thus could be assumed equal in the regression. Later periods, when cohorts of interest occupied age groups of interest, were considered important to preserve in the regression.

(3) Younger cohorts (Cohorts 8 and 9) were aged 35 to 44 and 25 to 34, respectively, in 1970. As in the choice of age constraints, these cohorts were considered to be less different than any other cohort pairs and could thus be assumed equal in the regression. In addition, they would not be in age groups of interest to this study until 1980 and 1990. Older cohorts occupied these age groups in 1970 and

it was useful to account for their differences, if present, in the regression.

Seven variables were studied with the regression technique: (1) residential density, (2) home ownership, (3) median home value, (4) apartment living, (5) monthly rental rates, (6) independent living (one-person households) and (7) ethnic composition. Weighted averages for these variables were computed according to the procedure described above and served as values of the independent variables in the regression analysis. These values were also plotted using the graphic technique described above. Given the rapid growth in the county over the thirty-year observation period, it was anticipated that changes in the values of the variables would not be due to only one of the three effects. Rather, the three effects were expected to interact, making it complex to identify the relative strength of any single effect. For this reason, seven different regressions were performed on each variable: one regression in which all effects were included; three regressions in which the effects of aging, cohort, and period were analyzed separately; and three regressions in which combinations (aging plus period, aging plus cohort, period plus cohort) were analyzed. In addition, these regressions were performed under each of the three equality constraints described previously. Thus, each variable was analyzed with a total of twenty-one regressions, with each regression tested for significance, as were the coefficients of the independent variables. The results were compared with the graphic interpretations to complete the analysis of trends.

Description and analysis consisted of examinations of the values of each cohort profile to identify differences and similarities at similar ages and census periods. Four cohorts, referred to in terms of numbers drawn from Figure 11 were of special interest. In 1970, those in Cohort 4 were 75 years of age or older and were identified as the old-old cohort. Those in Cohort 5 were between the ages of 65 and 74 and were identified as the young-old cohort. Those in Cohorts 6 and 7 were 45 to 54 and 55 to 64 years of age, respectively, and were identified as the middle-aged and late middle-aged cohorts. These four cohorts represented today's elderly citizens and those of the next generation. Differences between the trends of these cohorts, therefore, have particularly important implications for transportation planners.

Trends in Population Density

Residential density is a key descriptor of the population in an urban society. Density is often inversely related to income, and density influences the ease and the cost with which services may be delivered to a population group. There are certain stereotypes relating densities to aging. It is often thought that younger families of child-rearing ages consciously select suburban communities of lower density but then relocate to denser inner-city areas when the children are grown and when older age brings about a decline in income and in physical mobility. The differentiation between aging, period, and cohort effects is particularly useful when studying changes in residential density over time in Los Angeles County.

Figure 38 summarizes trends in the average densities at which cohorts resided from 1940 to 1970. The four cohorts of interest were found to differ considerably in the average densities at which they resided over the periods observed. Successively younger cohorts consistently resided at lower densities. In 1970 the oldest cohort resided at an average density of 16.3 persons per gross acre, while the average member of the cohort aged 65–74 resided at a density of about 15.9. Values for the middle-aged cohorts were 14.6 and 13.6 persons per gross acre, respectively. This pattern held for every observational period. The cohorts, therefore, did not share similar environments as measured by this variable. Younger cohorts tended to live in environments of lower densities than did older ones.

The figure also shows that, while successive cohorts consistently resided at lower densities, their patterns were not systematically affected by period influences. Cohorts

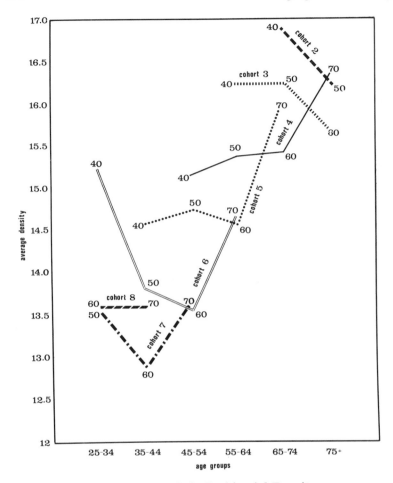

Figure 38. Trends in Residential Density

were observed to change differently at different time periods, with some cohorts showing increases in density while others decreased. This pattern was especially marked from 1940 to 1960. Between 1960 and 1970, however, cohorts were affected in a similar fashion with nearly parallel increases occurring in average density. These patterns suggested a cohort effect with a less significant period effect. The pattern of densities increasing with age was also suggestive of an aging effect in the trends.

These observations were confirmed in the multiple regression analysis of this variable. Age and cohort regressions were found significant at the 0.001 level, as were all interaction effects. In the regression of all independent variables, age and cohort coefficients were found significant, while only Period 4 (as suggested in the graphic representation) was found significant at the 0.05 level.

These findings suggested that, as each cohort aged, it tended to select areas of higher density, but that there were significant differences between the densities at which different cohorts resided. Younger cohorts resided at lower densities at particular ages than did older cohorts when they had been at those ages. This tendency should remain even if period effects are present and would imply that elderly populations of the future will be found at lower densities than are today's elderly.

Trends in Home Ownership

Researchers often note how important home ownership is to the aged. The privately owned home frequently represents the single most important financial asset in old age and is an important element in decisions concerning relocation. An understanding of trends in home ownership is, therefore, also important for anticipating the location of the elderly in the future.

Figure 39 shows cohort profiles of the percentage of occupied units which were privately owned. Marked differences were observed for all cohorts between census periods, especially between 1940 and 1950, when all cohorts moved sharply toward areas in which the number of homes owned was high. This trend was reversed after 1950 for the older cohorts and continued to decline even more sharply after 1960. In 1970 the average member of the old-old cohort resided in an area in which about 41 percent of all occupied units were privately owned. The average young-old cohort resided in an area in which this percentage was only slightly higher. Younger cohorts

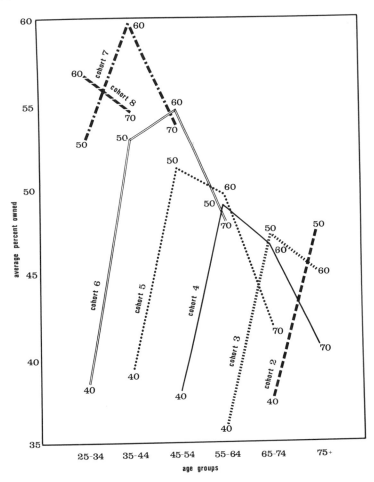

Figure 39. Trends in Home Ownership

typically resided in areas in which the ownership rate was over 50 percent.

When cohorts were compared at similar ages, widely different values were found at earlier ages, with the range narrowing considerably after 65 years of age. This narrowing of range beyond 65 suggested an aging effect which was confirmed by multiple regression analysis. When cohorts were compared at similar time periods, no significant differences were observed. For example, in 1940 the range for all cohorts was between 35.2 percent for those over 75 years of age and 38.2 percent for those 25 to 34. In 1970 this range was from 40.8 to 54.6 percent. The absence of any significant cohort effect was confirmed in the multiple regression analysis.

The major influence observed in these trends was a period effect. Cohorts were observed to respond similarly, with each moving after 1940 toward areas with a high proportion of homes owned but then moving after 1950 toward areas where a lower proportion was owned. This strong period effect was confirmed by multiple regression analysis, with each period in the regression found significant at the 0.01 level.

These data suggested that while age exerts some influence upon this variable, especially in later years, few generational differences can be expected. Sociohistorical influences, including probably the price of housing, may exert a greater influence. All cohorts were observed to reside in areas where fewer homes were owned after 1950. These trends further suggested that apartment living may become a more dominant residential pattern and that home ownership may become a progressively weaker influence on residential location in the future.

Trends in Housing Value

It was noted above that housing values may play an important role in the movement away from private residences, especially in old age. In Los Angeles County, many of the elderly and middle-aged reside in areas distinguished in part by home value. Higher home values among the middle-aged might suggest differences in financial resources and, as a consequence, different access to opportunities when entering retirement.

Figure 40 illustrates trends in the median home values of areas in which the cohorts resided after these values were adjusted for inflation using the Consumer Price Index. For all cohorts there were marked trends toward higher home values between 1940 and 1970. Each cohort followed a

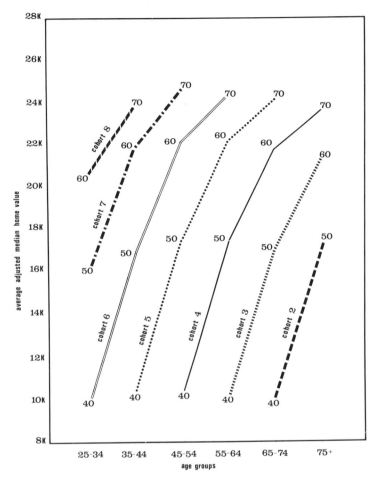

Figure 40. Trends in Housing Value

very similar profile, suggesting a strong period effect. This was confirmed by multiple regression analysis. Period variables, when regressed alone, explained over 99 percent of the variation and were significant at the 0.001 level. No significant aging or cohort effects were found in the regression.

In general, these trends suggested that homes became increasingly more expensive over time and that decisions of home ownership tended to be made independent of age. They also suggested that those elderly who owned homes were not segregated by age. Rather, they occupied homes in areas similar to those occupied by other age groups. These trends, coupled with the trends toward areas where fewer homes were owned, also suggested that recent home values may have prompted many persons to relocate in areas where apartment living was a more prominent residential pattern.

Trends in Apartment Living

The two comparisons above suggested that there may have been a significant trend toward residing in apartments, the result of both period and aging effects. Apartment living is associated with higher densities, which make delivery of services more efficient, and also with greater potential for mobility or relocation. If present, this mobility may make it difficult to forecast the location of the elderly in the future.

Figure 41 summarizes trends related to patterns of apartment living. The figure shows typical areas in which cohorts resided in terms of the percentage of occupied units located in structures containing five or more units. Since 1950, there has been a strong trend to reside in areas containing a higher percentage of apartments. As expected, this trend mirrored those trends associated with home ownership. Residency in apartment areas declined from 1940 to 1950, while residence in areas with high home ownership was increasing. After 1950 this trend reversed and more people began renting steadily. In 1970 the old-old cohort resided in areas in which apartments represented about 30.7 percent of all units. The young-old generation resided in areas where 28.8 percent of all units were in this category. The middle-aged and late middle-aged groups, on the other hand, resided in areas in which apartments represented 20.8 and 24.6 percent, respectively. All four cohorts generally followed similar patterns after 1940.

Comparisons made by age group showed that younger

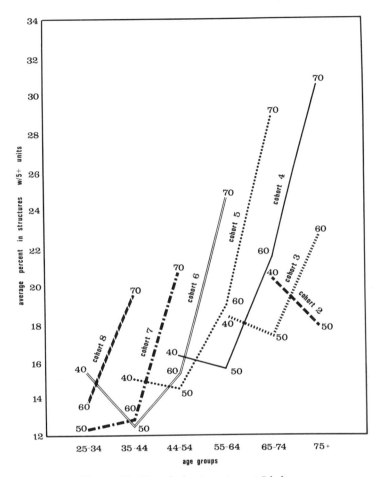

Figure 41. Trends in Apartment Living

age groups typically resided in areas with less apartment living, while older groups increasingly resided in areas where apartments were more common. Those 25 to 34 years of age, for example, tended to reside in areas where apartments represented between 12 and 15 percent of the housing. The old-old were consistently found to reside in areas in which this percentage was over 17 percent and, since 1960, over 22 percent. Those between 65 and 74 resided in areas with a slightly lower proportion of apartments than those areas characteristic of the old-old. These trends suggested a significant aging effect. This was confirmed by multiple regression analysis in which all age groups were found significant at the 0.01 level or greater.

When cohorts were compared at each census period, differences were also noted. Younger cohorts consistently resided in areas where apartments represented a smaller percentage of the total housing. This cohort effect was also confirmed by multiple regression analysis, with the effect of each cohort being found significant at the 0.05 level.

Comparisons by census period showed marked differences, with each cohort responding in similar manner for each period. As noted above, each cohort moved toward areas in which apartments were less common between 1940 and 1950, but reversed this trend after 1950, when they displayed nearly identical patterns. These patterns reflected a strong period effect for all periods. This effect was also confirmed, with each period in the regression found significant at the 0.001 level. When the data were regressed to determine only period effects, 52.6 percent of the variation was explained, and the multiple correlation coefficient was significant at the 0.001 level. Aging and period effects, in combination, explained 99.3 percent of the variation. Both coefficients were significant at the 0.001 level.

These data suggested a marked trend on the part of all cohorts toward apartment living—apparently the result of aging and sociohistorical events. While cohorts responded similarly to these influences, they did so from different initial positions. This seemed to suggest that future generations of the elderly will increasingly be found in apartments and that changes in the housing market and rental rates, rather than the aging process, will prove to be stronger influences on these trends.

Trends in Monthly Rental Rates

Rents, like housing values, reflect the financial resources available to individuals and, as a result, strongly influence location patterns.

Trends in the adjusted median rents which characterized the typical areas in which the cohorts resided are shown in Figure 42. In general, the profiles for all cohorts revealed a trend toward residing in areas with higher rental rates even after correction for inflation. These trends have been accelerating since 1950. The four cohorts of special interest showed slightly different values over time, with the middle-aged cohorts usually residing in areas with higher rents. This was especially true in 1960 and 1970.

When the trends were compared for similar ages, it was found that those of advancing age (especially 55 and over) had moved to areas with lower rents. Those between the ages of 35 and 54, however, characteristically resided in areas of higher rents than did those between the ages of 25 and 34. This trend probably reflected the increasing purchasing power that came with advancement in the labor force. These data were suggestive of an aging effect which was confirmed by multiple classification analysis. The younger age groups were found to be significant at the 0.001 level, while differences in the older age groups were found to be less and less significant.

Comparison of cohorts by census period suggested significant differences after 1960. Prior to that year, cohorts had occupied areas with similar monthly rental rates, while after 1960 they resided in areas with higher rents. In 1970, for example, the old-old typically resided in areas where the prevailing rent was about $107 per month. The young-old resided in areas with only slightly higher monthly rents (about $109 per month). Those aged 45 to 54 and 55 to 64 resided in areas where prevailing rents were $120 and $114 per month, respectively. These cohort differences were found to be significant in the regression analysis of all effects. When the data were regressed to determine the significance of cohort effects alone, however, these influences were not found to be significant.

Period effects, as can be observed in Figure 42, were pronounced. They were found significant for each obser-

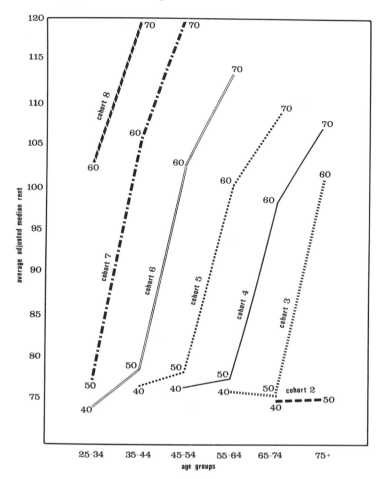

Figure 42. Trends in Monthly Rental Rates

vation period at the 0.001 level. When the data were analyzed to determine only the influence of period effects, it was found that 96.4 percent of the variation was explained by these effects and that the multiple correlation coefficient was significant at the 0.001 level.

These data demonstrated that, while advancing age tended to prompt location in areas with lower rental rates, the cohorts retained their differences. Sociohistorical events also strongly influenced these decisions, probably by significantly affecting the range of available rents. Areas in which cohorts resided were only slightly differentiated by the rental rate. In the future aging citizens may migrate toward areas with lower rents, but these areas may very well be different from those occupied by the elderly today. Above all, events which affect the monthly rental rate will strongly determine the residential pattern of rental areas.

Trends in One-Person Households

Gerontological literature consistently demonstrates that the elderly experience a loss of friends and family members through death and migration. Many elderly, therefore, reside alone. This weakening of the family network with age is often associated with increased dependence on public services, including transportation. Trends in this area are therefore important aspects in the planning and delivery of many services.

Figure 43 summarizes trends showing the percentage of the population which resided alone. The figure reveals that cohorts have increasingly resided, over time, in areas where a greater percentage of the population lived alone. The cohorts differed, however, in the areas which typified them. In 1970 the old-old cohort resided in areas in which 13.4 percent of the households were occupied by one person. Those 65 to 74 years of age resided in areas in which this percentage was slightly lower, at 12.4 percent. The middle-aged and late middle-aged, by comparison, resided in areas where individuals constituted only 8.4 and 10.3 percent of all households.

Comparisons of cohorts at similar ages revealed that this percentage increased with advancing age and that aging was a significant influence. Characteristically, younger age groups resided in areas in which fewer persons resided alone. As they aged, however, cohorts were increasingly found in areas where more persons resided alone. These later differences in age groups were found to be significant in the multiple regression analysis of all effects. When the

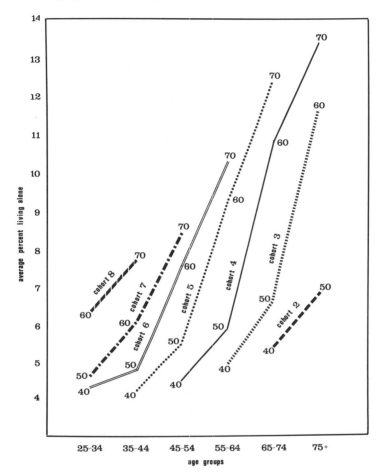

Figure 43. Trends in One-Person Households

data were regressed to find the effect which age alone had on the variation, however, aging was not found to be a significant determinant.

Comparisons of cohorts at each observation period suggested differences, especially among the younger cohorts. Multiple regression analysis of all effects revealed that, while several cohorts were significantly different, cohort effects alone were not significant determinants of the variation in the data.

When the data were examined for period effects, however, there were marked differences. Each cohort tended to have similar patterns on this variable throughout the periods observed. From 1940 to 1950 all cohorts tended to reside in areas in which few households were occupied by single individuals, due, perhaps, to a shortage of housing during that time, resulting in households of multiple generations. After 1950, however, each cohort showed rapid changes, which continued from that point until 1970. This strong period effect was confirmed by the regression analysis, with all periods in the regression found significant at the 0.001 level. The multiple correlation coefficient produced when the data were analyzed for the effects of period alone was 0.644 and was significant at the 0.001 level.

These data suggested that, as anticipated, aging had some effect on the percentage of households occupied by single individuals. Age was not, however, the major correlate with location in such areas. Rather, these areas seemed more distinguishable on the basis of historical events. Important in its own right was the fact that each cohort showed a greater tendency to reside in areas in which larger percentages of households were occupied by primary individuals. These data would seem to suggest that living alone is becoming more prevalent among all cohorts and that, in future periods, the adjustments now accompanying old age may be less dramatic.

Trends in Racial Composition of Residential Areas

Figure 44 illustrates cohort profiles of the percentage of the population which was white. It shows that over time there was a strong and persistent trend toward racial integration. This trend was observed for all cohorts, and the four cohorts of special interest showed similar patterns throughout the periods observed. The areas characteristic of each cohort showed strong similarities for each of the four census periods observed.

When the data were compared by age group, few differ-

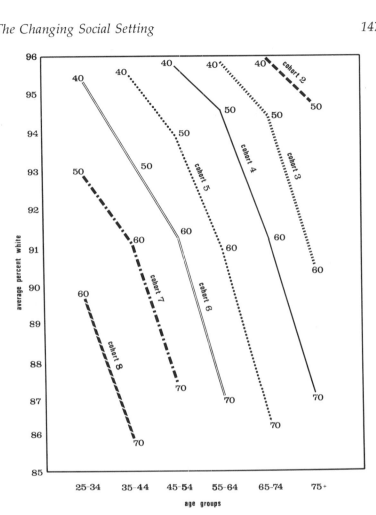

**Figure 44. Trends in Racial Composition
of Residential Areas**

ences were observed. In 1970, for example, the youngest
age group (23 to 34 years) resided in areas which were
about 85 percent white. The old-old age group, on the
other hand, resided in areas which had mean values of 87
percent white. In 1960 these same age groups resided in
areas which were 95 and 96 percent white, respectively.
This pattern was found for all periods. There was, however, a slight tendency for the older age groups to be
found in less integrated areas. These older age groups

were found to be significant in the multiple classification analysis at the 0.01 level. This aging effect was not found to be significant, however, when the data were analyzed for the effects of aging alone.

When cohorts were compared for differences at each census period, each cohort was found to be unique, but the cohort effect alone was not found to be a significant determinant of the variation in the trends.

As expected, period effects in the multiple classification analysis were found to be the best determinant of the variation in the data. They were found to explain 90.3 percent of the variation when the data were regressed to determine the influence of these effects alone. The multiple correlation coefficient was significant at the 0.001 level.

These data suggested that all cohorts were similarly influenced by period effects, resulting in more racially heterogeneous areas, but that the older age groups tended to reside to a greater extent in areas having a higher percentage of white residents. While there were some differences among cohorts, they were not sufficient to explain the variation in the trends. These data further suggested that, in the future, subpopulations of the elderly may be less distinguishable by racial characteristics. If these trends continue, the ethnic elements of lifestyles may become less important.

Conclusions

The longitudinal analysis performed over four census periods demonstrated that social trends among today's elderly are the result of a composite of aging, period, and cohort effects. In almost every case, the patterns provided by the graphical method of analysis were interpretable and consistent with the regression technique.

Many analysts and policymakers concerned with the problems and needs of the elderly tend to attribute most of these problems to the effects of aging. The clear presence of both cohort and period effects indicates, however, that the circumstances of the elderly are derived from some important influences which are independent of as well as dependent upon the process of aging. The high degree of correspondence between the elderly and middle-aged lifestyle groups confirmed that the aging process alone did not influence the lifestyle patterns of the elderly. The impacts of wars, depressions, technological changes, and variables in the housing market are period effects which certainly impact today's elderly. In addition, similar period influences will be significant in determining the social situation of the elderly in the future. Cohort effects were also found to be present, indicating that each generation of elderly can be expected to maintain an element of cultural and social uniqueness which will accompany and modify those experiences directly associated with the aging process.

Several trends were observed to mirror and/or reinforce each other in the graphic and multiple regression analysis. There was a trend away from areas of high home ownership and toward areas where apartment living was more common. This trend was found to be strongly influenced by period effects and resulted in similar responses by all cohorts. Cohorts, however, were influenced by these effects as the result of different initial conditions, which will potentially result in still different conditions. Hence, the future elderly may continue to move toward apartment living but will probably not be found in the same areas or in the same concentrations as are today's elderly.

Increases in the cost of privately owned homes and in monthly rents were observed to affect all cohorts in a similar manner. These trends suggested that the elderly of the future may be different from those of today and that this difference will be based on their ability to absorb these costs. It is probable that the process of aging will have only a minor impact on these trends.

In the future aging will continue to exert a significant effect on the occurrence of one-person households among the elderly population. Again, however, these single households will probably not be found in areas unique to that population. Rather, the elderly will share areas with persons from other cohorts also dwelling alone. In addition, the trauma of living alone may be reduced as younger cohorts mature, since they were observed to have dwelled increasingly in areas characterized by more persons living alone.

Race will probably become a less important element of lifestyle among elderly generations of the future. Trends toward more racially mixed areas of residence were observed throughout the period of study.

Early in this chapter, the analysis of residential density patterns after 1940 showed that the total population, the elderly population, and each cohort tended to undergo suburbanization. By combining the analysis of the seven lifestyles among the middle-aged and the graphical and regression analysis, it is possible to reach some conclusions about probable trends in residential patterns among the elderly during the coming decades. In general, the next elderly generation will reside at higher densities than its cohort presently occupies in middle age, but at lower densities than those which typified the inner-city elderly of 1970. The reasons for this can be found partly in the related expectations that a higher proportion of the future elderly will reside in apartment units than is the case today. The elderly who moved to the suburbs in earlier years will, in general, remain in their single-family homes. It is important to observe, however, that the suburbs of Los Angeles have become more and more densely populated, as forces in the housing market have caused a decline in single-family homes and increasing construction of suburban apartments. Thus, those who move to the suburbs between now and the turn of the century are more likely to dwell in apartments and condominiums at moderate densities than in single-family homes at lower densities. The cohort effects that gave rise to suburbanization of the elderly over the past few decades are now interacting with the period effect of escalating housing costs in the 1970s and eventually, will give rise to a suburban, but more densely settled, elderly population.

For transportation planning, these trends suggest a less concentrated elderly population which will increasingly reside in areas with those of other ages. Services intended for the elderly individual living alone will benefit others who share the same areas and also live alone. In general, programs and policies designed on the basis of age alone will be less desired and effective in the future. Programs and policies will be more responsive and will reflect the impacts of sociohistorical events and the differences which exist between today's elderly and those of the next generation.

Chapter 6
The Future Population and Residential Location of the Elderly

*T*rends toward diversity and suburbanization among the elderly have been well established by the analysis presented in the first five chapters. These findings provide a sufficient basis from which to argue that current transportation policy is not appropriately sensitive to the heterogeneity of its elderly clients and does not match the provision of service to evolving needs. Even more graphic evidence of impending change, however, is found in explicit forecasts of the residential locations and travel patterns of the elderly of the future. Such forecasts for Los Angeles County are presented in this chapter and the next in order to illustrate in concrete terms the logical consequences of trends documented in earlier chapters. Policy recommendations based on these forecasts, and the foregoing analysis, will be presented in the final chapter.

Because forecasts of population and travel have been widely misused and severely criticized in the field of transportation planning, some interpretation and an expression of caution seem appropriate at this point. Transportation planners have been criticized because they have justified entire highway and transit networks upon the basis of similar forecasts. The networks which have been built are now viewed as the tools with which those forecasts were transformed into self-fulfilling prophesies. Critics argue that such forecasts should have been viewed more selectively and that planners should have inquired whether the scenarios promised by their forecasts were, in fact, appropriate or desired. If they were not, efforts should have focused upon diverting the trends in order that the forecasts would never become realities rather than focusing on plans to meet the travel demands that were forecast. The projections which follow are intended only to provide concrete illustrations of the likely outcomes of continuing trends. All forecasts assume certain forms of stability which, if interrupted, can easily invalidate them, and the estimates provided here are no exceptions. They are not intended to be the basis for specific planning or scheduling of transit routes. They merely project what the future will be like with the continuation of the current policy environment, planning priorities, and social and demographic trends. It is hoped that they will thus be used to arrive at clearer planning objectives and policy initiatives, which may in turn bring about a future for older Americans which differs, perhaps markedly, from that portrayed in these scenarios. The success of these forecasts will not be dependent upon the accuracy which they will have attained by the target years. Rather, it will depend upon a sincere effort by planners, policymakers, and interested citizens to debate their implications, mobilize resources to accommodate some of these implications, and divert the trends in other respects.

Because it was found in earlier chapters that the seven lifestyle areas give rise to significantly different travel patterns, and because these lifestyle groupings appeared stable over time and in comparisons of the middle-aged population with the elderly, estimates of the population were prepared for each of the areas. It was found that alternative assumptions about migration into and from Los Angeles County could have more significant impacts upon the results than other parameters of the forecast. For this reason, three different scenarios involving high, medium, and low net migration rates for the population groups under study were employed. This chapter describes the population forecasting technique and presents results of applying that technique to the three migration scenarios. These results are compared with available population estimates by public agencies in order to insure that they are reasonable. The estimates produced in this study do seem reasonable in light of similar data from a number of public agencies, and the forecasts under varying assumptions of migration rates became the basis for the travel forecasts included in Chapter 7.

Population Forecasting Methodology

The cohort-survival method of population forecasting was selected as most appropriate for this study. Techniques based upon graphical or mathematical extrapolation of past population trends in the aggregate were deemed generally unreliable for time periods greater than five to ten years.[1] These approaches were especially unreliable for application to Los Angeles County because they were concluded to be unresponsive to the significant changes in age-specific migration rates which could be expected to characterize this area during the forecast period.[2] Methods other than the cohort-survival technique would have been simpler and easier to apply. These would employ the application of trends in ratios of the study area's population to larger jurisdictions. Such ratio techniques might have been adequate to arrive at gross population totals for the study area during the next thirty years. The assumptions underlying the application of ratio techniques were considered inadequate, however, to produce useful estimates of population which were specific to the seven lifestyle areas and also specific to the ages of the population subgroups.[3]

1. State of California, Department of Finance, Financial and Population Research Section, *Population Projections for California Counties 1975–2020,* Report No. 74 P-2 (1974), p. 1.

2. Van Beuren Stanbery, *Population Forecasting Methods: A Report on Forecasting and Estimating Methods,* prepared for the U.S. Department of Commerce, Bureau of Public Roads, Urban Planning Division (1952, revised and condensed 1964), pp. 18–25.

3. Ibid., pp. 25–29.

The cohort-survival method was deemed most appropriate because it produces age- and sex-specific estimates of future populations. This method takes into account the population at the start of the forecasting period as well as the three components that change this base figure—births, deaths, and migration. It was thought that more accurate predictions could be made by using specific rates of change for individual population components than by using rates of change for the population as a whole.[4] For example, a more accurate forecast can be made by applying appropriate survival rates to each age cohort rather than by applying a county-wide average survival rate to all cohorts.

The cohort-survival technique was employed to estimate the elderly population for the seven lifestyle groups in 1990 and 2000. The lifestyle group was taken as the appropriate unit of aggregation for several reasons. First, and most important, it was determined in Chapter 3 of this study that travel behavior varied in a statistically significant manner across the lifestyle groups. Because the population forecasts were to be used to estimate future travel by the elderly, it seemed essential to base these forecasts upon population characteristics closely associated with travel behavior. Second, it was considered unreasonable to project population over a time period as long as thirty years for disaggregate units of analysis, such as individual census tracts. If highly aggregative units of analysis were not employed, forecasting errors might have exceeded the magnitudes of the forecasted variables. The seven lifestyle areas, in addition to their association with travel patterns, provided satisfactorily high levels of aggregation.

The cohort survival method as applied in this study involved several steps, which are summarized as follows:

Step 1. Population data for Los Angeles County were retrieved from the United States Census. The population over age 35 in the 1970 census was subdivided into specific age and sex cohorts for each of the seven lifestyle areas.

4. Ibid., p. 29.

Age groups 35 and over were chosen because they will constitute the entire elderly population (those 65 and older) in the year 2000.

Step 2.   The age of each cohort was advanced through one ten-year forecast interval. During each interval, some members of each cohort can be expected to die. Age specific survival rates were applied to compute the number of survivors expected to remain among the cohort total. Ten-year survival rates, shown in Table 25, were calculated using five-year survival rates projected by the U.S. Bureau of the Census.[5]

Step 3.   Total net migration was projected and distributed by age and sex. These migration figures were then added to or subtracted from the appropriate surviving cohort memberships to determine future populations of the respective lifestyle areas.

There were no satisfactory measures of migration rates either into or out of Los Angeles County or from one lifestyle area to another within the county. Yet migration rates and the assumptions that underlie the projected quantity of migration were perhaps the most critical elements in the forecasting model.

A residual migration method was employed in this study. After examining 1960 and 1970 census data, it was possible to derive a basis for projecting migration over the forecast period. Using the 1960 population data, survival

5. U.S. Department of Commerce, Bureau of the Census, Series P-25, No. 601 (October 1975), p. 130, Table B–1. To illustrate how survival rates were obtained for ten year periods, the calculation of the 1980–1990 survival rate for males aged 45 to 49 in 1980 is taken as an example:

	1980–85	1985–90
45–49	.957876	.959086
50–54	.934549	.935645

The probability of surviving until 1985 for those 45 to 49 in 1980–1985 is .957876. In 1985–1990 this subcohort will be aged 50 to 54. The probability of survival (to age 55 to 59) through 1990 for those 50 to 54 in 1985–1990 is .935645. Thus, the probability of surviving from 1980–1990 is the product of the two five-year rates or: (.957876) (.935645) = .896232.

Table 25. Projected Survival Rates* by Age and Sex

Age-Sex Cohorts	(1) 1970-75	(2) 1975-80	(3) 1970-80 (1)x(2)	(4) 1980-85	(5) 1985-90	(6) 1980-90 (4)x(5)	(7) 1990-95	(8) 1995-2000	(9) 1990-2000 (7)x(8)
M 35-39	.982354	.972836	.955669						
M 40-44	.972170	.957040	.930406						
F 35-39	.989523	.984169	.973858						
F 40-44	.983780	.976437	.960599						
M 45-49	.956037	.933383	.892349	.957876	.935645	.896232			
M 50-54	.932087	.899862	.838750	.934549	.902657	.843577			
F 45-49	.975784	.965977	.942585	.976954	.967433	.945138			
F 50-54	.964984	.959870	.917574	.966701	.953072	.921336			
M 55-59	.897673	.852301	.765088	.901113	.855962	.771318	.904110	.859358	.776954
M 60-64	.850293	.790463	.672125	.854666	.794360	.678912	.857725	.797309	.683872
F 55-59	.949078	.930779	.883382	.951968	.934272	.889397	.954186	.937323	.894380
F 60-64	.928775	.895951	.832137	.932769	.901080	.840499	.935786	.905365	.847228
M 65-69	.788015	.710259	.559695	.791870	.714944	.566143	.795494	.719784	.572584
M 70-74	.709817	.605016	.429451	.713014	.613883	.437707	.718197	.621615	.446442
F 65-69	.892498	.832189	.742727	.898076	.839789	.754194	.903118	.847452	.765349
F 70-74	.826786	.733118	.606131	.836506	.744716	.622959	.844353	.754904	.637405
M 75-79	.600375	.500000	.300188	.609724	.500000	.304862	.616921	.500000	.308461
M 80-84	.500000	.500000	.250000	.500000	.500000	.250000	.500000	.500000	.250000
F 75-79	.726062	.600000	.435637	.738872	.600000	.443323	.748855	.600000	.449313
F 80-84	.600000	.600000	.360000	.600000	.600000	.360000	.600000	.600000	.360000

* A survival rate is simply the proportion of the population in any cohort which can be expected to live through the period shown at the head of the appropriate column.

rates were applied to five-year cohorts, and the resulting figures were compared with 1970 data. The difference between the two figures was a measure of in- or out-migration during the decade of the 1960s. Hence, net migration determined in this manner included movements into and out of the county, as well as those from one lifestyle area to another.[6] Some error was involved in these estimates, because current survival rates were applied and assumed valid for the 1960–1970 period. This probably overstated actual survival during the period; therefore, in-migration may be slightly understated for those lifestyles experiencing it, while out-migration may be slightly overstated. These small imprecisions were not important because the migration matrix obtained was used only as a guide or base, from which future migration was to be estimated. By analyzing Table 26 by lifestyle area (down the columns) and by age (across the rows), and by incorporating judgments about future county growth, three alternative migration scenarios were formulated. Because migration may vary considerably, the use of high, medium, and low migration scenarios enabled the impact of such variations to be understood.[7]

6. As an example to illustrate this procedure, the calculations for the male 45 to 49 cohort in the black lifestyle area are shown below:
   a) The 1960 population for males 45 to 49 was 20,150.
   b) The survival rate for males 45 to 49 was .892349.
   c) Application of the survival rate to the population yields:
$$(20,150) \ (.892349) = 17,981$$
   d) The 1970 population of males 55 to 59 was 13,458.
   e) Thus, with no migration, 17,891 males should have aged into the 55 to 59 category during the decade. This 1970 census indicates that there were only 13,458 in this cohort. Therefore, it is concluded that 4,523 individuals have migrated away from this lifestyle area during the decade.
   f) Using the same procedure, 4,545 females in this cohort were found to have migrated out, making a total of 9,068 out-migrants aged 45 to 49 in this lifestyle area (see Table 26).

7. The population forecasts were performed by differentiating the population by sex. However, for simplicity of presentation, the remaining tables in this chapter have added the sexes together. In the case of the calculations shown in the previous footnote, 9,068 out-migrants are reported rather than the two separate figures for males and females.

Although net migration appeared to be small for the 1960–1970 period, population groups aged 35 and older exhibited a net migration out of the county of approximately 32,000 people. For the county as a whole, net in-migration for the decade amounted to approximately 253,000, while the county's total population rose by almost one million people during the same period. Because there was net out-migration among those over 35, the county's growth was attributable to a combination of natural increase (births minus deaths) and substantial in-migration of persons under 35. Examination of birth and death statistics showed that natural increase contributed approximately 741,000, or about three-fourths of the total population increase during the decade.[8] Conversations with staff members in the Population Research Section of the County Department of Regional Planning confirmed these inferences regarding the age characteristics of migrants. For the county as a whole, it appears that the current trend is for the middle-aged and the elderly to leave, while families headed by young adults tend to migrate into or remain within Los Angeles County because of its continued role as an employment center.

Data in Table 26 indicate that migration patterns varied considerably from one lifestyle area to another among the age groups involved in this study. Between 1960 and 1970, about 20 percent of the residents of the black community migrated out of that area, while among the new suburbanites net migration into the area constituted nearly 30 percent of the 1960 population. All other lifestyle areas varied between these two extremes. In the black community net migration was actually considerably larger than the total net population change between 1960 and 1970. The large outward migration was offset somewhat by the many black residents who entered the group by reaching the age of 35 during the decade of the 1960s. Nearly three-fourths of the growth in population among the institutionalized during the 1960s was due to migration, while only about

8. U.S. Department of Commerce, Bureau of the Census, Series P-25, No. 461, (June 28, 1971), p. 10.

Table 26. Migration by Age and Lifestyle Area, 1960–1970

Age Groups	Spanish American	New Suburbanites	Black Community	Central City Dwellers	Early Suburbanites	Financially Secure	Institutionalized	All Lifestyle Groups
35–39	8,275	18,998	− 9,718	1,690	−16,333	957	1,065	4,934
40–44	7,344	16,844	− 8,581	1,584	−14,403	907	930	4,625
45–49	3,313	13,648	− 9,068	576	− 5,524	−2,860	557	− 510
50–54	2,317	10,457	− 7,775	− 1,556	− 5,999	−2,604	431	− 4,729
55–59	59	8,384	− 7,180	− 5,441	− 3,157	−2,398	− 160	− 9,893
60–64	− 19	6,380	− 5,690	− 4,640	− 2,699	−1,979	− 51	− 8,698
65–69	− 716	4,937	− 5,524	− 7,976	− 1,140	− 839	− 234	−11,492
70–74	− 215	3,394	− 3,241	− 4,391	510	− 245	− 97	− 5,305
75–84	310	2,673	− 2,477	− 3,225	1,133	764	38	− 784
Net Migration for Ages 35–84	20,668	85,715	−59,254	−24,531	−48,632	−8,297	2,479	−31,852
1960 Population over Age 35	210,432	307,090	297,818	676,587	881,507	319,504	16,435	2,709,373
1970 Population over Age 35	275,282	529,629	259,413	634,996	985,050	341,243	19,668	3,045,281
Population Change 1960–1970 over Age 35	64,850	222,539	−38,405	−41,591	103,543	21,739	3,233	355,908
Net Migration As Percent of 1960 Population over 35	9.8%	27.9%	− 19.9%	− 3.6%	− 5.5%	− 2.6%	15.1%	− 1.2%
Net Migration As Percent of 10-Year Population Change among Those over Age 35	31.9%	38.5%	154.3%	60.0%	− 47.0%	−38.2%	76.7%	− 9.5%

Note: It was assumed that there was zero net migration among those over age 85 in order to arrive at these figures. The numbers of individuals over age 85 in each lifestyle group were very small.

one-third of the growth in the Spanish-American and new suburban lifestyle areas was due to migration. This wide variation in migration patterns demonstrates the importance which should be attached to the migration scenarios when considering future population shifts among the lifestyle areas.

Step 4.   When employing cohort-survival techniques, the population of the youngest cohort is normally estimated at this point by utilizing fertility rates of women in child-bearing age groups. Since this study was concerned with the future elderly population, the need for birth rates was eliminated. All those in the target population were alive in the base year of 1970.

Step 5.   Steps 1 through 4 were then repeated for the next two forecast periods, reaching the horizon dates of the forecast, 1990 and 2000.

Every population forecast is, of course, a judgmental exercise, especially with regard to migration. All three components of regional population change — births, deaths, and migration — are dependent upon a variety of factors, including economic activity in the region, its housing and labor markets, amenities which it features, and the climate which it offers. Because of the many variables to which population changes may be sensitive, any forecast is based on a set of assumptions. Some of these assumptions may be termed "macro" since they deal with the larger context within which forecasts are made. Examples of this type of assumption are: (a) that the social, economic, and political institutions and organizations of the region and its surroundings will remain stable throughout the forecast period; (b) that there will be no occurrence of all-out war; (c) that there will be no occurrence of large-scale disasters such as earthquakes, drought, fires, epidemics, and famine. Deviations from such assumptions will render any population forecast inaccurate since these deviations far outweigh any "micro" assumptions internal to the forecast itself.

More specific assumptions are of greater interest to the forecaster, since it is these assumptions which form the "rational" basis of the forecast. Typical of these assumptions are: (a) that the state of medical technology and the resulting death rates will not change drastically in the near future; (b) that the age and sex composition of in- and out-migrants will remain stable; (c) that the factors influencing decisions concerning residential and business location within the study area will experience no dramatic changes. Many such assumptions were made in this study. They will be enumerated in the following section.

Population Forecast Scenarios

Utilizing the forecast survival rate table and the 1960–1970 migration matrix, it was possible to produce three forecasts of the 1990 and 2000 elderly population. Differences among these scenarios were attributable solely to varying assumptions regarding migration. Net migration out of the county by the population 35 years and older was projected under all three scenarios, consistent with current general trends in the age composition of migrants into and out of Los Angeles.

Although the county experienced rapid population growth in the early 1960s, that growth appeared to diminish during the latter part of the decade. Current estimates generally show a stablization of population. However, this levelling off of aggregate population obscures significant demographic changes occurring within the county by age categories. As noted previously, population growth was largely accounted for by natural increase and in-migration of young adults. This growth was partially offset by out-migration of approximately 32,000 people among those 35 and older between 1960 and 1970. It would be misleading, however, to assume that out-migration will continue at the overall 1960–1970 rate, since aggregate population growth varied systematically during the period, from strong in-migration at the beginning to strong out-migration at the end of the decade. Over the decade, these two elements appeared to have approximately balanced each other. It is probable, therefore, that the overall figure for out-migration during the decade of 1960–1970 understates the current rate of out-migration.

Migration rates of the 1960s were thus viewed as the lowest possible estimate of future rates of out-migration for purposes of this projection. Utilizing Table 26 and incorporating assumptions of future Los Angeles County growth, it was possible to derive the following migration figures:

Scenario	1970–80	1980–90	1990–2000
Low	− 52,000	− 51,500	− 41,500
Medium	−142,500	−112,500	− 75,500
High	−194,000	−151,500	−103,000

[The specific components (by age and lifestyle area) comprising these figures are documented in the following sections.]

These figures were not strictly comparable to other migration forecasts available for the county, since they applied only to persons 35 and older. Two other available population forecasts incorporated estimates for out-migration for the county population as a whole. The County Department of Regional Planning has estimated that net out-migration among all age groups will total 458,000 during the period 1970–1980, 370,000 during 1980–1990, and zero for 1990–2000. In its statewide forecast, the California State Department of Finance estimated substantially higher out-migration for Los Angeles County among all age groups: 400,000 for the period 1970–1975 alone, gradually diminishing to 110,000 in the period 1995–2000.

In Table 27 the results of these two alternate forecasts for the age groups in this study are compared to the estimates resulting from the three scenarios discussed above. Figures from the SCAG-76 forecast are also included for comparison; the SCAG-76 estimates relied heavily on the aforementioned Department of Finance forecast, however, so they should not be considered as independent estimates. Table 27 shows that for the total county elderly population, the Department of Finance consistently forecast the lowest estimate, while the Los Angeles County Planning Department consistently forecast the highest. The three forecast scenarios generated in the present study consistently fell between these two extremes.

All forecasts concurred that there will be net out-migration among the elderly during the next decades, but all pointed to an increasing number of county residents aged 65 and older in the years 1990 and 2000. If future transportation needs of the elderly are to be ascertained, on the basis of previously analyzed associations between travel behavior and lifestyle characteristics of the elderly, population changes within individual elderly lifestyle areas need to be examined. Assumptions regarding future population changes in each lifestyle area are discussed in the following presentations of the three forecast scenarios.

Low Migration Scenario

The lowest out-migration among persons 35 and older was forecast to be 52,000 during 1970–1980, 51,500 during 1980–1990, and 41,500 during 1990–2000. The components comprising these aggregate ten-year totals are shown in Table 28. By comparing the rows with one another, one may examine the forecast migration subtotals by age. Similarly, by comparing the columns, one may examine migration assumptions by lifestyle area.

Generally, the youngest cohort analyzed (35–44) was assumed to migrate out of the county at a low rate. Net out-migration for this cohort was forecast to be approximately 12,000 for the 1970–1980 decade. Out-migration will increase in the middle-aged cohorts (those 45 to 54 and 55 to 64), reaching a high of over 20,000 out-migrants during the 1990–2000 period. Out-migration among the elderly (the 65 to 74 and 75+ cohorts) was projected to be smaller than that of the middle-aged cohorts over the forecast period. The elderly cohorts (65 to 74 and 75+) were still estimated, however, to migrate out in greater numbers than the youngest (35 to 44) cohort.

Table 27. Population Forecast Comparisons

		State of California, Dept. of Finance (D-100)	SCAG-76	L. A. County, Dept. of Regional Planning	Low Migration Scenario	Medium Migration Scenario	High Migration Scenario
1990	M 65-74	179,350	184,700	241,917	250,100	232,100	217,500
	F 65-74	282,160	290,000	339,740	353,900	331,700	318,000
	M 75+	109,240	112,200	123,895	126,500	112,500	102,600
	F 75+	205,150	211,200	297,560	250,300	228,400	213,600
	TOTAL	775,900	798,100	1,003,112	980,800	904,700	851,700
2000	M 65-74	149,580	151,000	218,419	234,600	211,200	197,100
	F 65-74	242,170	244,300	305,556	321,500	291,300	271,800
	M 75+	116,590	116,300	152,908	155,700	137,700	120,600
	F 75+	240,000	239,400	313,676	314,300	289,000	267,900
	TOTAL	748,340	751,000	1,060,559	1,026,100	929,200	857,400

Table 28. Migration Forecasts: Low Migration Scenario
(Figures in Thousands)

		Spanish-American	New Suburbanites			Black Community	Central City Dwellers	Early Suburbanites	Financially Secure	Institutionalized	Net		
			1970-1980	1980-1990	1990-2000						1970-1980	1980-1990	1990-2000
Young	35-39	4	10			-7	0	-14.5	0.5	0	-7		
	40-44	4	8			-5	0	-12.5	0.5	0	-5		
Middle-Aged	45-49	1.5	7	3.5		-6	0	-4.5	-2	0	-4	-7.5	-12
	50-54	0.5	5	2.5		-4	0	-5	-1.5	0	-5	-7.5	-10
	55-59	0	5	3	1	-4	-5	-2.5	-1.5	0	-8	-10	-12
	60-64	0	3.5	2.5	1	-3.5	-4	-2	-1.5	0	-7.5	-8.5	-10
Elderly	65-69	0	2.5	1	0.5	-3	-7.5	-0.5	0	0	-8.5	-10	-10.5
	70-74	0	1	0.5	0	-1.5	-4	0	0	0	-4.5	-5	-5.5
	75-84	0	1	0.5	0	-1.5	-2	0	0	0	-2.5	-3	-3.5
	Total Net Migration										-52	-51.5	-41.5

Many assumptions regarding age were made in forecasting population changes by lifestyle area. Members of the Spanish-American community, especially the older cohorts, were seen as being relatively stable over the forecast period. Population growth was assumed to occur among those under 35 through natural increase, in-migration, and the aging of populous, younger cohorts.

Immigration was assumed to continue to contribute to population growth in the new suburban areas, as new housing continues to attract new residents. This trend will slow, however, as new housing becomes less available and previously new homes grow older. Within this lifestyle group, in-migration was estimated to be greatest among the youngest cohorts and to diminish gradually among the older cohorts. This reflects the finding that migrants to the new suburban area were typically younger middle-aged families (many of whom may have migrated away from the early suburban community).

The black lifestyle group was forecast to continue the basic trend of out-migration exhibited during the previous decade. In accord with 1960–1970 trends, migration was assumed to be largest among the younger cohorts, diminishing with age. The assumption for this group was that population will increase through births and the in-migration of young adults, while those over 35 will continue to migrate out. Although the elderly will migrate out to a slight degree, they were forecast to remain a relatively stable component of the total black population.

Future central-city dwellers were estimated to be mainly young adults aged 25 to 34 who will migrate in. These young people will only partly replace older residents, who will tend to migrate out. This out-migration was estimated to be largest for the 55 to 64 cohort and to diminish gradually with age. The number of persons in the middle-age cohorts (35 to 44, 45 to 54) was assumed to remain fairly constant during the period, in accord with 1960–1970 evidence.

The financially secure were also expected to reflect growth among younger cohorts, though to a lesser degree than will be the case with new suburbanites. Slight out-migration was expected from the middle-aged cohorts in accord with the 1970–1980 experience. The older cohorts were assumed to remain stable and to continue residency in this community.

Because of the special nature of the institutionalized lifestyle area, demographic changes within it were not considered to be of major significance to this forecast. Net migration was assumed to be zero and the resulting elderly population residing in these fourteen census tracts amounted to less than 1 percent of the forecast elderly population of the county.

Medium Migration Scenario

The low migration scenario, although forecasting slightly higher out-migration in comparison with that experienced in the 1960–1970 period, nonetheless employed conservative estimates of current and future migration. The medium migration scenario utilized similar assumptions regarding the distribution of total migration, but estimated higher out-migration and lower in-migration than that experienced during the 1960–1970 decade.

The result of these changes, displayed in Table 29, yielded net out-migration figures among those 35 and older of 142,500 during 1970–1980, 112,500 during 1980–1990, and 75,500 during 1990–2000. Several assumptions combined to produce this projected increase in out-migration. The small in-migration previously forecast for the Spanish-American community was reduced to zero, and it was assumed that in this area the population 35 and older would show no net in-migration. Similarly, the in-migration of the new suburban lifestyle area was revised downward, reflecting somewhat slower population growth. As in the first scenario, the institutionalized population was projected to remain stable. For the other four lifestyle areas, out-migration estimates were adjusted upward to levels slightly higher than the estimates of the low migration scenario in their respective age categories. These adjustments may not be unreasonable in view of the

Table 29. Migration Forecasts: Medium Migration Scenario
(Figures in Thousands)

		Spanish-American	New Suburbanites 1970–1980	New Suburbanites 1980–1990	New Suburbanites 1990–2000	Black Community	Central City Dwellers	Early Suburbanites	Financially Secure	Institutionalized	Net 1970–1980	Net 1980–1990	Net 1990–2000
Young	35–39	0	8			-10	0	-16.5	0	0	-18.5		
	40–44	0	6			-10	0	-15	0	0	-19		
Middle-Aged	45–49	0	5	2.5		-10	-1.5	-6	-4	0	-16.5	-19	
	50–54	0	3	1.5		-8	-2.5	-6.5	-4	0	-18	-19.5	
	55–59	0	3	1	0	-7	-7	-4	-3	0	-18	-20	-21
	60–64	0	2	0.5	0	-6	-6	-3	-3	0	-16	-17.5	-18
Elderly	65–69	0	0	0	0	-6	-9	-1.5	-1	0	-17.5	-17.5	-17.5
	70–74	0	0	0	0	-3.5	-6	-1.5	-1	0	-12	-12	-12
	75–84	0	0	0	0	-3	-4	0	0	0	-7	-7	-7
Total Net Migration											-142.5	-112.5	-75.5

fact that recent trends, especially those since the mid-1960s, have exhibited accelerating migration out of Los Angeles.

High Migration Scenario

The high migration scenario forecast that those lifestyle areas currently exhibiting very high levels of out-migration will continue to do so. The principal components of this group are the central-city and early suburban communities and, to a lesser extent, the financially secure area. Under this scenario, assumptions for the remaining four communities remained identical to the medium migration scenario. It was felt that migration totals for these four subpopulations were unlikely to be more extreme than those previously forecast and could not be adjusted either upward (black community) or downward (Spanish-American and new suburban areas) with any degree of confidence. Again, the institutionalized group was assumed to remain at zero net migration.

As shown in Table 30, these adjustments resulted in a net out-migration of 194,000 during 1970–1980, 151,500 during 1980–1990, and 103,000 during 1990–2000. As in the medium migration scenario, the kinds of assumptions regarding the age characteristics of migrants remained similar to those of the low migration scenario. The three forecast scenarios differed in the total volume of the migrant population.

The results of the three forecasts for 1980, 1990, and 2000 are shown in Tables 31 through 33, respectively. These tables show not only county-wide totals by age as reported in Table 27, but also cohort totals in each of the seven lifestyle groups. In addition, for 1990 and 2000 the total elderly population in each lifestyle is displayed in the bottom row of the tables.

Comparison of Population Forecasts with Housing Market Projections

A population forecast which has predicted substantial growth within a particular area should be consistent with

Table 30. Migration Forecasts: High Migration Scenario
(Figures in Thousands)

		Spanish-American	New Suburbanites 1970-1980	New Suburbanites 1980-1990	New Suburbanites 1990-2000	Black Community	Central City Dwellers	Early Suburbanites	Financially Secure	Institution-alized	Net 1970-1980	Net 1980-1990	Net 1990-2000
Young	35-39	0	8			-10	- 1	-20.5	-1.5	0	- 25		
	40-44	0	6			-10	- 1	-18.5	-1.5	0	- 25		
Middle-Aged	45-49	0	5	2.5		-10	- 2.5	- 9	-6	0	- 22.5	- 25	
	50-54	0	3	1.5		- 8	- 3.5	- 9	-6	0	- 23.5	- 25	
	55-59	0	3	1	0	- 7	- 9	- 6.5	-6	0	- 25.5	- 27.5	- 28.5
	60-64	0	2	0.5	0	- 6	- 8.5	- 5	-6	0	- 23.5	- 25	- 25.5
Elderly	65-69	0	0	0	0	- 6	-12	- 2.5	-2	0	- 22.5	- 22.5	- 22.5
	70-74	0	0	0	0	- 3.5	- 8	- 2.5	-2	0	- 16	- 16	- 16
	75-84	0	0	0	0	- 3	- 5.5	- 1	-1	0	- 10.5	- 10.5	- 10.5
	Total Net Migration										-194	-151.5	-103

Table 31. Low Migration Scenario:
Population by Lifestyle Area and Age, 1990–2000

	Spanish-American 1990	Spanish-American 2000	New Suburbanites 1990	New Suburbanites 2000	Black Community 1990	Black Community 2000	Central City Dwellers 1990	Central City Dwellers 2000
65–74	55,300	68,300	132,600	147,400	35,800	30,100	103,700	82,200
75+	34,500	44,500	67,300	103,500	22,700	23,400	78,800	74,400
Total	89,800	112,800	199,900	250,900	58,500	53,500	182,500	156,600

	Early Suburbanites 1990	Early Suburbanites 2000	Financially Secure 1990	Financially Secure 2000	Institutionalized 1990	Institutionalized 2000	Total 1990	Total 2000
65–74	206,800	170,600	65,900	54,000	3,900	3,500	604,000	556,100
75+	123,200	165,800	47,900	55,400	2,400	3,000	376,800	470,000
Total	330,000	336,400	113,800	109,400	6,300	6,500	980,800	1,026,100

Table 32. Medium Migration Scenario: Population by Lifestyle Area and Age, 1990–2000

	Spanish-American 1990	Spanish-American 2000	New Suburbanites 1990	New Suburbanites 2000	Black Community 1990	Black Community 2000	Central City Dwellers 1990	Central City Dwellers 2000
65–74	52,800	60,800	125,400	140,900	24,000	12,400	96,500	75,500
75+	34,500	42,900	61,800	97,100	10,800	12,100	69,700	64,300
Total	87,300	103,700	187,200	238,000	34,800	24,500	166,200	139,800

	Early Suburbanites 1990	Early Suburbanites 2000	Financially Secure 1990	Financially Secure 2000	Institutionalized 1990	Institutionalized 2000	Total 1990	Total 2000
65–74	201,900	162,600	59,300	46,800	3,900	3,500	563,800	502,500
75+	118,200	159,000	43,500	48,300	2,400	3,000	340,900	426,700
Total	320,100	321,600	102,800	95,100	6,300	6,500	904,700	929,200

Table 33. High Migration Scenario:
Population by Lifestyle Area and Age, 1990–2000

	Spanish-American 1990	2000	New Suburbanites 1990	2000	Black Community 1990	2000	Central City Dwellers 1990	2000
65–74	52,800	60,800	125,400	140,900	24,000	12,400	86,300	67,900
75+	34,500	42,900	61,800	97,100	10,800	12,100	58,800	47,100
Total	87,300	103,700	187,200	238,00	34,800	24,500	145,100	115,000

	Early Suburbanites 1990	2000	Financially Secure 1990	2000	Institutionalized 1990	2000	Total 1990	2000
65–74	193,000	148,100	50,100	35,300	3,900	3,500	535,500	468,900
75+	111,800	148,900	36,100	37,400	2,400	3,000	316,200	388,500
Total	304,800	297,000	86,200	72,700	6,300	6,500	851,700	857,400

independently prepared housing forecasts which have predicted growth in construction activity. Similarly, a forecast of declining population growth for a particular area would, in general, be inconsistent with a projection of substantial growth in the area's housing stock. For this reason, the foregoing population projections and their assumptions regarding future locational changes within Los Angeles County were examined for their consistency with available projections of housing market activity. The forecast of housing market activity employed here was the most recent one available from the Southern California Association of Governments (SCAG).[9] Patterns of forecast population growth, in general, corresponded very well with housing units that were expected to be added in the future.

The Spanish-American lifestyle area was forecast to be relatively stable for age groups 35 and older, with most population growth occurring among the under 35 cohorts. Since much of the population increase is expected to occur through natural increase, little new housing activity is expected in this area. Housing projections show the lowest growth rates for this community, principally the east-central statistical area of the SCAG forecast. The largest growth rates in housing expected are for the Antelope Valley and Malibu areas, both of which were classified as being in the new suburban community. Consistent with these housing data, the new suburban area was forecast to grow in almost all age categories and under all three scenarios. The financially secure area was projected to grow in population, although the elderly component was forecast to remain relatively stable. Projected housing data showed that, in relation to the rest of the county, the rate of new housing for this lifestyle area would be moderately high, although not as high as the aforementioned new suburban community. Moderately high growth rates in housing were projected for the central-city area as well.

9. Southern California Association of Governments, *SCAG-76 Growth Forecast Policy* (Los Angeles: Southern California Association of Governments 1976), pp. 33–45.

Although this population forecast predicted out-migration among those 35 and over, the moderately high growth rate in housing was not inconsistent with population figures. Despite moderate out-migration, the remaining elderly are expected to be joined by young adults migrating to the central areas. The remaining lifestyle areas, namely the black and the early suburban communities, will be characterized by an increasingly young adult population and more and more out-migration among those 35 and older. Growth rates in housing were projected by SCAG to be moderate to low in relation to the county as a whole. Housing growth rates for the institutionalized, characterized by a small population and localized in isolated spots throughout the county, were difficult to analyze. But, because of the characteristics of this area, demographic changes were not considered to be of major significance to the population forecast.

Overall, the SCAG forecast and the present population forecast were found consistent, providing an additional degree of confidence in their use. It is regrettable that no housing data were sufficiently detailed so as to allow a preferred choice among the three population forecast scenarios.

Summary and Conclusions

For this study the most appropriate population forecasting method was determined to be the cohort-survival method, which specifically accounted for the three components of regional population change—births, deaths, and migration. Because the focus of the study was the elderly population, the birth component was safely ignored. Projected survival rates were obtained from the Census Bureau. Finally, migration by age and by sex was estimated through application of the residual migration method.

By utilizing the residual migration method and census data, and by employing assumptions about future demographic changes in the county, three forecast scenarios were obtained. These three forecasts, after having been summed up over all areas, compared reasonably with population forecasts of the California Department of Finance and the County Department of Regional Planning. Moreover, this particular forecasting method yielded a population projection for the seven areas of interest to this study. These projections by community were then compared to and found consistent with available housing projections for the county.

The principal finding of this demographic study suggested that the middle-aged and the elderly will continue to migrate out of Los Angeles County in the future. Despite this out-migration, the elderly population in the county can be expected to grow by 1990 and 2000. Transportation policy will therefore need to address the problems posed by an increasing elderly population distributed unevenly among a variety of lifestyles. The next chapter will estimate the implications of this population distribution for transportation planners by developing forecasts of future travel by the elderly.

Chapter 7
The Future Travel Patterns of the Elderly

*T*he final analytical task consisted of developing a forecast of probable travel by the elderly of the future for a variety of purposes and a number of modes. This forecast builds directly upon the distributions of population in the years 1990 and 2000 which were arrived at in Chapter 6. The caveats which applied to those forecasts are thus even more applicable here. These projections are not intended to serve as the basis of operational transportation planning; rather, they are meant to be scenarios against which strategic policy alternatives can be evaluated in general terms. Major trends in the data, such as sweeping differences between lifestyles, emerge as being significant. The specific numbers which constitute elements of the forecasts are not necessarily highly accurate nor of great technical significance. The findings of Chapter 3 revealed that travel patterns of today's elderly vary systematically with differences in lifestyle. When combined with the population projections of Chapter 6, these findings form the building blocks for the following forecasts of travel by senior citizens.

The Travel Forecast

The trip generation forecasting technique chosen was a form of cross-classification analysis. The more widely used technique, multiple linear regression, was explored but was judged to be unsuitable for application to this research. Because the successful use of multiple linear regression demanded consistent, reliable projections of several socioeconomic variables which might be used as independent variables, emphasis was initially placed upon determining the availability of such projections through 1990 and 2000. Because of their association with travel, variables of particular interest were median income, automobile ownership, and housing status. Several forecasts of these variables were collected from public agencies. These forecasts were not consistent with each other, however, because they were based on varying population projections and diverging scenarios regarding future directions for Los Angeles County. In addition, several agencies were in the process of revising their forecasts in order to reflect demographic changes that had occurred in the county within the past decade. Statistically satisfying regression equations could have been fit using the origin-destination data of the 1967 Los Angeles Regional Transportation Study (LARTS). When used for forecasting, however, these equations would have been only as good as the forecasts of the independent variables which they utilized. Because of the great differences among estimates of these variables, the errors that might arise from the utilization of these forecasts would be too great to be tolerated. Consequently, multiple linear regression was rejected as a tool for trip generation forecasting.

Attention was then directed toward the cross-classification technique.[1] In using this technique, the independent variables deemed to be of greatest significance in influencing travel behavior, such as persons per dwelling unit and number of automobiles owned, are cross-classified in tabular form. Within the tables the differing mean trip rates are entered corresponding to specific values of the independent variables. For example, in

1. U.S. Department of Transportation, Federal Highway Administration, Urban Planning Division, *Trip Generation Analysis* (Washington, D.C.: U.S. Government Printing Office, 1975).

Table 34. Example of a Trip Rate Cross-Classification Table

Average Total Trips Per Dwelling
Unit Per Day

Characteristic i	Characteristic j			
	j_0	j_1	j_2	j_3
i_0	x_{00}	x_{01}	x_{02}	x_{03}
i_1	x_{10}	x_{11}	x_{12}	x_{13}
i_2	x_{20}	x_{21}	x_{22}	x_{23}
i_3	x_{30}	x_{31}	x_{32}	x_{33}

Table 34, members of a household with characteristics i_3 and j_2 make an average of x_{32} trips per day. Forecasts can be made for future trips by forecasting the number of future households with characteristics i_3 and j_2. As will be explained later, the only forecast needed for this analysis was the population forecast of Chapter 6. Forecasts of population and travel are thus consistent with each other, a consistency which would have been unattainable had multiple regression been used under the circumstances discussed above.

Use of this technique involved three assumptions. One was that households with similar values of the cross-classified variables exhibit similar travel behavior. All households with characteristics i_3 and j_2 were assumed to make the same number of trips per day. Although this assumption may be unrealistic when applied to a population in the aggregate, in this study the county population had been disaggregated into six lifestyle areas[2] and separate cross-classifications could be carried out for each. By clustering people into different lifestyles, it was possible to consider separately groups that were more homogeneous

2. The institutionalized group was again not considered due to insufficient data.

than they would have been if forecasts had been made on a county-wide basis.

Appropriate application of cross-classification required that the independent variables chosen for cross-classification were the most significant in determining travel behavior. The choice of appropriate independent variables was thus critical. Of the many variables available, two have repeatedly appeared in past studies, such as the Puget Sound Regional Transportation Study,[3] LARTS,[4] and the Chicago Area Transportation Study (CATS).[5] These variables—the number of automobiles available to members of a household and the size of the household itself—have proven to be of the greatest significance in explaining and predicting travel behavior. Additional evidence to support the importance of these two variables can be found in a national household survey conducted by the University of Michigan to determine the most important factors influencing trip generation.[6] That study also found that the two most important variables were family size and automobile ownership. Of these latter two variables, automobile ownership was deemed to be of greater importance in this study. Since only the last stage of the family life cycle was being considered, variation in family size was minimal. An elderly household is likely to consist of one or two people, while a middle-aged or young adult household may consist of from two to four or more persons, due to the greater likelihood of children being present. Support for this assumption is found in research by CATS. It found that among households headed by an el-

3. Puget Sound Regional Transportation Study, *Staff Report No. 16* (1964).

4. Los Angeles Regional Transportation Study, *The LARTS Transportation Model: Description and Assumptions*, Technical Report Series tr/2 (Los Angeles: State of California, Division of Highways, District 07, 1974).

5. Chicago Area Transportation Study, *1970 Travel Characteristics: Trip Generation*, CATS 372–49 (October 1976).

6. John Lansing and Eva Mueller, *Household Trip Production: Results of a Nationwide Survey* (Ann Arbor: University of Michigan, Survey Research Center, 1967).

derly person, 90 percent of these were one- or two-person households. Average household size was found to be 1.8 persons per household.[7]

A third assumption is that the mean travel rates (x_{ij}) associated with the cross-classified variables will remain relatively stable over time. Several studies examining the temporal stability of travel rates have given support to this last assumption. Smith and Cleveland report that in Detroit mean daily trip rates for households with more than one automobile were only about 10 percent higher in 1965 than in 1953.[8] Households with no cars exhibited travel rates about 20 percent lower in 1965 than in 1953. Because underreporting was suspected among those households reporting no trips, however, nontravelers were then excluded from the analysis, and this 20 percent decrease was transformed into a range from a 3.9 percent decrease to an 8.7 percent increase in travel. Smith and Cleveland also found that slightly higher travel rates prevailed in suburban areas than in the central city, a divergence which increased over the twelve-year period as central-city travel rates fell slightly, while those in suburban areas grew slightly. These results are confirmed by CATS, which documents changes in Chicago from 1956 to 1970.[9] Overall, in Chicago the travel rates per household increased from 6.21 to 6.88 per day, or an approximate 11 percent rise over the fourteen-year period. Households owning no automobiles traveled at approximately 25 percent lower rates in 1970 than in 1965. Households owning three or more cars exhibited travel rates approximately 15 percent higher, while households with one or two cars ranged from a 3 percent decrease to a 10 percent increase. Changes in travel rates varied with density, as low density suburban rates increased approximately 32 percent while

7. Chicago Area Transportation Study, *1970 Travel Characteristics*, pp. 37, 58.

8. Robert L. Smith, Jr., and Donald E. Cleveland, "Time Stability Analysis of Trip-Generation and Predistribution Modal-Choice Models," *Transportation Research Record* 569 (1976), pp. 76–86.

9. Chicago Area Transportation Study, *1970 Travel Characteristics*, pp. 31–56.

high density inner-city rates decreased approximately 13 percent. The fact that the changes varied with population density suggested that it was wise to consider different trip rates for different lifestyle areas. Densities varied considerably among lifestyle areas in Los Angeles: from 2.00 persons per gross acre in the new suburban lifestyle area to 6.62 persons per gross acre in the Spanish-American lifestyle area. Finally, Downes and Gyenes studied changes in trip generation rates in Reading, England, from 1962 to 1971. They found that home-based trips had representative errors of 10 to 15 percent of the mean trip rate at the zonal level. Stratification by trip purpose and mode resulted in errors of approximately 10 to 30 percent. When 1962 rates were used to forecast 1971 trips, the forecasting accuracy of the trip rates was equal to or slightly greater than the accuracy indicated by the foregoing errors. The authors concluded that there was considerable stability of travel rates in the nine-year period because the indicated variation about the mean rates amounted to only a few percent of those mean values.[10]

Cross-classification analysis is the approach to trip generation currently recommended by the U. S. Department of Transportation. It is preferred because, in comparison with regression analysis, it makes efficient use of survey data, it is valid for forecasting as well as in the base year, it is easily monitored and updated, and it is straightforward and understandable.[11] Since the analysis may assume many different forms, the specific methodology utilized in this study is described in the following paragraphs.

Description of Cross-Classification Forecast

The methodology employed consisted of six steps. First, the average household size for each lifestyle area was determined from 1970 U.S. Census data. These figures were

10. J.D. Downes and L. Gyenes, *Temporal Stability and Forecasting Ability of Trip Generation Models in Reading*, Transport and Road Research Laboratory Report No. LR 726 (Crowthorne, England: Department of the Environment, 1976).

11. U.S. Department of Transportation, Federal Highway Administration, Bureau of Public Roads, *Guidelines for Trip Generation Analysis* (Washington, D.C.: U.S. Government Printing Office, 1967), p. 21.

then used in conjunction with the population forecasts of Chapter 6 to yield the projected number of households in each lifestyle area in 1990 and 2000. The third step again utilized 1970 census data to determine automobile owner- ship rates per household by lifestyle area. The projected number of households was then allocated to categories of automobile ownership. The fifth step involved the 1967 LARTS data which yielded travel rates for each lifestyle area. Finally, the projected number of households owning automobiles was multiplied by the trip rates to produce the travel estimates for 1990 and 2000. Each of the six steps is presented in greater detail in the sections which follow.

Step 1: Determination of Average Household Size. The first step was to determine the average household size for each lifestyle area. Census data for households which in- cluded elderly persons were retrieved for each lifestyle area. These data, combined with the population data used in Chapter 6, were used to calculate the number of persons per household headed by an elderly person in each life- style area.[12] These results are given in Table 35.

Step 2: Aggregation of Forecast Population into Households. Using the rates of persons per household in Table 35, it was possible to calculate the number of households headed by elderly persons in 1990 and 2000 for each life- style area. The population forecasts of Chapter 6 were ad- justed to include only the elderly population residing in households headed by an elderly person. This count of persons for each lifestyle area was then divided by the appropriate persons per household, which yielded the projected number of future households headed by elderly persons, assuming family size will remain constant over time. These household projections for 1990 and 2000, for

12. Because available census data were organized in such a way that the number of automobiles owned is attributed to the household by the age of its head and not to individuals within the household, only households headed by elderly are considered in this calculation. Since about 90 percent of the elderly reside in these households, this proce- dure was deemed appropriate. The remaining 10 percent are reintro- duced into the discussion of future travel near the end of this chapter.

Table 35. Persons per Elderly-Headed
Household by Lifestyle

Lifestyle Area	Persons per Household
Spanish American	1.82
New Suburbanites	1.81
Black Community	1.41
Central City Dwellers	1.18
Early Suburbanites	1.54
Financially Secure	1.55

each of the three scenarios and for each of the six lifestyle areas, are shown in Table 36.

Step 3: Determination of 1970 Rates of Automobile Ownership. Next, the number of automobiles available in 1970 per household headed by the elderly and the middle-aged was determined using a special tabulation of the U.S. Census. A matrix of this type must be multiplied by a matrix of tripmaking rates per household to yield projected amounts of travel in the future. In earlier chapters, it was concluded that the elderly of the future will have a greater availability of automobiles than do today's elderly. While conventional thought holds that many elderly today do not have cars because these people are old, it has been shown that cohort differences explain why these people do not have cars to a greater extent than do aging effects. The predominance of automobile travel among today's middle-aged population suggests that it is unrealistic to expect automobile ownership of the future elderly to be similar to that of today's elderly. It was therefore hypothesized that automobile ownership among the elderly of the future would be more widespread than it is among today's older population. Acknowledging, however, that aging does play some role, it was further assumed that future automobile ownership among the elderly would be less than current automobile ownership is among the middle-aged. Hence, when projections of future travel behavior were made, they were bounded by estimates representing upper and lower limits to the quan-

Table 36. Projected Count of Households Under
Three Scenarios to 2000 by Lifestyle

Lifestyle Area	Migration Scenario	1990	2000
Spanish American	Low	45,020	56,540
	Medium	43,760	51,980
	High	43,760	51,980
New Suburbanites	Low	94,830	119,020
	Medium	88,810	112,910
	High	88,810	112,910
Black Community	Low	35,000	32,010
	Medium	20,820	14,660
	High	20,820	14,660
Central City Dwellers	Low	140,790	120,810
	Medium	128,210	107,850
	High	111,940	88,720
Early Suburbanites	Low	186,270	189,880
	Medium	180,680	181,530
	High	172,050	167,640
Financially Secure	Low	65,190	62,670
	Medium	58,890	54,480
	High	49,380	41,650

tity of travel. The upper limit was based on current rates of automobile ownership among the middle-aged, while the lower limit was based on current ownership patterns of the elderly.

Table 37 shows the 1970 distribution of households by lifestyle area according to the number of automobiles available per household. The upper panel presents the data for the 1970 elderly population, while the lower panel contains information on the middle-aged in that year. Below the raw number of households in each category is the percentage distribution for each age-lifestyle combination. The last column gives county-wide averages. Examination of this table reveals that in each lifestyle group fewer of the middle-aged are without cars and more of

Table 37. Percentage Distribution of Elderly-Headed and Middle-Aged-Headed Households by Number of Automobiles Owned and Lifestyle Area (1970)

		Spanish-American	New Suburbanites	Black Community	Central City Dwellers	Early Suburbanites	Financially Secure	Los Angeles County Totals
Elderly (65+)	Number of Households	29,520	41,359	35,786	150,175	103,906	44,463	406,674
	Percent of Households Owning:							
	0 cars	55.2%	28.2%	48.8%	48.6%	31.4%	20.5%	39.7%
	1 car	35.5%	52.9%	40.1%	42.1%	51.7%	49.5%	45.7%
	2+ cars	9.3%	18.9%	11.1%	9.3%	16.9%	30.0%	14.6%
Middle-Aged (45-64)	Number of Households	51,657	147,533	76,211	203,330	286,522	109,277	875,996
	Percent of Households Owning:							
	0 cars	27.7%	3.6%	23.9%	18.0%	5.3%	2.7%	10.7%
	1 car	44.7%	33.3%	46.2%	49.2%	38.6%	26.8%	39.7%
	2+ cars	27.6%	63.1%	29.9%	32.8%	56.1%	70.5%	49.6%

them own two or more cars per household than do the elderly. Among lifestyles, the Spanish-American, black, and central-city areas show the highest rates of those without cars in both the middle-aged and elderly age groups. For both age groups, fewer of the new suburban, early suburban, and financially secure residents are without cars. The new suburban, early suburban, and financially secure lifestyle areas include higher percentages of households owning two or more automobiles than does the county as a whole, while among the Spanish-American, black, and central-city areas, proportions of households having access to two or more cars fall below the county-wide average.

Step 4: Allocation of Projected Households to Categories of Automobile Ownership. The data from Tables 36 and 37 were combined to yield a projection of the distribution of future households among the three categories of automobile ownership, by assuming that the percentage distributions of households within categories will remain constant over time. Tables 38, 39, and 40 show the automobile ownership characteristics of households for 1990 and 2000 for the low, medium, and high migration scenarios, respectively. The tables are divided to show low ownership rates, which are based on the current ownership rates of the elderly, and high ownership rates, which are based on current ownership rates among the middle-aged.

Step 5: Determination of Mean Tripmaking Rates. Next, a matrix of mean travel rates was obtained for each lifestyle area from the data collected in 1967 by LARTS.[13] The distribution of the 3,827 households in the LARTS sample which included elderly people is shown by lifestyle areas and by automobile ownership characteristics in Table 41. Although 1970 census data and 1967 LARTS data are not strictly comparable, given the three-year gap, examination of Table 41 reveals that automobile ownership characteris-

13. Los Angeles Regional Transportation Study, *LARTS Base Year Report* (Los Angeles: State of California, Division of Highways, District 07, December 1971).

Table 38. Distribution of Projected Households into Auto Ownership Categories by 1970
Elderly and Middle-Aged Auto Ownership Rates: Low Migration Scenario

	Forecast Year	Spanish-American	New Suburbanites	Black Community	Central City Dwellers	Early Suburbanites	Financially Secure
Projected Total Households	1990	45,020	94,830	35,000	140,790	186,270	65,190
	2000	56,540	119,020	32,010	120,810	189,880	62,670
Low Ownership Rates — Households Owning:							
0 cars	1990	24,851	26,742	17,080	68,424	58,489	13,364
	2000	31,210	33,564	15,621	58,714	59,622	12,847
1 car	1990	15,982	50,165	14,035	59,272	96,302	32,269
	2000	20,072	62,961	12,836	50,681	98,168	31,022
2+ cars	1990	4,187	17,922	3,885	13,094	31,479	19,557
	2000	5,258	22,495	3,553	11,235	32,090	18,801
High Ownership Rates — Households Owning:							
0 cars	1990	12,471	3,414	8,365	25,342	9,872	1,760
	2000	15,662	4,285	7,650	21,746	10,063	1,692
1 car	1990	20,124	31,579	16,170	69,269	71,900	17,471
	2000	25,273	39,634	14,789	59,439	73,294	16,796
2+ cars	1990	12,425	59,837	10,465	46,179	104,498	45,959
	2000	15,605	75,101	9,571	39,625	106,523	44,182

Table 39. Distribution of Projected Households into Auto Ownership Categories by 1970 Elderly and Middle-Aged Auto Ownership Rates: Medium Migration Scenario

	Forecast Year	Spanish-American	New Suburbanites	Black Community	Central City Dwellers	Early Suburbanites	Financially Secure
Projected Total Households	1990	43,760	88,810	20,820	128,210	180,680	58,890
	2000	51,980	112,910	14,660	107,850	181,530	54,480
Low Ownership Rates							
Households Owning:							
0 cars	1990	24,156	25,044	10,160	62,310	56,734	12,072
	2000	28,693	31,841	7,154	52,414	57,000	11,168
1 car	1990	15,535	46,981	8,349	53,977	93,411	29,151
	2000	18,453	59,729	5,879	45,405	93,851	26,968
2+ cars	1990	4,069	16,785	2,311	11,923	30,535	17,667
	2000	4,834	21,340	1,627	10,031	30,679	16,344
High Ownership Rates							
Households Owning:							
0 cars	1990	12,122	3,197	4,976	23,078	9,576	1,590
	2000	14,398	4,065	3,504	19,413	9,621	1,471
1 car	1990	19,560	29,574	9,619	63,079	69,742	15,783
	2000	23,235	37,599	6,773	53,062	70,071	14,600
2+ cars	1990	12,078	56,039	6,225	42,053	101,362	41,517
	2000	14,347	71,246	4,383	35,375	101,838	38,409

Table 40. Distribution of Projected Households into Auto Ownership Categories by 1970 Elderly and Middle-Aged Auto Ownership Rates: High Migration Scenario

	Forecast Year	Spanish-American	New Suburbanites	Black Community	Central City Dwellers	Early Suburbanites	Financially Secure
Projected Total Households	1990	43,760	88,810	20,820	111,940	172,050	49,380
	2000	51,980	112,910	19,660	88,720	167,640	41,650
Low Ownership Rates — Households Owning:							
0 cars	1990	24,156	25,044	10,160	54,403	54,024	10,123
	2000	28,693	31,841	7,154	43,118	52,639	8,538
1 car	1990	15,535	46,981	8,349	47,127	88,950	24,443
	2000	18,453	59,729	5,879	37,351	86,670	20,617
2+ cars	1990	4,069	16,785	2,311	10,410	29,076	14,814
	2000	4,834	21,340	1,627	8,251	28,331	12,495
High Ownership Rates — Households Owning:							
0 cars	1990	12,122	3,197	4,976	20,149	9,119	1,333
	2000	14,398	4,065	3,504	15,970	8,885	1,125
1 car	1990	19,560	29,574	9,619	55,075	66,410	13,234
	2000	23,235	37,599	6,773	43,650	64,709	11,162
2+ cars	1990	12,078	56,039	6,225	36,716	96,521	34,813
	2000	14,347	71,246	4,383	29,100	94,046	29,363

Table 41. Distribution of the LARTS Sample by Lifestyle Area and
Auto Owning Characteristics

Autos Owned	Spanish-American	New Suburbanites	Black Community	Central-City Dwellers	Early Suburbanites	Financially Secure	Total
0	62.7%	33.1%	49.0%	59.4%	39.5%	28.4%	45.3%
1	32.3%	51.4%	42.4%	35.2%	48.7%	51.8%	44.0%
2+	5.0%	15.5%	8.6%	5.4%	11.8%	19.8%	10.7%
Number Sampled	220	393	255	1124	1328	485	3805*
Percent of Sample	5.7%	10.3%	6.7%	29.4%	34.7%	12.7%	99.4%*

*The institutional lifestyle area, excluded from this analysis because of data insufficiency,
was represented by only 22 households, bring the total to 3,827 (100%).

tics in the LARTS sample are in close agreement with the complete census enumeration shown in Table 37. Table 41 also shows that the sample households were distributed in such a way that a sufficient number of households were sampled for each cell of the matrix.

From this LARTS sample, it was possible to calculate trip rates per household per day. These rates, shown in Table 42, are stratified by area, automobile ownership, and trip purpose in the upper portion of the table and by life-style area, automobile ownership, and mode of travel in the lower portion. Examination of Table 42 confirms the commonly held assumptions regarding the relationship between the amount of travel undertaken by a household and the number of automobiles that it owns. In general, rates of trips by households according to the purpose of the trip show that as automobile ownership increases the amount of travel also increases. This pattern is strongest in the personal business, leisure, and work trip categories. The trip rates for shopping purposes show a mixture of increases and decreases with rising automobile owner-ship. Lower trip rates for households with an increasing number of cars are partially explainable by the quantity of goods that a shopper is able to carry in one trip. Shoppers with cars can carry much more in each trip than those using buses, thus eliminating some shopping trips. Household trip rates by mode reveal that as automobile ownership increases automobile driver trips increase, while transit passenger trips decrease. Trip rates by the automobile passenger mode in general fall with the acqui-sition of a second car, since those who formerly rode as passengers are now more likely to have direct access to an automobile and to drive.

Step 6: Projection of Future Travel Behavior. Table 42 was multiplied by the appropriate number of projected house-holds categorized by their characteristics of automobile ownership (Tables 38 to 40). Travel rates were utilized three times, since each migration scenario was rep-resented. Projected trips were summed up over au-tomobile owning categories and entered into Tables 43

Table 42. Household Tripmaking Rates per Day by Trip Purpose and Mode, by Lifestyle Area, and by Auto Ownership Characteristics

		Spanish-American			New Suburbanites			Black Community			Central-City Dwellers			Early Suburbanites			Financially Secure		
Autos Owned		0	1	2+	0	1	2+	0	1	2+	0	1	2+	0	1	2+	0	1	2+
Trip Purpose	Personal Business Trips	0.33	0.97	1.18	0.36	0.88	1.02	0.35	1.24	0.86	0.41	1.15	1.60	0.33	1.33	1.43	0.49	1.48	1.69
	Leisure Trips	0.07	0.25	0.09	0.12	0.57	0.66	0.05	0.31	0.45	0.09	0.56	0.72	0.13	0.59	0.64	0.09	0.77	0.85
	Work Trips	0.03	0.35	0.82	0.05	0.41	0.87	0.11	0.26	0.68	0.05	0.20	0.67	0.05	0.35	0.74	0.15	0.31	0.61
	Shopping Trips	0.13	0.42	0.36	0.12	0.76	0.56	0.13	0.28	0.32	0.14	0.73	0.73	0.19	0.86	0.78	0.19	0.89	0.59
Trip Mode	Auto Driver	0.00	1.28	1.91	0.14	2.22	2.80	0.08	1.56	2.36	0.01	2.02	2.77	0.04	2.27	3.01	0.04	2.59	3.23
	Auto Passenger	0.21	0.38	0.36	0.39	0.52	0.30	0.18	0.35	0.27	0.21	0.52	0.97	0.46	0.74	0.52	0.44	0.77	0.50
	Transit Passenger	0.29	0.21	0.18	0.08	0.02	0.00	0.38	0.07	0.00	0.38	0.10	0.03	0.14	0.02	0.03	0.33	0.06	0.00

through 45. These three tables allow a comparison by life-style area of trips in each forecast year, by each travel category, for the low, medium, and high migration scenarios, respectively. The high and low estimates of travel are also represented based on the automobile ownership rates of today's elderly and middle-aged. These tables show that the predominant reason for making a trip is forecast to be for personal business. This is generally true for all lifestyle areas, in all scenarios, and in both forecast years. There will be fewer trips for the purposes of work, shopping, and leisure, and their relative importance with respect to other purposes will vary across lifestyle areas. Most trips in the future will be taken by the au-

Table 43. Travel Behavior by Trip Purpose, Mode, and Lifestyle Area: Low Migration Scenario

Forecast Year	Travel Variable	Auto Owning Rate*	Spanish-American	New Suburbanites	Black Community	Central City Dwellers	Early Suburbanites	Financially Secure
	Personal Business Trips	Low	28,645	72,052	26,722	117,167	192,398	87,357
		High	38,297	90,053	31,979	163,935	248,317	104,390
	Leisure Trips	Low	6,113	43,632	6,953	48,778	84,569	42,673
		High	7,022	57,902	10,140	74,321	110,583	52,676
	Work Trips	Low	9,773	37,497	8,170	24,048	59,924	23,938
		High	17,606	65,176	12,240	46,061	102,988	33,715
1990	Shopping Trips	Low	11,450	51,370	7,393	62,407	118,487	42,797
		High	14,546	57,919	8,964	87,825	145,218	42,999
	Auto Driver	Low	28,454	165,292	32,430	156,683	315,698	147,281
		High	49,491	238,127	50,591	268,092	478,147	193,768
	Auto Passenger	Low	12,799	41,892	9,035	57,891	114,537	40,506
		High	14,739	35,703	9,992	86,136	112,086	37,207
	Transit Passenger	Low	11,317	2,239	7,472	32,321	11,058	6,346
		High	10,080	336	4,311	17,942	5,955	1,629
	Personal Business Trips	Low	35,973	90,434	24,440	100,539	196,127	83,982
		High	48,097	113,024	29,247	140,671	253,130	100,355
	Leisure Trips	Low	7,676	54,763	6,359	41,855	86,208	41,024
		High	8,618	72,672	9,275	63,773	112,726	50,640
	Work Trips	Low	12,273	47,063	7,471	20,635	61,087	23,013
		High	22,112	66,031	11,195	39,524	104,983	32,412
2000	Shopping Trips	Low	14,380	64,475	6,762	53,551	120,782	41,144
		High	18,269	72,693	8,199	75,360	148,033	41,336
	Auto Driver	Low	35,735	207,458	29,659	134,447	321,817	141,588
		High	62,155	298,870	46,271	230,045	487,414	186,278
	Auto Passenger	Low	16,074	52,579	8,264	49,676	116,757	38,941
		High	18,511	44,811	9,137	73,911	114,259	35,768
	Transit Passenger	Low	14,212	2,811	6,835	27,734	11,273	6,101
		High	12,658	422	3,942	15,396	6,071	1,566

*The low auto owning rate is based on the current elderly ownership rates while the high auto owning rate is based on the current middle-aged rates.

Table 44. Travel Behavior by Trip Purpose, Mode, and Lifestyle Area: Medium Migration Scenario

Forecast Year	Travel Variable	Auto Owning Rate*	Spanish-American	New Suburbanites	Black Community	Central City Dwellers	Early Suburbanites	Financially Secure
1990	Personal Business Trips	Low	27,841	67,480	15,896	106,698	186,624	78,915
		High	37,225	84,336	19,024	149,288	240,865	94,302
	Leisure Trips	Low	5,941	40,862	4,136	44,420	82,029	38,549
		High	6,826	54,227	6,032	67,679	107,265	47,585
	Work Trips	Low	9,499	35,117	4,860	21,899	58,127	21,625
		High	17,114	61,039	7,281	41,946	99,897	30,457
	Shopping Trips	Low	11,130	48,111	4,399	56,830	114,929	38,662
		High	14,139	54,242	5,332	79,978	140,859	38,844
	Auto Driver	Low	27,657	154,802	19,291	142,684	306,222	133,048
		High	48,106	223,011	30,095	244,138	463,797	174,726
	Auto Passenger	Low	12,441	39,233	5,375	52,718	111,100	36,592
		High	14,327	33,437	5,944	78,438	108,722	33,612
	Transit Passenger	Low	10,999	2,944	4,445	29,434	10,727	5,733
		High	9,797	847	2,564	16,340	5,777	1,472
2000	Personal Business Trips	Low	33,072	85,792	11,193	89,756	187,503	73,006
		High	44,218	107,221	13,394	125,580	241,997	87,240
	Leisure Trips	Low	7,057	51,951	2,912	37,366	82,417	35,662
		High	8,108	68,941	4,247	56,932	107,769	44,022
	Work Trips	Low	11,284	44,647	3,422	18,423	58,400	20,005
		High	20,329	77,603	5,126	35,284	100,366	28,176
	Shopping Trips	Low	13,220	61,165	3,097	47,807	115,472	35,767
		High	16,796	68,961	3,755	67,277	141,523	35,934
	Auto Driver	Low	32,853	196,808	13,583	120,028	307,666	123,085
		High	57,144	283,528	21,190	205,368	465,978	161,934
	Auto Passenger	Low	14,778	49,879	3,785	44,348	111,623	33,851
		High	17,018	42,510	4,185	65,983	109,235	31,094
	Transit Passenger	Low	13,066	3,742	3,131	24,759	10,777	5,303
		High	11,636	1,077	1,806	13,744	5,803	1,361

*The low auto owning rate is based on the current elderly ownership rates while the high auto owning rate is based on the current middle-aged rates.

tomobile driver mode regardless of lifestyle area, migration scenario, or forecast year. Similarly, public transit will be the least utilized of the three modes analyzed in this study, if the assumptions inherent in the forecasts prove to be valid over time.

Table 46 summarizes the approximate range of modal shares incorporated in the more complex and complete tables which precede it. For each of the six lifestyle areas, this table incorporates a range of estimates of modal shares in order to reflect the variation introduced by the use of three migration scenarios and both high and low estimates of automobile ownership.

Although public transit will be the least utilized mode, it

Table 45. Travel Behavior by Trip Purpose, Mode, and Lifestyle Area: High Migration Scenario

Forecast Year	Travel Variable	Auto Owning Rate*	Spanish-American	New Suburbanites	Black Community	Central City Dwellers	Early Suburbanites	Financially Secure
1990	Personal Business Trips	Low	27,841	67,480	15,896	93,157	177,711	66,172
		High	37,225	84,336	19,024	130,343	229,359	79,073
	Leisure Trips	Low	5,941	40,862	4,136	38,782	78,113	32,324
		High	6,826	54,227	6,032	59,091	102,140	39,901
	Work Trips	Low	9,499	35,117	4,860	19,120	55,350	18,132
		High	17,114	61,039	7,281	36,622	95,126	25,539
	Shopping Trips	Low	11,130	48,111	4,399	49,618	109,441	32,417
		High	14,139	54,242	5,332	69,829	134,132	31,874
	Auto Driver	Low	27,657	154,802	19,291	124,577	291,597	111,561
		High	48,106	223,011	30,095	213,156	441,644	146,775
	Auto Passenger	Low	12,441	39,233	5,375	46,029	105,794	30,682
		High	14,327	33,437	5,944	68,485	103,529	28,184
	Transit Passenger	Low	10,999	2,944	4,445	25,698	10,214	4,808
		High	9,797	847	2,564	14,266	5,501	1,234
2000	Personal Business Trips	Low	33,072	85,792	11,193	73,834	173,155	55,814
		High	44,218	107,221	13,394	103,306	223,481	66,694
	Leisure Trips	Low	7,057	51,951	2,912	30,739	76,140	27,264
		High	8,108	68,941	4,247	46,833	99,522	33,655
	Work Trips	Low	11,284	44,647	3,422	15,154	53,932	15,294
		High	20,329	77,603	5,126	29,026	92,686	21,540
	Shopping Trips	Low	13,220	61,165	3,097	39,326	106,635	27,343
		High	16,796	68,961	3,755	55,344	130,694	27,472
	Auto Driver	Low	32,853	196,808	13,583	98,735	284,123	94,099
		High	57,144	283,528	21,190	168,940	430,322	123,797
	Auto Passenger	Low	14,778	49,879	3,785	36,481	103,082	25,880
		High	17,018	42,510	4,185	54,279	100,876	23,772
	Transit Passenger	Low	13,066	3,742	3,131	20,368	9,952	4,055
		High	11,636	1,077	1,806	11,307	5,359	1,041

*The low auto owning rate is based on the current elderly ownership rates while the high auto owning rate is based on the current middle-aged rates.

Table 46. Percent of Forecast Travel by Mode

	Spanish-American	New Suburbanites	Black Community	Central City Dwellers	Early Suburbanites	Financially Secure
Auto Driver	51-64%*	81-88%	66-80%	62-72%	69-79%	75-83%
Auto Passenger	19-23%	15-17%	16-18%	22-23%	19-25%	17-19%
Bus Passenger	15-18%	.4-1%	9-12%	7-9%	1-2%	1-3%

*Incorporation of three migration scenarios and two different rates of auto ownership results in an approximate range of modal shares rather than a single percentage estimate.

will nonetheless be an important one in the future, especially for certain lifestyle areas. In terms of absolute numbers, most public transit trips will be taken in the central-city, Spanish-American, and early suburban lifestyle areas. Fewest transit trips will occur in the black, financially secure, and new suburban lifestyle areas. Since the travel differentials between lifestyle areas are predominantly a function of the size of the areas' elderly population, it is more meaningful to examine the percentage of total trips that will be made by way of public transit within each lifestyle area. Table 46 reveals that the three lifestyle groups that will have the heaviest rates of public transit use are the Spanish-American, black, and central-city lifestyle areas. Public transit use for these three areas will be roughly 16.5, 10.5, and 8 percent of trips, respectively, using the midpoints of the ranges shown in the table. Those who will depend least on public transit will be the new suburban, early suburban, and financially secure areas, which will use it for approximately 0.7, 1.5, and 2 percent of their trips, respectively.

All trips, regardless of purpose or mode, were summed up for each lifestyle area. This total number of projected trips per day, rounded to the nearest hundred, is presented in Table 47. For each scenario and for each forecast year the high and low estimates of future travel are shown. For example, the black elderly, under the medium migration scenario in 1990, are projected to make between 29,300 and 37,700 trips per day. The large differences in projected trips between lifestyle areas are, to a great extent, a function of the size of the projected elderly population. Although differentials in travel rates contribute to these differences in projected trips, they are a small contributor when compared to the effects of the absolute sizes of the projected population on the number of future trips.

Given the high and low travel estimates of all previous tables, more weight should be given to the upper estimate. This is true for two compelling reasons. As previously mentioned, it is unrealistic to believe that the elderly of the future will have patterns of automobile ownership similar

Table 47. Summary Table of Projected Total Trips, 1990 and 2000

Scenario	Forecast Year	Spanish-American	New Suburbanites	Black Community	Central=City Dwellers	Early Suburbanites	Financially Secure	L.A. County
Low	1990	56,000 77,500	204,600 271,100	49,200 63,300	252,400 372,100	455,400 607,100	196,800 233,800	1,214,400 1,624,900
	2000	70,300 97,300	256,700 340,400	45,000 57,900	216,600 319,300	464,200 618,900	189,200 224,700	1,242,000 1,658,500
Medium	1990	54,400 75,300	191,600 253,800	29,300 37,700	229,800 338,900	441,700 588,900	177,800 211,200	1,124,600 1,505,800
	2000	64,600 89,500	243,600 322,700	20,600 26,500	193,400 285,100	443,800 591,700	164,400 195,400	1,130,100 1,510,900
High	1990	54,400 75,300	191,600 253,800	29,300 37,700	200,700 295,900	420,600 560,800	149,000 176,400	1,045,600 1,399,900
	2000	64,600 89,500	243,600 322,700	20,600 26,500	159,100 234,500	409,800 546,400	125,200 149,400	1,023,400 1,369,000

Note: The two entries in each cell represent low and high estimates of future travel.

to those of today's elderly. If the future elderly are physically able to continue driving and if they are financially able to retain their automobiles, it is likely that they will exhibit greater rates of automobile ownership than do the current elderly. The second argument for weighting the upper estimate more heavily stems from the method of analysis utilized in this study. Because the organization of available data categorized the number of automobiles owned on the household level and not on the individual level, this analysis was similarly executed on the household level. To accomplish this, only those elderly residing in households headed by an elderly person were included in the analysis. Elderly persons living with their middle-aged children were not included since this was categorized as a household headed by a middle-aged person. Because of difficulty in attributing the number of automobiles available to an elderly person in this situation, it was decided to exclude them from the immediate quantitative forecast which produced Table 47. Since the number of elderly persons not residing in elderly-headed households comprised approximately 10 percent of the elderly population in 1970, this is strong evidence to place more credence in a higher travel estimate.

The two arguments above strongly emphasize a travel estimate that is considerably higher than the low estimates provided in this study. There is also a reason for emphasizing a lower travel forecast than the high estimates of Table 47. Since the high estimates were based on the automobile ownership rates of the current middle-aged population, they did not reflect any effects that the aging process may have as middle-aged cohorts become old. The elderly certainly have higher incidences of disabilities, which can physically limit their mobility and affect their choice of mode. Because many old people are disabled, their travel behavior is not likely to match the higher rates of the middle-aged population. It is difficult, however, to determine how many disabled elderly exist. Even if the number were known with some confidence, information regarding the abilities of the elderly to use various modes of travel remains to be discovered. Without these kinds of data, it is difficult to ascertain to what extent the high travel figure is overestimated.

Several sources were investigated in an attempt to estimate the number of persons who become disabled as they move from middle into old age. Revis has reported on a National Health Survey, conducted by the United States Department of Health, Education, and Welfare (HEW), which estimates the number of those in the United States who suffer from various degrees of physical limitation. According to this report, 4.5 percent of those aged 45 to 64 are unable to carry on a major activity.[14] This proportion rises to 16.3 percent of the elderly group, a change of 11.8 percent with age. Many in this disability category may have severe difficulties using the automobile and public transit, while some are likely to be housebound or bedfast. The survey also reports that 12.1 percent of the 45 to 64 age group have limitations in major activities but can nonetheless manage to engage in them. This is contrasted with 21.6 percent of the 65+ group for the same disability category, a change of 9.5 percent with age.[15] Abt Associates also estimated the population with transportation handicaps but in slightly different terms. Finding regional variations in the location of the handicapped within the United States, Abt Associates provided statistics by region. It is unfortunate that the age groups considered do not coincide with the categories used by HEW and in this study, as data in the Abt study are presented for the groups 18 to 64 and 65+. Abt Associates estimate that 0.9 percent of the 18 to 64 age group residing in the West cannot use public transit, while 8.2 percent of the elderly are similarly restricted. Further, 1.1 percent of the younger

14. Major activity is defined as the ability to work, keep house,˙ or engage in school or preschool activities.

15. U.S. Department of Health, Education, and Welfare, Public Health Service, National Health Survey, *Limitations of Activity and Mobility Due to Chronic Conditions*, Series 10, No. 96 (1972), Table 1, p. 15, cited in Joseph S. Revis, *Transportation and the Disabled* (Washington, D.C.: Institute of Public Administration, 1976), p. 13.

group can use public transit but with difficulty, while the comparable figure for the older group is 6.1 percent.[16] Thus, as people become elderly, an additional 5 percent are estimated to have difficulty using public transit and an additional 7.3 percent are estimated to become non-users of public transit. Since the younger group is defined as 18 to 64 rather than 45 to 64, rates of handicapped incidences are likely to be higher if only the group 45 to 64 were to be considered. The percentage changes with age cited above are therefore likely to be overstated. Nevertheless, the figures cited by both HEW and Abt Associates support a future travel estimate that is somewhat lower than the highest one presented in this study.

Projected Changes in Travel Behavior

The implications of projected travel can best be evaluated in comparison with current travel inventories. By examining current data, areas of increasing or decreasing travel by the elderly may be determined, which will aid in assessing the requirements of future transportation systems. Household data classified by automobile ownership characteristics were obtained from the 1970 census and multiplied by LARTS trip rates of Table 42. The results are displayed in Table 48 for all of the travel variables and for each lifestyle area. The bottom row of the table shows the total amount of travel for each lifestyle area, rounded to the nearest hundred.

By comparing current to projected travel behavior, certain trends in modal shifts may be detected. Because of a growing elderly population and their higher propensity to own automobiles, compared with today's older people, the elderly of the future are forecast to exhibit dramatic increases in automobile drivership. The most dramatic increase in driving will be in the new suburban lifestyle area,

16. Abt Associates, Inc., *Estimation of Transportation Handicapped Population*, p. 42, cited in *Transportation Problems of the Transportation Handicapped*, Vol. 1, "The Transportation Handicapped Population, Definitions and Counts," Crain and Associates, eds. (Washington, D.C.: U.S. Department of Transportation, 1976), p. 44.

Table 48. 1970 Travel Behavior by Trip Purpose and Mode, and by Lifestyle Area

		Spanish-American	New Suburbanites	Black Community	Central City Dwellers	Early Suburbanites	Financially Secure	Total L.A. County Trips
Trip Purpose	Personal Business Trips	18,777	31,412	27,328	124,991	107,304	59,561	369,400
	Leisure Trips	2,122	19,019	7,106	52,035	47,164	29,091	156,500
	Work Trips	6,407	16,337	8,345	25,666	33,402	16,322	106,500
	Shopping Trips	7,506	22,397	7,558	66,566	66,088	29,178	199,300
Trip Mode	Auto Driver	18,649	72,037	33,142	167,150	176,030	100,397	521,900
	Auto Passenger	8,391	18,273	9,240	61,764	63,899	27,622	186,300
	Transit Passenger	7,421	1,372	7,743	34,474	6,170	4,335	62,800
	Total Trips	34,800	89,200	50,300	269,300	254,000	134,200	831,800

which may exhibit a 300 to 400 percent increase over 1970 levels. Again, it is important to recognize that the largest part of this increase will be attributable to growth in this population subgroup, and a lesser part of the increase will be derived from changes in rates of automobile ownership and travel. Areas showing a possible doubling of current automobile driver trips are the Spanish-American and early suburban lifestyle areas. The central-city dwellers and the financially secure will also show increases but will probably not double current levels. The black lifestyle area may show slight increases in automobile driver trips, but, if net out-migration is accelerated, this area may experience a slight decrease in trips by this mode.

Increases in automobile passenger trips are also likely to occur in the future. The greatest increase is forecast to be in the new suburban lifestyle area, which may double and possibly triple current automobile passenger trips. The Spanish-American, early suburban, and financially secure areas will also show increases in trips made by this mode, but increases will not be as dramatic. Little change is projected in this travel category in the central-city and black lifestyle areas. Automobile passenger trips may decline, however, in the black lifestyle area with increasing out-migration.

The only two lifestyle areas projected to show an increase in those riding public transit are the Spanish-American and early suburban lifestyle areas. In large part, this is due to the expected growth in the elderly population in both areas. The new suburban and financially secure lifestyle areas will likely show little change in transit ridership despite a forecast of increasing population growth among the elderly. Central-city dwellers and the black community are projected to exhibit decreases in public transit ridership among the elderly. This is largely attributable to a declining future elderly population.

A comparison of estimated total future travel as a proportion of current volumes is shown in Table 49 for all scenarios and forecast years. Analysis of this table reveals that the most dramatic increase in total travel will occur

Table 49. Forecast Proportional Changes in Travel over Current Volumes

Scenario	Forecast Year	Spanish American	New Suburbanites	Black Community	Central City Dwellers	Early Suburbanites	Financially Secure	L.A. County
Low	1990	1.61 / 2.23	2.29 / 3.04	0.98 / 1.26	0.94 / 1.38	1.79 / 2.39	1.47 / 1.74	1.46 / 1.95
	2000	2.02 / 2.80	2.88 / 3.82	0.89 / 1.15	0.80 / 1.19	1.83 / 2.44	1.41 / 1.67	1.49 / 1.99
Medium	1990	1.56 / 2.16	2.15 / 2.85	0.58 / 0.75	0.85 / 1.26	1.74 / 2.32	1.32 / 1.57	1.35 / 1.81
	2000	1.86 / 2.57	2.73 / 3.62	0.41 / 0.53	0.72 / 1.06	1.75 / 2.33	1.23 / 1.46	1.36 / 1.82
High	1990	1.56 / 2.16	2.15 / 2.85	0.58 / 0.75	0.75 / 1.10	1.66 / 2.21	1.11 / 1.31	1.26 / 1.68
	2000	1.86 / 2.57	2.73 / 3.62	0.41 / 0.53	0.59 / 0.87	1.61 / 2.15	0.93 / 1.11	1.23 / 1.65

Note: The two entries in each cell represent low and high estimates of proportional changes in travel over current volumes. A value of 1.00 indicates no change from present travel volumes, while lower numbers represent declines and larger numbers indicate increases in travel.

in the rapidly growing new suburban lifsetyle area. The amount of travel by the elderly in the future will be double and probably triple 1970 levels. The forecast also shows a likely doubling of current travel in the Spanish-American and the early suburban lifestyle areas. The remaining three lifestyle areas show smaller changes. The financially secure are likely to exhibit only slight increases in travel. The central-city dwellers may undertake approximately the same number of trips as they do at present, but the possibility exists that their actual number of trips may decrease. (This will be the case if a large number of central-city elderly migrate away from this lifestyle area.) The black elderly will make about the same number of trips in the future as at present, if the current rate of migration from their lifestyle area is diminished. If migration accelerates, however, this lifestyle area will experience a decrease in total travel by its senior citizens.

For the county as a whole, travel by the elderly will increase until the turn of the century but is unlikely to double in magnitude over 1970 levels. The minimum amount of forecast travel, however, represents an approximate increase of 25 percent over current levels. Generalizing overall migration scenarios, forecast daily trips are likely to grow from approximately 832,000 to anywhere from 1,200,000 to 1,400,000. This represents roughly a 50 to 75 percent increase in travel over 1970 levels.

Summary and Conclusions

Cross-classification analysis was employed in order to produce a travel estimate for the elderly population in 1990 and 2000. The methodology employed allowed the forecast to be internally consistent and thus more reliable. Using as inputs 1970 census data, 1967 LARTS data, and the population forecast of Chapter 6, the analysis produced high and low estimates of future travel based on current rates of automobile ownership among the middle-aged and the elderly.

The analysis demonstrated that, regardless of lifestyle area, most trips will be made for personal business. In addition, trips taken by the elderly in the future will be predominantly by the automobile driver mode, while public transit will be the least utilized of the modes considered in this study. Nevertheless, public transit will remain an important mode of travel particularly for the Spanish-American, black, and central-city lifestyle areas.

In comparison with 1970 volumes of travel, forecast trips for 1990 and 2000 will be approximately 50 to 75 percent greater in number. The most dramatic increase among modes will be in the automobile driver category. The increase in total volume of travel will not be constant across all lifestyle areas. This is because some rapidly growing areas will experience great increases in travel while some areas undergoing net out-migration and a declining elderly population will experience decreases in travel by older people. Similarly, increases in the amount of travel by particular modes will not be constant across all lifestyle areas. Future changes in choice of mode will be affected by the projected growth or decline of the elderly population, along with differing abilities to meet transportation needs with the private automobile. These variations in forecast travel behavior by lifestyle area must be considered in evaluating alternatives for meeting the future mobility needs of the elderly.

Chapter 8
Meeting the Changing Transportation Needs of Older Americans

*T*his study has analyzed the diverse lifestyles of the elderly of the future in Los Angeles County. It has also examined a detailed inventory of transportation services currently available to each of several lifestyle groups among the elderly. Building upon this research, this final chapter will suggest policy directions which might be taken to meet the transportation needs of the elderly through the year 2000. The empirical analysis which formed the basis for these recommendations dealt exclusively with the case study of Los Angeles County. It is difficult, therefore, to assess the extent to which the findings are unique to Los Angeles or how they might apply to other settings as well. The policy recommendations discussed in this chapter are based upon the expectation that elderly residents of other metropolitan areas are as diverse as the elderly of Los Angeles and that their diversity has spatial as well as social dimensions. It is expected that a variety of lifestyles and cultures would be found in applying this technique to other locations, but it is not assumed that the seven particular lifestyle groups found in Los Angeles would be found elsewhere. Other ethnic and cultural groups would certainly be influential in cities having histories quite different from that of Los Angeles. In addition to the heterogeneity that will exist among older residents, however, it is also expected that the trend toward suburbanization and low density living found in this study would be present in most American metropolitan areas, though perhaps to different degrees. During the past three decades, the development of suburbs oriented toward the automobile has truly been a national phenomenon. Although the process of suburbanization undoubtedly characterizes older populations throughout the country, levels of public transit service and patterns of automobile ownership and use vary widely from place to place. The policy recommendations thus incorporate the premise that a wide variety of service levels and styles of transit service are necessary to support diversity both within and between regions. Federal legislation has already established the precedent of setting policies at the national level to meet the transportation needs of the elderly. The observations and proposals made in this chapter, therefore, have relevance at the federal as well as metropolitan levels.

Recapitulation of Major Conclusions from Los Angeles

This research has pointed to a future elderly population which is diverse in its lifestyles and associated travel patterns. In part, these diverse travel patterns reflect the fact that lifestyle groups have patterns of activity which differ significantly from one another. In addition, the diverse travel patterns also reflect differences in transportation services available in various areas of the county. Table 50 summarizes the findings by indicating, for each lifestyle area, the major trends expected in population and travel patterns through the turn of the century, along with the major characteristics of existing transportation services available in each group. These findings suggest policy directions for satisfying the mobility needs of the elderly in the future. A major conclusion is that transportation services are not currently sensitive to the various travel behaviors exhibited by the elderly in the different lifestyle areas, nor are these services likely to improve in the future unless there are substantial modifications in policy.

Table 50. Summary of Findings for Los Angeles County

	Spanish American	New Suburbanites	Black Community	Central-City Dwellers	Early Suburbanites	Financially Secure
Population Forecast	increases	doubles, possibly triples	decreases	decreases	increases	increases
Travel Forecast						
Auto Driver	doubles	triples, possibly quadruples	slight increases	increases	doubles	increases
Auto Passenger	increases	doubles	little change	little change	increases	increases
Bus Passenger	increases	little change	decreases	decreases	increases	little change
Total Trips	doubles	triples	decreases	little change	doubles	increases
Current Inventory of Services						
Bus	high	low	high	high	average	low
Taxi: Fares	high	varies	high	varies	varies	low
Quality	high	low	high	average	low	average
Specialized Services	average	average	high	low	high	average

In Los Angeles buses and specialized transportation service will continue to be important. Increased service by both of these modes may be necessary for the Spanish-American and early suburban lifestyle areas in order to accommodate a growing population with increased demands for public transportation. For areas of projected declines in population and public transit ridership, (such as the black and central-city lifestyle areas), important trade-offs may have to be made. In the black lifestyle area, both bus and specialized providers currently give high levels of service. In the face of declining ridership by the elderly, one or both types of service may be reduced somewhat in the future while still providing adequate mobility to those without cars and the disabled. Central-city residents currently have relatively high levels of bus service but low levels of specialized service. They may have to continue to rely predominantly on conventional transit in the face of declining population, unless innovative and cost-effective paratransit systems can be devised.

For areas of population growth in which a very large proportion of future trips will be satisfied by the private automobile, both bus and specialized services are now provided at low levels. As a consequence, these communities (the new suburban and financially secure) seldom use public transportation. The design of specialized and conventional services for these areas will present some difficulties. The elderly, like other population groups in these locations, will continue to have high levels of automobile ownership, and housing will continue to be provided at relatively low densities. It will be difficult to justify significant expansions of public transportation in areas having these characteristics. The automobile therefore will continue to be the principal form of transportation serving the elderly. This will present a special problem for the very old, the handicapped, and those elderly without cars, for they will be living in areas so dominated by the automobile that there will be a danger of these people becoming increasingly isolated. Public policy must not forget to incorporate ways of meeting their travel requirements.

The widespread use by the elderly of conventional taxi service did not appear promising, because service was found to be best where residents are least likely to afford the fares and worst in areas of greatest affluence. Taxis are thus likely to be utilized primarily for occasional emergency trips, unless fare structures and quality of service are dramatically altered. Possibilities for more innovative use of this potentially flexible mode of transportation will be addressed later in this chapter.

It is clear that current transportation services for the elderly are not specifically tailored to their differences in lifestyles. Many reasons for this were identified in Chapter 4. Services are provided to communities defined by political boundaries rather than by lifestyle differences, and most transit services are designed for the entire population, rather than the elderly specifically, within that area. Even modes that should be the most sensitive to varying needs, such as specialized paratransit services, did not appear to be tailored to needs unique to specific lifestyles. Future transportation planning should be more sensitive to the various travel behaviors of elderly residents— behaviors that arise from large differences in automobile ownership, family income, and family settings. Services should be provided that are more carefully tailored to the needs and preferences associated with elderly lifestyles, subject, of course, to the usual planning considerations of efficiency and resource limitations.

The Problem of Interpreting Transportation Needs

The relationship among available transportation services, observed travel behavior, and transportation needs is complex and difficult to interpret. One problem is that the availability of services is an important determinant of observed behavior. In the language of economics, observed behavior represents the interaction of the supply of available services with the demand for travel. Hence, such behavior cannot be strictly interpreted as evidence of either the supply of or demand for travel operating alone. Another problem is the fact that economic notions of travel demand, determined by such factors as income and travel costs, are confused with subjectively conceived notions of mobility needs, many definitions of which can be equally compelling.

While demand represents those services actually purchased by an individual, given his or her income and the prices of traveling via different modes, this may not conform to one's notion of how much travel the individual needs. The need may only represent the travel necessary for a person to nourish himself and care for his health, or it may extend to include social visits, personal business trips, or recreational travel. No single one of these definitions is intrinsically correct.

This study makes no attempt to define an elderly person's travel needs in terms of some arbitrary number of trips by different modes or for different purposes. Instead, it argues that elderly persons are entitled to the mobility necessary for them to maintain adequate nourishment and good health, conduct personal business, engage in social relationships, and pursue recreation. While this is an abstract goal, it can guide decisions governing transportation programs serving the elderly if it is considered in conjunction with the inventory of automobile travel, along with conventional and specialized transit services reported previously. Meeting this goal implies providing additional service to those lifestyle groups whose current travel requirements related to their personal health and basic social activity are not being met.

As an illustration, it was noted that the elderly Spanish-American population of Los Angeles County is characterized by extremely low income and limited access to automobile travel. This group receives bus service slightly better than the county average, and, while it is served by taxi service of the best quality measured for the county, that service is available only at fares which are likely to be prohibitively high. These services are supplemented by a moderate number of small-scale specialized transportation operators, who together supply only a small number of trips in comparison with this group's population without cars. In contrast, the financially secure elderly, characterized by high incomes and high rates of automobile ownership, are poorly served by bus transit. While receiving taxi service of only average quality, this group enjoys the lowest taxi fares sampled. Specialized transportation service to this group is limited, yet it appears reasonably good when compared to the large number of cars among its members, and it is generally available without charge.

If the basic mobility needs of both these lifestyle groups are to be met, elderly Spanish-Americans must be provided with more extensive travel services. Yet the major public effort to serve the mobility needs of the elderly, through supplying specialized demand-responsive services, does not appear to have been as successful in serving Spanish-Americans as it has in increasing mobility among the most affluent and those who depend least upon public transit. An equal commitment to the mobility needs of these two groups would require providing more service to the Spanish-American group. Policy analysis of a sort not incorporated in the present study would be needed to develop a more complete understanding of how existing institutions fail to meet this requirement.

Guidelines attached to each federal program supporting transportation for the elderly define its eligible clients; these are the basic standards of mobility need as defined by public policy. Some programs, such as those funded under Section 16(b) (2) of the 1964 Urban Mass Transportation Act, as amended in 1970, merely require that clients be elderly or handicapped. Others require that clients be unemployed, including programs under Title IX of the 1965 Older Americans Act. Still others require that clients be malnourished or in dangerously poor health. In administering these restrictions at the local program level, however, it is important that some flexibility be retained which permits local services to be tailored to persons within eligible user groups who have the least access to other travel alternatives. In local administration of this type, knowledge of the travel patterns of elderly persons among different lifestyles and the inventory of their current access to mobility presented by the present research should both prove useful.

Current National Priorities for Meeting the Transportation Needs of the Elderly

The national commitment to meet the transportation needs of the elderly is substantial and is growing in significance. It is characterized by a lack of coordination among a number of federal agencies which participate, sometimes resulting in legal proceedings to settle disputes over questions or jurisdiction and administrative procedure. For purposes of discussion, current national policy for providing better transportation to senior citizens can be distilled into three major program areas. First, in recognition of the relative economic need of older citizens, federal law now requires that any transit operator receiving federal operating assistance under Section 5 of the Urban Mass Transportation Act (as amended) may not, during off-peak hours, charge the elderly more than one-half of the regular fare applied to general transit users during peak hours.[1]

A second major area of national involvement in transportation policy which significantly impacts the elderly is the removal of physical barriers which limit access to service by handicapped and elderly persons with reduced physical mobility. The extent of the national commitment to this policy is made evident in the following quotation from a publication of the Urban Mass Transportation Administration (UMTA):

The requirements include such things as improved handrails and stanchions, nonslip flooring, lighting in the bus step well, priority seating signs for elderly and handicapped persons,

1. U.S. Department of Transportation, Urban Mass Transportation Administration, *Transportation Assistance for Elderly and Handicapped Persons* (Washington, D.C.: Office of Public Affairs, Urban Mass Transportation Administration, 1977), pp. 3–4.

warning strips next to boarding platforms and other hazard warnings in transit-related buildings. In addition to the above requirements for the currently available transit bus, all newly designed, full-sized transit buses advertised for bid and purchased with UMTA funds after February 15, 1977, will be required to have front door step risers not exceeding eight inches in height . . . . and up to September 30, 1979, UTMA has required that manufacturers offer, as an option, a wheelchair accessibility package consisting of a level-change mechanism (lift or ramp), sufficient front door and passageway clearances to permit a wheelchair to reach a securement location in the bus and one securement device to hold a wheelchair in place. All buses offered for bid with Federal assistance after September 30, 1979, will be required to meet new bus specifications. These specifications include: a bus floor height of not more than 22 inches, capable of kneeling to 18 inches above the ground, and a ramp for boarding.[2]

The third major area in which a national commitment has been made to provide transportation service to the elderly is the financial support granted to specialized paratransit services operated by transit authorities, social service agencies, and voluntary organizations across the country. In Chapter 5 it was already mentioned that such services are now being offered by thousands of organizations. Saltzman observed that these "human service agency" transportation projects were usually initiated using funds from agencies not primarily involved in transportation.[3] They employed monies available under programs funded by recent amendments to the Social Security Act of 1935, the Older Americans Act of 1965, the Urban Mass Transportation Act of 1964, the National Mass Transportation Assistance Act of 1974, the Housing and Community Development Act of 1974, and other legislation.[4] Because of the diverse legislative origins of these

2. Ibid., pp. 2–3.

3. Arthur Saltzman, "Coordinating Transportation for Human Service Agency Clients," paper presented at the International Conference on Transport for Elderly and Handicapped Persons, Cambridge, England, April 1978. Forthcoming in conference proceedings.

4. Richard K. Brail, James W. Hughes, and Carol A. Arthur, *Transportation Services for the Disabled and Elderly* (New Brunswick, N.J.: Center for Urban Policy Research, Rutgers University, 1976), pp. 145–50.

programs, they are administered by agencies within at least three federal departments and by more than one bureau or agency within each of those departments. Saltzman estimated that in 1976 as much as one billion dollars was spent nationally in providing special transportation services for all human service agencies, and that an annual growth rate of 13 to 18 percent was expected through 1978, with the rate of growth slowing to about 8 percent per year after that. The growing importance of these services is illustrated by the findings of John Crain. He surveyed 1900 social service agencies in the San Francisco Bay area and discovered that about half of these agencies either owned and operated their own vehicles or purchased transportation services for their clients.[5] In spite of this rapid growth, coordination among agencies providing transportation for their clients is virtually nonexistent, and there is still little evidence of cooperation between such social service agencies and operators of conventional transportation services.

The results of the present study indicate that these three major directions that federal programs are taking are collectively inadequate to meet the wide range of transportation needs which characterize various lifestyle groups. Emphasis upon fare reductions helps that proportion of the elderly population which is in financial need but does little to improve service to those who receive service that is infrequent, spatially sparse, or low in quality. Indeed, the requirement of reduced fares might actually inhibit improved service in some areas by allowing the service providers to recover only a small proportion of their costs from the fare box. Several of the lifestyle groups were, of course, characterized by a lack of financial need. On the basis of equity, then, it must be questioned, for example, why the financially secure as well as the needy elderly should receive fare subsidies. Similarly, the emphasis upon the reduction of physical barriers will provide increased travel opportunities for those elderly (and

5. John Crain and Associates, eds., *Paratransit Survey Component of MTC Special Transit Service Needs Study,* prepared for the Metropolitan Transportation Commission, Berkeley, California, April 1974.

younger) persons who are handicapped. Yet few elderly are severely handicapped, and handicapped people comprise only a small proportion of the market for public transportation. These changes in the physical plant by which public transportation is provided will add so significantly to the capital cost of public transportation systems that an important question must be raised. Given the variety of needs revealed in the present case study, does it seem wise to concentrate resources to such an extreme in capital equipment which assures accessibility to a small proportion of the elderly population and an even smaller proportion of the total population? It is especially important to ask this question because programs to improve physical accessibility are being implemented in parallel with specialized door-to-door paratransit services, which often operate in areas where conventional bus service is also available. It would seem that federal dollars are being used to foster two parallel programs—specialized services and accessible line-haul transit service—in identical service areas in which the total proportion of the population in need of either program is quite small. Yet the variety of service needs implied by the variation in lifestyles among the elderly goes largely unrecognized under current programs.

The Goals of Transportation Policy for the Elderly

Policies regarding transportation for the elderly should be directed toward several objectives. Primarily, they should seek to provide each aged person with at least the minimal level of mobility necessary to function in society. Second, the services necessary to ensure this level should be produced at the lowest possible cost to the public. In turn, this requires that programs specifically aimed at elderly persons should be coordinated with transportation policies serving other groups or goals. Finally, programs should be adaptable to changing needs among the elderly population over time, as well as being open to different strategies for meeting those needs.

Guaranteeing a Basic Level of Mobility

In both urban and suburban areas, a minimal level of access to transportation is essential to the maintenance of personal health, adequate nutrition, and necessary social relationships. Each person should receive this basic level of mobility on the same grounds that basic levels of nourishment, clothing, and shelter are provided at public expense when private resources cannot provide them. Federal policies governing the supply of transportation services at public expense currently reflect a commitment to the distribution of those services so as to offer each person who does not now enjoy it this basic opportunity to travel.[6] This implies that elderly persons, as well as other groups needing transportation, should be provided travel services in proportion to their inability to provide this basic level for themselves. Aged people have needs for transportation assistance which depend on the services currently available to them and those necessary to guarantee health, transact personal business, and maintain social contacts. For example, an elderly person unable to convey himself or herself to a hospital or clinic for periodic health care can legitimately claim a need for transportation, just as he or she can claim a right to public support through food stamps to ensure adequate nutrition.

Providing Cost-Effective Services

Where travel services are provided through public investment, they should be produced at the lowest cost necessary to meet the objective of ensuring a minimum standard of mobility among the elderly. Because a substantial amount of public resources is already committed to providing transportation, the viability of expanded or new programs will depend in part on how efficiently added investments can be made to serve their target populations. Public acceptance of new government expenditures serv-

6. Ronald F. Kirby and Robert G. McGillivray, "Alternative Subsidy Techniques for Urban Public Transportation," *Transportation Research Record* 589 (1976), p. 25.

ing the disadvantaged is also likely to depend on how cost effectively they promise to achieve their objectives.

Among the most serious problems facing transit policymakers around the world is the continuously deteriorating financial position of the public transit industry. Transit deficits are rising precipitously and portend drastic cutbacks in service, extensive subsidies from already overburdened public treasuries, or some combination of these. For example, as recently as 1967 the national total of transit revenues exceeded total operating costs. By 1975, however, operating expenses nationally were 180 percent of revenues, and the operating deficit was more than 1.5 billion dollars.[7] It is estimated that the total national transit deficit increased between 1975 and 1976 by 15 percent, and that it rose by another 9 percent during 1976 and 1977.[8] In Los Angeles the Southern California Rapid Transit District (SCRTD) met its operating costs from fare-box revenues in 1969, but by 1977 its collections could cover only about one-third of the cost of operations. In Chicago, New York, and London there have been significant fare increases and service reductions in the face of escalating costs, and increased subsidies have also been necessary. These measures, in turn, only intensified a continuing trend toward declines in ridership. In 1967 the American transit industry carried 6.6 billion passengers, but in 1975 it carried only 5.6 billion.[9]

There are several explanations for these alarming trends in transit finance. One factor is the transfer of most transit operations from private to public ownership over the past two decades. When private operators become insolvent, they curtail service and eventually close down entirely. Public ownership, however, has usually resulted from a desire to keep unprofitable services in operation in order

7. American Public Transit Association, *Transit Fact Book*, 1976-1977 edition (Washington, D.C.: American Public Transit Association, 1977).

8. Ralph E. Rechel, *Contemporary Issues and Problems in Financing Services for the Transportation Disadvantaged* (Washington, D.C.: Institute of Public Administration, September 1977), pp. 13–14.

9. American Public Transit Association, *Transit Fact Book*.

to provide mobility to those citizens without cars and jobs to unionized public employees. Thus, public acquisition of transit operations, and the subsequent retention of unprofitable routes, is one important factor in this cost escalation. Another factor has been the escalation of employee wages and fringe benefits within the transit industry. Labor constitutes more than three-fourths of the total operating cost of most transit operations. The fact that the average transit employee in the United States received pay increases of 52 percent between 1970 and 1975 is without question a significant cause of the operating cost crisis which the industry faces.[10] Also, the cost of fuel has doubled during the last five years, and, while fuel constitutes a smaller proportion of operating budgets than does labor, this also contributes to the spiral of increasing costs.

To a greater extent each year, the costs of transit operations are met by public subsidies. In the United States, the federal capital and operating subsidy to public transit operators grew from 676 million dollars in 1974 to 1.7 billion dollars in 1976, with 2.5 billion budgeted for 1977. Thus, in 1976 the federal government spent more supporting the transit industry than had been collected in fare box revenues during the entire three-year period of 1970 through 1972![11] Yet federal subsidies covered only 9 percent of the national transit bill in 1977, with state subsidies providing 12 percent and local government subsidies covering another 20 percent. Projections for the next five years show no changes in these trends.[12] When faced with such mounting deficits, transit operators must carefully consider the cost implications of providing service for senior citizens.

The evolution of national policies for providing mobility to the elderly will take place within a policy environment strongly dominated by concerns for this problem of cost

10. Ibid.

11. Harold F. Hammond, "Urban Transit and Federal Support," *Traffic Quarterly* 30 (1976), pp. 487–88.

12. Martin Wachs, "Transportation Policy in the Eighties," *Transportation* 6 (June 1977), pp. 103–19.

escalation. The extension of public transit service and the retention of service on the least economically productive routes are most often justified on the basis of providing service to those dependent upon it, usually assumed to include many elderly and handicapped persons. Yet transit operators claim that these patrons do not cover the average costs of the services provided to them. The elderly receive the privilege of reduced fares and constitute only a small portion of the total transit market. When transit authorities do extend or continue services primarily for the benefit of those dependent upon them, they are likely to be concerned that specialized transportation services operated by social service agencies often compete with them and skim away some of their elderly and handicapped. Finally, transit operators, when faced with the added expense and administrative burden of achieving full accessibility for wheelchairs, are likely to raise their voices in complaint. They see themselves as forced to provide extensive changes in their capital equipment to accommodate a small proportion of their patrons who receive most of their rides at fares reduced far below cost. While federal dollars help to bear the costs of meeting accessibility requirements, this is of little consolation for three reasons. First, every federal dollar spent on capital expenditures for achieving accessibility is seen by the transit operators as a dollar which would have been spent on other service expansions or equipment replacement had it not been for the federal accessibility requirements. Second, dollars spent by transit operators on tailoring services to the elderly and handicapped are seen as squandered to the extent that other federal dollars provide rides for members of the same market segment through transportation programs offered by social service agencies. Finally, it can be pointed out that the entire annual federal expenditure on transportation programs for the elderly is tiny in comparison with the need and in comparison with the implications of federal requirements for full accessibility. The American Public Transportation Association has estimated the cost of converting the existing bus fleet to make it accessible to be over one billion dollars and the cost of insuring accessibility on existing rail systems to be over five billion dollars. They claim that the cost to comply with accessibility regulations will exceed the entire estimated UMTA capital assistance program for the next twelve years,[13] while to date the entire annual federal expenditure on programs for the elderly and handicapped is smaller than UMTA's program to provide downtown people movers in only four cities.[14]

Although the transit industry is likely to have significantly overestimated the costs of compliance with accessibility requirements, the implications of cost escalation are clear. During the coming decades, it is probable that transit operators will seek to decrease service and to serve only their most productive markets. This will occur as costs continue to increase in the absence of any significant overall shift from the automobile to public transportation. In the face of pressure to consolidate and reduce the proliferation of service, it seems impossible over the next decade to continue a set of specialized transportation services by social service agencies which are uncoordinated with each other and with the increasingly costly service operated by public transit authorities. The extent to which coordination is really possible is presently unknown, and the payoffs in cost-efficiency which can result from more effective coordination may be smaller than many hope for.[15] Yet, in a political environment dominated by concerns for conservation of resources and control of cost escalation, programs for the elderly will have to be more carefully coordinated if they are to remain politically viable

13. American Public Transit Association, "Comments of the American Public Transit Association on Behalf of Public Transit Operators re Proposed Rule Concerning Coordination of Federal Agency Enforcement of Section 504 of the Rehabilitation Act of 1973," (Washington, D.C.: American Public Transit Association, August 1973).

14. Joseph S. Revis, *Transportation for Older Americans—1976: Progress, Prospects, and Potentials* (Washington, D.C.: Institute for Public Administration, 1976), p. 13, Table 6.

15. Institute of Public Administration, "Coordinating Transportation for the Elderly and Handicapped: A State of the Art Report" (Washington, D.C.: Office of Service and Methods Demonstrations, Urban Mass Transportation Administration, U.S. Department of Transportation, November 1976).

and fundable. New or expanded programs serving the
mobility needs of the elderly must be integrated with other
transportation policies. Efficient provision of service requires minimizing overlap among user groups, preventing
duplication of capital investments having the same purpose, and avoiding complex restrictions on operating practices of suppliers of transportation services.[16] In order to
meet these requirements, programs to improve mobility
among the aged must be coordinated with those serving
other groups needing transportation, which can include
elderly members, such as the handicapped, those requiring medical or nutrition services, and the poor. In addition, potential conflicts with programs directed toward
other goals of transportation policy, such as air quality
improvement, transportation system management, increased labor productivity, and transit supply deregula-
tion, must be minimized if services are to be provided cost
effectively.

Preserving Program Flexibility

It is also important to formulate policies which allow
flexibility over time in adapting to changing patterns of
travel need among target populations. This is likely to require granting substantial local administrative flexibility in
interpreting the travel needs of an area's elderly population within the broad restrictions accompanying each
program. Flexibility also demands an awareness that
strategies which are promising over the long run may differ from those which are useful in the short run. Hence,
while technological advances in the automobile or relaxa-
tions in regulation of suppliers of transportation service
may improve the mobility of the elderly over the long run,
integration of small-scale specialized services or price subsidies for use by those aged who use existing taxi and bus
services may be productive in the more immediate future.

16. Ronald F. Kirby and Francine L. Tolson, *Improving the Mobility of
the Elderly and Handicapped Through User-Side Subsidies,* Publication UI-
5050-4-4 (Washington, D.C.: Urban Institute, 1977), pp. 7–14.

Service Coordination Through a
Local Transportation Authority

To meet both objectives of providing for each aged person's basic right to mobility and doing so cost effectively, closer coordination of existing programs supplying transportation to the elderly appears to be necessary. This finding is documented by the response of specialized service operators to the survey conducted as part of this research, as well as by other research. One promising way to integrate the efforts of these operators and substitute more efficient forms of transportation service is to establish a single local authority which would specifically integrate funding from available sources. That authority would then act as a centralized supplier of specialized demand-responsive transportation to the county's elderly population.

The Need for Increased Coordination
Among Specialized Service Suppliers

Research reported in Chapter 4 indicated that operators of specialized transportation services tend to cooperate neither with each other nor with suppliers of conventional transit and taxi service. Operators frequently reported serving identical areas or user groups without specific knowledge of how effectively others did so. Agencies serving the same area occasionally were each empowered only to serve single client groups residing in that area or to provide travel for only specific purposes. In some cases an operator could provide a trip originating in its service area but was barred from serving the return trip if it originated outside that area. Further, many suppliers of specialized service were restricted from allowing patrons to combine other trip purposes with the primary purpose they served. In most cases the sharing of equipment, drivers, or maintenance among suppliers appears to have been discouraged or prohibited.

This lack of coordination hindered the efforts of suppliers to meet the travel needs of their elderly clients, in some cases even placing outright hardship on users. For example, a person requiring travel for several purposes might have been required to arrange a separate trip for each purpose even if all travel was to be done on the same day. Each trip would typically have to originate and end at the person's home, and each would have required reservations up to several days in advance. It is clear that such uncoordinated operations are not only economically inefficient but are likely to be ineffective in assuring the mobility which is the objective of each program.

The findings from research conducted for this study are supported by those of other investigators. Kirby and Tolson cite administrative conflict among service providers as an impediment to efficient and effective attempts to serve mobility needs of client groups.[17] One form in which this conflict emerges is the outright refusal of operators to supply service outside their designated areas or target groups even when they could conveniently do so. While often done in the purported interests of their respective client groups, such refusals may often be based on administrative restrictions. Whatever the motivation, refusal to coordinate efforts to provide service clearly hinders meeting the goals of serving travel needs and doing so cost effectively.

Saltzman argues that the most significant failure in coordinating strategies to provide transportation service occurs at the local program level.[18] He cites several barriers to needed coordination. One important barrier is the hesitancy of local organizations providing service to relinquish control over funds or administrative autonomy. As a result, the objectives of transportation programs become locally reinterpreted as being the continuation of disjointed, autonomous organizations rather than an effort to serve the mobility needs of clients. Even those programs that mandate coordination among agencies to which they disburse funds typically specify a minimum or undefined

17. Ibid.
18. Arthur Saltzman, "The Benefits of Cooperation Among Human Service Agency Transit Operators in Rural Areas," Ph.D. dissertation proposal, University of California, Irvine (1977), pp. 5–9.

level of cooperation, for which they provide no mechanism or incentives of enforcement.

Saltzman affirms the findings of this research that restrictions on uses of funds written into program legislation inhibit cooperation among local transportation agencies. For example, an agency will usually refuse to allow its vehicles to serve the clients of other areas or programs, even where this can be done cheaply or conveniently, because the agency interprets its operating charter as precluding it. Operators' reluctance to share or exchange service may have also been aggravated by conservative interpretations of funding restrictions offered by federal program administrators. Such barriers to coordinated use of funds not only induce inefficient service but are also likely to limit the effectiveness with which service needs are met.

A report prepared by the National Cooperative Highway Research Program cites as particular problems both overall funding limitations and restrictions on uses of funds from federal programs serving those who need transportation.[19] These problems interact to produce a pattern of small, fragmented operators of specialized transportation services. Acting independently, they tend to duplicate services to users or service areas in some cases, while in other cases they can completely overlook groups in need of additional services. This study also cites other barriers to coordinating local agencies supplying travel services. Differing requirements of user eligibility—age, income, health, etc.—prevent the coordinated use of resources available under different programs. Conflicts between specialized service suppliers and public transportation operators can preclude both from meeting travel needs. Insurance coverage restrictions can also reduce the effectiveness and increase costs of meeting these needs.

A report by the Institute of Public Administration to the

19. National Cooperative Highway Research Program, *Transportation Requirements for the Handicapped, Elderly, and Economically Disadvantaged* (Washington, D.C.: Transportation Research Board, 1976), pp. 36ff.

United States Administration of Aging concurs in these findings.[20] This report cites a survey of thirty-two state and Area Agencies on Aging (AAAs) created under the Older Americans Act, in which five categories of problems were reported. These included funding problems, client group restrictions, operating difficulties with actual transportation systems, organizational problems (such as uncertainty regarding service areas), and conflicting administrative efforts with federal and state government. Each of these was seen as making programs funded through AAAs unnecessarily costly and ineffective in meeting travel needs among the elderly population. Operators of travel services saw the integration of programs, which the removal of these barriers would permit, as a means of achieving increased capacity to serve the needs of their clients as well as greater operating efficiency.

It is clear that several independent research efforts agree that there needs to be closer coordination of fragmented local efforts to provide mobility to the elderly. This is likely to require several adjustments: integration of existing specialized service operations in order to reduce the overlap between service areas and target clientele now characterizing their efforts; elimination of cumbersome restrictions on operating and service boundaries which virtually require inefficient and duplicative practices; relaxation of restrictions on expenditures, which in some cases lead to excess capital purchases and unnecessary duplication of vehicle fleets and which in other cases completely preclude purchase or lease of equipment; and efforts to smooth the impact upon elderly users of divergent funding cycles of programs currently financing transportation services.

Program coordination further requires integrating the provision of specialized transportation services with the imposition of special equipment requirements on public transit operators in order to provide vehicle accessibility for these users. These two approaches are currently being pursued independently to meet the mobility needs of ap-

20. Revis, *Transportation for Older Americans — 1976*, pp. 20–23.

proximately 20 percent of the elderly who are "transit handicapped" and unable to utilize conventional public transit service.[21] Buses accessible to the transit handicapped are costly for transit operators to provide. They may be an ineffective and wasteful attempt to serve this group if, at the same time, the commitment to provide specialized, demand-responsive travel at public expense continues.

Achieving Coordination Through a
Local Transportation Authority

More coordinated efforts to meet the travel needs of the elderly might be provided through a regional agency which would integrate the current functions of local suppliers of specialized services. Such an agency would participate directly in financing, supplying, and distributing transportation services. It would integrate funding from the diverse federal sources available to finance services for the aged with locally available funding sources. The latter would include matching shares and direct subsidies provided by municipal and county governments, as well as contributions from social service agencies, senior citizens' organizations, or other groups concerned with the transportation problems of the elderly. It would employ these combined resources in the direct provision of specialized transportation services using equipment it owned or leased, as well as the purchase of services from existing suppliers, such as bus and taxi operators.

The proposed agency would be empowered to enter into contractual agreements governing the purchase and delivery of transportation services. Contracting with existing service providers such as taxi companies or public transit authorities presents a strong potential source of increased effectiveness. In the interest of supplying services efficiently, the organization would combine the stock of vehicles, driver staffs, service areas, and eligible clientele of existing special service suppliers, perhaps assuming their reservation and scheduling functions as well. This

21. U.S. Department of Health, Education, and Welfare, *Facts on Aging* (Washington, D.C.: U.S. Government Printing Office, 1970).

would likely be advantageous where existing operators are restrained from operating in a more efficient and effective manner because of low utilization of vehicles, legally restricted service areas, and overlapping user groups.

Concurrently, the proposed agency would be empowered to contract with local municipalities, social service agencies, and formal senior citizens' organizations for the supply of transportation services to their respective elderly residents or memberships. These services would be made available to such groups on the basis of available federal and local funding earmarked for serving different groups.

Such an agency would also be authorized to accept grants, loans, or other forms of monetary assistance directly from the federal government, although some funding might reach the agency indirectly. For example, in the case of Los Angeles, financing received under Title III of the Older Americans Act might be channeled to the transportation agency through the local AAA, currently the designated local sponsor of programs funded under this section. It would also have the authority to assemble local funding shares from governments or service organizations where they are required to qualify for matching federal financing. Because the local agency would operate in a primarily coordinative capacity, seeking more effective application of the existing federal commitment to transportation for the elderly, it would be eligible to receive federal funding restricted to receipt by nonprofit sponsors [such as under Section 16(b)(2) of the 1964 UMTA Act].

The travel services supplied directly or purchased by the proposed local transportation agency could then be allocated to the target population groups at which the funding sources employed are directed: patients in medical clinics or hospitals, users of nutrition centers, visitors to senior citizens' centers, etc. The agency would be responsible for adhering to eligibility requirements under each program from which it received funds. Operating within these guidelines, it could retain flexibility in directing services to the members of those eligible groups having the greatest needs for mobility. It could also supply specific types of services which are likely to be most effective in serving different lifestyle groups. Hence, in administering federal transportation programs at this level, the local agency would have responsibility parallel to that retained by public housing authorities, which specify and administer standards for determining the eligibility and financial contribution expected of tenants of projects under its jurisdiction.

Under current legislation, public transit operators such as SCRTD and the municipal bus companies are required to offer reduced fares to senior citizens who ride at peak hours. They are also required to acquire buses which are accessible to the handicapped. These programs are often operated in geographic areas in which specialized transportation services are also being offered to the elderly, usually with public subsidies. Federal dollars are thus being used to support several competing programs. A local transportation authority could, to some extent, mitigate the inefficiency which stems from this situation. For example, where SCRTD or the municipal bus companies had excess vehicle capacity, probably during off-peak hours, they could enter into agreements with the local transportation authority to provide some of the specialized services under its jurisdiction. Rather than continuing the proliferation of small and inefficient systems involving a few vehicles, this type of arrangement would allow idle equipment and drivers to recover some of the costs which they must incur under existing federal legislation by offering some of the specialized transportation service for the elderly. In some cases, high operating costs which characterize transit operators bound by union agreements would preclude such agreements by the conventional transit operators to offer specialized services. The local authority would not, however, be required to enter into such agreements if it could achieve similar service levels at lower cost by purchasing services from other operators.

An illustration of how the local transportation authority would operate may be helpful. The City of Inglewood, California, now operates a demand-responsive transportation service using a single van owned by the city. It transports senior citizens to and from a multipurpose activity center on the basis of telephone reservations—only one call per trip. Under the arrangement proposed here, the City of Inglewood could make a much wider array of services available for its older citizens by entering into a contract with the transportation authority. For example, the city could arrange with the authority to continue to supply specialized service to its handicapped senior citizens on an advance reservation basis. It might also arrange for demand-responsive, dial-a-ride service for some of its elderly population previously served by the city's van. The transportation authority could provide this service using funding earmarked for providing the elderly with access to any of the services available at the city's senior citizens' center. It could do so, for example, by contracting with the taxi franchise serving Inglewood to respond to calls for service from elderly residents there. Alternatively, if a group of aged residents required occasional transportation to the center on a regularly scheduled basis, the transportation authority might provide that service to the city on a subscription basis, using a van or other vehicle it operated.

Such an arrangement would offer several advantages. The opportunity for an expanded segment of the city's elderly to take advantage of the social services it offers would be provided. Users whose travel is now confined to the City of Inglewood would be able to reach services lying beyond that city's borders. In these ways the city's financial commitment to its elderly would be more efficiently employed. The burden of applying for and renewing grants as well as the uncertainty of whether or not funding programs would continue to finance its van service, would be diminished. Finally, the reservation and dispatching functions required by the city's current van operation would be partly transferred to better trained and experienced suppliers and would be partly substituted for by more immediate demand-responsive travel requiring no advance reservation and dispatching. Both the elderly recipients of this type of service and the city should benefit as a result.

Organizational Options for a
Local Transportation Authority

While the concept of a local authority acting as a supplier of transportation services to the elderly is a promising avenue toward coordinating efforts to serve their mobility needs, the specific form of this organization needs clarification. At least three alternative methods for implementing a local authority are available: it could be chartered as an extension of an existing social service agency, as an adjunct of an existing public transportation operator, or as a new independent body. Each of these alternatives has clear advantages but also presents distinct drawbacks. Further research will be needed to clarify these strengths and weaknesses, as well as other possible approaches to establishing the proposed authority, but they can be outlined briefly here.

One interesting possibility is the chartering of such a local transportation authority as an extension of an existing agency committed to serving travel or other needs of the aged population. While legally remaining a branch of local government, the proposed organization would be brought under the jurisdiction of a body having both interest and experience in fulfilling service needs of the elderly. In the state of Massachusetts, for example, some twenty smaller and medium-sized cities have for some time been operating small transportation systems for senior citizens under their local Councils on Aging.[22] In the case of Los Angeles, a logical organization might be the county-wide AAA. This agency was established under the Older Americans Act of 1965 specifically to disburse funds for the provision of various services to the elderly. In this capacity, some 20 percent of the total federal support for transportation for fiscal year 1975 provided under Title III of the Older Americans Act was channeled to operators of transportation projects through local AAA's. Hence,

22. Diogo Teixeira and Karla H. Karash, "An Evaluation of Councils on Aging Dial-a-Ride Systems in Massachusetts," *Transportation* 4 (June 1975), pp. 105–22.

expansion of the disbursement function already served by these agencies may be a strategic point at which to intervene in implementing the transportation service brokerage concept advocated here. Because these agencies are chartered to administer public assistance for the various service needs of the aged, they may also be a logical place in which to vest administration of policies designed to serve more effectively the diverse mobility needs of the elderly population.

This same orientation toward providing social services for the elderly could, however, present some problems if the local AAA were designated as transportation authority for the elderly. Because it serves the needs of the elderly exclusively, the AAA might lack perspective concerning how important improved mobility is for the elderly as compared with other transportation policy objectives, including meeting the needs of other disadvantaged groups. This could lead to its advocating transportation service levels for the aged which are inordinately high in comparison to those received by other groups, or which are achievable only at extreme cost. In addition, the agency's lack of experience or expertise as a transportation operator might cause it to face many of the same obstacles to providing cost-effective travel service now encountered by individual social service agencies which operate specialized demand-responsive services.

A second strategy might be to incorporate the functions of the proposed local authority within an existing transportation authority. In the case of Los Angeles this body would logically be SCRTD, the principal supplier of public transportation to the county. This strategy shares an obvious advantage with the previous one, in that no new organization would have to be established. Further, vesting the recommended brokerage function in the regional transit authority is probably the most promising way to coordinate efforts to improve the mobility of the elderly. By combining public transit, taxi, and specialized demand-responsive service SCRTD would face an incentive to supply needed service to eligible elderly clients using the mode which most cost effectively met their varying needs. It could also draw upon its considerable experience in supplying and distributing transportation services to achieve more efficient delivery of transportation services to the elderly who lack such services.

This approach does have some potential disadvantages, however. Chief among these is likely to be excessive emphasis on the costs at which a transit district is able to deliver service. Unless its receipt of federal and local matching funds earmarked for supporting transportation for the elderly is contingent upon continuing demonstration that the mobility needs of these groups are being met, service quality may be sacrificed in the interest of cost reduction or operational efficiency. While conventional transit authorities might be cost conscious to the point that services for the elderly could suffer, Saltzman notes that in many instances their operating costs can actually exceed those of the uncoordinated social service agencies. Unionized bus drivers employed by conventional transit authorities earn substantially higher wages than do most drivers employed by social service agencies. Even if the specialized services were to be provided by a separate division of a transit company, it is likely that wages would have to be increased to match union scale. Under Section 13(c) of the Urban Mass Transportation Act, transit employees who are assigned to federally funded programs must not have their welfare decreased by virtue of their participation in the programs. Thus, while transit operators might be able to provide more efficient and coordinated operations than would local service agencies, it is not at all certain that they could do so at lower cost.[23]

Another potential problem is reflected in the attitudes of heads of human service agencies toward the takeover of their transportation services by a conventional transit authority. Crain found that most agencies would prefer not to be in the transportation business themselves if an efficient and compassionate alternative provider of service existed. Yet most agency directors surveyed in the San Francisco region believed that existing transit authorities

23. Saltzman, "Coordinating Transportation for Human Service Clients."

would not be sensitive or responsive to their clients.[24] In addition, if the existing public transit authority is to be relied upon to assume a brokerage function in delivering services to the elderly, the question must be addressed as to whether it would assume a similar function in meeting the needs of other groups without transportation. It seems likely that the authority could act equally effectively as an intermediary in the delivery of services to the poor, the handicapped, youth, and other groups. While this is not a drawback to the possibility of its serving the elderly, it does indicate that a much wider base of research remains to be assembled before unified service to all groups needing transportation can be seriously considered.

A few systems for both the elderly and handicapped have already been instituted under the auspices of the local transportation authorities. A demonstration project called "Project Mobility" is currently being operated by the Metropolitan Transit Commission in the Minneapolis and St. Paul area. Using local and federal funding, the transit authority there is providing persons who qualify with door-to-door service using medium-sized accessible vehicles, driven by unionized drivers from the authority's regular staff. The fare charged for service is only ten cents per ride above the regular transit fare. In Pittsburgh, Pennsylvania, a somewhat different sort of project is presently in the planning stages. Here, the Port Authority of Allegheny County, the local transit authority, is planning to function as a service broker for transportation for the elderly and handicapped, rather than operating the service using its own vehicles and drivers. It will accept bids from taxi companies, school bus companies, and other paratransit service operators to provide door-to-door service to eligible clients within certain subareas of the metropolitan area. Services will also be available between the contract subareas. The service providers who obtain the contracts will have to adhere to the Port Authority's rules regarding client eligibility and will have to follow preestab-

24. Crain, *Paratransit Survey Component*.

lished fare policies. The Port Authority will have control over overall operating and management functions as well as responsibility for collecting and disbursing funds.[25] Although the project was still in the planning stages as this book went to press, it is being watched very closely as a potential model of coordination of services to the elderly and handicapped. It should be noted that in both the Twin Cities and Pittsburgh cases, the services operated by the local transit authority are not exclusive. In both cities, social service agencies and municipalities may continue to operate their own specialized services for the elderly. In both of these cases, an attempt is being made to offer coordinated service of such fine quality and cost efficiency that private and public agencies will decide to rely upon them rather than providing their own competing services. How successful such efforts at coordination are must be evaluated at a later date, since they are so new and have yet to be fully implemented.

A third alternative would be to establish the proposed local transportation authority as a newly chartered, independent branch of regional or county government or, possibly, as a private, nonprofit organization. This could occur upon the adoption of state legislation empowering counties to create agencies which would subsume existing transportation programs serving the elderly or allowing the creation of nonprofit organizations for this purpose. This would follow the precedent of public housing authorities, local agencies created to construct and operate low-cost shelter under early federal housing programs. Specifically, such legislation should allow counties to charter public or nonprofit corporations, which would operate as branches or extensions of government. Their existence would thus be under the ultimate jurisdiction of the state, although they would preserve considerable operational

25. Alfred Blumstein *et al.*, "Project Design for a Coordinated Paratransit Service for Elderly and Handicapped Persons in Allegheny County, Pennsylvania," paper presented at the Workshop on Transportation for the Elderly and Handicapped, sponsored by the Transportation Research Board, held at Elkridge, Maryland (September 1977).

flexibility at the local level if the housing authority precedent were adhered to. Two current illustrations of this
type of system are the Older Americans Transportation
System serving over ninety counties in Missouri and an
independent state-wide transportation system for elderly
and handicapped citizens of Delaware.

In chartering such transportation authorities, a state
would delegate to the agency significant responsibilities
for its operations. These would include the power to
purchase or lease capital equipment and operate it in order
to supply transportation services directly. If empowered to
negotiate contracts, the local agency could purchase
transportation services from existing suppliers on a one-
time, continuing, or subscription basis using available federal and other financing sources. In those cases in which
the precedent of the housing authority was followed, the
transportation agency could make direct contracts with
other branches of government and private parties, extending its range of potential suppliers to include transit
districts, franchised taxi operations, and other service
suppliers established in the future. The Delaware Authority for Specialized Transportation (DAST) was created by
the state legislature to provide service throughout the
state. Through purchase of service contracts, local governments, the United Fund, and many private agencies
contract with DAST to transport their clients. According to
Saltzman, these agencies reported that in most cases the
cost to the agencies was found to be far lower than was the
case when they were providing their own services.[26]

One clear advantage of this strategy is that it assigns
service coordination and delivery to a body which is not
solely concerned with either the availability of social services to the elderly or the efficient provision of transit
service to the area as a whole. This would appear to make
more realistically attainable the effective provision of services to the elderly at reasonable costs. On the other hand,
it does present complications by introducing another

26. Saltzman, "Coordinating Transportation for Human Service
Clients."

decision-making body into the service delivery process already characterized by a seriously fragmented decision chain.

There are several distinct ways in which organizations can be structured to fulfill the coordinating functions argued for in previous sections. Each features particular strengths, each has potentially severe drawbacks, and none is clearly dictated. Future research concerning the travel needs of groups lacking mobility should explore the brokerage concept advanced here, including the study of what type of organization can most effectively implement the concept.

Federal agencies that provide financial support for transportation sponsored by social services have recently become quite interested in research and experimentation dealing with coordination. A recent working agreement between the Administration on Aging and UMTA holds open the prospect for coordinating the funding programs of the two agencies.[27] The Office of Human Development Services of HEW has chosen five sites for experiments where it will fund coordinated transportation programs for social service agencies.[28] Early reports from coordinated efforts conducted solely at the initiative of local governments have given impetus to such federally sponsored experiments. In Chattanooga, Tennessee, for example, some forty service providers reported that they substantially lowered cost per client mile while improving service when they pooled their resources into a single radio-dispatched system. The system was providing service at a cost of 61 cents per passenger mile, while the forty agencies were experiencing average costs before coordination of $2.93 per passenger mile.[29]

27. U.S. General Accounting Office, *Hindrances to Coordinating Transportation of People Participating in Federally Funded Grant Programs*, Vol. 1 (Washington, D.C., October 1977).

28. Saltzman, "Coordinating Transportation for Human Service Clients."

29. Dolli Cutler, "Interagency Cooperation: A Federal Perspective," in Douglas J. McKelvey, ed., *Proceedings of the First National Conference on Rural Public Transportation* (Greensboro: North Carolina A and T State University, June 1976).

Despite this growing interest and indications of early success, service coordination is not likely to be easily achieved, nor is it a panacea which will appeal to every agency. Many organizations will continue to prefer the visibility of their private, brightly identified vehicles. Many small organizations will happily continue to find it possible to operate voluntary services without any form of public support. In some locations the barriers to coordination will prove insurmountable. There is a clear trend toward larger, integrated or coordinated systems for the elderly, however, and on balance it is probable that the benefits of this transition will outweigh the costs.

Meeting Mobility Needs Through User-Side Subsidies

The current federal commitment to serving the travel needs of the elderly is implemented through subsidies to mass transit systems and payments to local agencies or governments operating specialized transportation services. Capital and operating grants are available to urban public transit operators under the Urban Mass Transportation Act (as amended). These grants enable transit suppliers to provide service at lower costs than would be possible without subsidies, while making transit vehicles more accessible to elderly patrons. Under some fifty other programs, the federal government encourages local branches of social service agencies or municipal governments to operate demand-responsive transportation serving the aged. Most or all of the costs of operations are financed under these programs, many of which provide transportation to make their primary services more accessible to elderly clients. Both of these approaches can be characterized as provider or supply-side subsidies aimed at meeting the needs of the elderly.

Increasing attention has recently been given to a user- or demand-side approach to serving the elderly as well as other groups needing transportation. By targeting subsidies on the users of transportation services, this approach serves the same objectives as provider-side programs: reducing the cost of service to users, making available service of a higher quality and improving its usefulness to recipients. Generally, user-side subsidies would allow eligible recipients to use existing transportation systems at costs below those ordinarily charged by their operators. When recipients utilized their services, suppliers would be reimbursed by the sponsoring public agency for the difference between their normal fare and the revenues collected from subsidized users. This could occur where the sponsoring agency sells to users vouchers or tickets at costs below their worth to transportation suppliers. Users would pay for services using these vouchers, which would in turn be redeemed by suppliers for payment from the sponsor. The vouchers could be any evidence that trips had actually been made by eligible recipients, ranging from actual tickets to records kept by the service operator.[30]

Arguments for User-Side Subsidies

The primary argument favoring increased reliance on user-side subsidies holds that they promote efficient use of transportation resources.[31] Because choice among travel modes is vested in the user, suppliers will compete to offer service levels and fares which attract riders. Users will select transportation which most closely meets their desired service characteristics at the lowest fare, promoting more productive use of resources by transportation suppliers.

User-side subsidies appear to offer a further important advantage in that they permit a closer matching of service supply to travel needs than does the supply-side intervention alone. Kirby and Tolson argue that they offer sponsoring agencies the flexibility to determine which users will be subsidized, for what modes and purposes of travel, and to what extent.[32] Because subsidies can be offered to users

---

30. Kirby and Tolson, *Improving the Mobility of the Elderly and Handicapped*, p. 15.

31. Kirby and McGillivray, "Alternative Subsidy Techniques," p. 27.

32. Kirby and Tolson, *Improving the Mobility of the Elderly and Handicapped*, p. 17.

in proportion to their travel needs, and suppliers are rewarded for serving subsidized patrons just as with other riders, public agencies can induce a closer match between need and actual availability of service than now appears to prevail. There are, of course, problems in interpreting the needs of potential subsidy recipients discussed previously. But within the broad guidelines as to need offered by federal transportation programs supporting the elderly, the research reported in this study should facilitate a closer understanding of how needs vary within the aged population. When combined with the flexibility offered by demand-side subsidies, this knowledge should permit public agencies to target more effectively travel assistance to groups that merit it.

As an illustration, this research has identified two subgroups of the elderly population in Los Angeles County which would be suitable targets of a user-side subsidy program. Members of both the black and Spanish-American elderly lifestyle groups are characterized by low incomes and limited automobile ownership, causing them to rely to a greater extent than other groups on public transportation for their travel needs. Although the black lifestyle group is served comparatively well by specialized demand-responsive operators, such service to the county's Spanish-American elderly is limited. Both groups are served well by taxi and public transit services according to the findings of this research, yet at fares many are likely to find prohibitively expensive given their limited incomes.

To gain access to basic personal services, engage in shopping and business, and maintain social relationships, members of these lifestyle groups may require expanded opportunities to travel. User-side subsidies made available to them, for example, under federal transportation assistance programs for which they now qualilfy, could substantially improve their mobility by allowing them to use buses and taxis at reduced fares. The agency sponsoring the subsidy could reimburse suppliers of these services in proportion to the number of riders served through ticket redemption or through record keeping and reporting by suppliers themselves. In this manner the travel needs of specific elderly groups could be more effectively served while efficient use of transportation resources is promoted.

Current Experience with User-Side Subsidies

Although experience with demand-side subsidies for travel is limited to date, there are some examples of the ways in which they might be administered.[33] In Great Britain, user-side subsidies are well established in providing for the transportation needs of handicapped persons. People who are physically disabled may apply to the Department of Health and Social Security for a "mobility allowance" of about twenty dollars per month, with decisions as to the legitimacy of claims being decided by doctors. The recipient of this benefit is free to determine the modes and frequencies of travel, and the benefit is not dependent upon the actual travel choices. If the handicapped person is able to drive, he or she may qualify for a small three-wheeled, one-passenger vehicle, available from centers which distribute artificial limbs and prosthetic devices. One may accept either the mobility allowance or the small vehicle, but not both. The eligible citizen who is physically qualified for either the mobility allowance or the car may exercise a free choice between the options.[34] In the United States some locally initiated programs and two sponsored by UMTA subsidize taxi rides for persons deemed qualified. In Oak Ridge, Tennessee, residents over 60 years old may use a ticket which they purchase from the city for 25 cents in lieu of the first $1.00 fare for a taxi ride. They must meet the remainder of the fare in cash, while the taxi operator can redeem the tickets for payment by the city. Elderly and disabled residents of Los Gatos, California, can redeem one 50 cent taxi ticket for a trip anywhere within the city limits, using up to ten

33. Ibid., pp. 19–23.
34. Great Britain, Department of Health and Social Security, *Mobility Allowance*, Leaflet NI 211 (January 1976).

tickets per month. The local taxi operator is paid $2.10 in city revenue sharing funds for each ticket collected.

UMTA sponsored programs in Danville, Illinois (through the Office of Service and Methods Demonstrations), and Oklahoma City (under a Section 5 operating assistance grant) subsidize shared-ride taxi service for elderly and disabled persons. Under the Illinois program a rider pays 25 percent of the normal taxi fare in cash and signs a voucher which the taxi operator redeems with the city for the remaining fare. Each rider is subject to a $20.00 monthly limit of subsidized taxi service; eligible users identify themselves with a card issued by the city. Over 20 percent of Danville taxi riders now represent subsidized users, and service quality is reported to be high.

Other programs allow eligible users access to a wider variety of service. Elderly and handicapped residents of New Jersey are allowed half-fare travel on all intrastate and some interstate bus and rail lines during off-peak hours. Riders pay half of the fare in cash and submit a ticket certifying their eligibility, which the provider later redeems with the State Department of Transportation for payment of the difference. A statewide program in West Virginia allows elderly residents with low incomes to buy an $8.00 monthly allotment of travel tickets for a price which depends on income. Public transit and taxicab operators, as well as interstate bus and rail services, accept these tickets at face value for payment of fares. This program also provides subsidies to selected transportation suppliers to allow them to purchase new equipment and expand service.

Another UMTA demonstration project under development in Montgomery, Alabama, will offer elderly and disabled citizens travel at half fare using conventional bus transit or shared-ride taxi service. Users will pay their half of the fare in cash; taxi operators will redeem signed vouchers with the city for the remaining half, while the city's transit system will be reimbursed based on its on-board record keeping of rides by subsidized users. A similar demonstration project in Lawrence, Massachusetts, will offer half-price bus and taxi travel to that city's elderly and handicapped residents. It will employ tickets sold to users at half of face value but accepted at full face value for fare payment. Taxi and bus operators will redeem collected tickets with the city for payment.

Unfortunately, there is little information on the costs and effectiveness of these programs in serving those who need transportation. They do illustrate, however, considerable local flexibility in determining eligibility for subsidies, type of travel to be funded, and extent of the subsidy to be offered. This type of adaptability is important in tailoring programs which can serve the travel needs of specific groups. These programs also indicate that, where existing transit service is good, it can be effectively utilized to serve these specific groups, thus offering an attractive alternative to federal funding of specialized demand-responsive services.

Administering Demand-Side Subsidies Through a Local Transportation Authority

The proposed local transportation authority offers a useful mechanism for the regional administration of demand-side subsidy programs in selected communities. The authority would be empowered to collect federal funds under programs which permit their disbursement directly to elderly persons. For example, these could include state and local revenue sharing funds, which have already been used to support elderly travel subsidies, and grants under certain sections of the Urban Mass Transportation Act. The precedent for use of operating assistance grants available under Section 5 of that act has been established in a subsidized taxi service pilot program in Oklahoma City.

In neighborhoods where it was deemed appropriate, coupons for taxi use could then be distributed to the elderly residents well served by taxis. In Los Angeles, this would include the Spanish-American, black, and central-city lifestyle groups identified in this study. A certain maximum number of coupons could be made available to any one person in any time period. Up to that number, eligible recipients could be charged for the tickets based on their incomes such as is done under the West Virginia program discussed above. Those with higher incomes would be charged a higher percentage of the face value of the tickets. The problem of wide geographic dispersion of these groups of elderly might be overcome by distributing the tickets through senior citizens' centers operated by the City of Los Angeles and several other cities in the county, through commercial banks (as has proven successful in the New Jersey program), or through places of employment.

The local transportation authority could then contract with taxi franchises serving the areas occupied by these elderly to respond to their calls and accept the tickets at face value as fare payment. Through redemption with the authority, taxi operators would recover the full cash value of the tickets, probably supplemented by a small premium to cover their costs of participation in the program (ticket collection and redemption, accounting treatment of subsidized ridership, etc.). Although the brokerage program now being planned in Allegheny County is not yet fully operational, it would appear to incorporate several of these principles in its preliminary design. This is only one of several possible arrangements, but it does illustrate a mechanism for more fully serving the travel needs of important groups. It offers an effective supplement—and a probable partial replacement—for current publicly supported attempts to meet those needs through an uncoordinated set of small-scale specialized transportation operations. Although user-side subsidy programs need not be restricted to use of taxi service, the local transportation authority would not provide similar subsidies for use of service which it provided directly, since its incentive to operate efficiently would be weakened. User-side subsidies and contracts with taxi operators would be employed in some communities, while the authority might directly provide specialized services in others, depending upon local conditions characterizing both the demand and supply sides.

Whether or not a program of user-side subsidies for transporting elderly persons is ever adopted on a large scale, a review of their possibilities does point out one critical flaw in current transportation policy. Reduced fare programs for elderly and handicapped people, and capital investments which will make transit systems more physically accessible are requirements which exist today simply as a condition for the receipt of federal transit subsidies. The requirements for investment do not vary with the number of elderly passengers carried, and the subsidies do not increase if an operator carries larger numbers of elderly riders. Thus, the current system provides no direct incentive for effectiveness on the part of the transit operator, and, since elderly passengers pay fares which amount to far less than the cost of a ride, transit operators are not likely to pursue vigorously new transit markets among the elderly. Under a program of demand-side subsidies, however, payments to the transit operator would increase with patronage, and an incentive to provide more and attractive service to older riders would exist. It is possible, of course, to provide such an incentive structure without adopting a full system of demand-side subsidies.[35] In England, for example, reduced fares are provided for elderly persons at the discretion of local governments, rather than as an element of national policy. When local authorities decide to provide "concessionary" fares, they make payments to the transit operators to cover the cost of fare reductions. Transfer payments from governments can form a significant source of income to the transit companies and can provide an incentive to offer attractive services to older travelers.[36] A significant disadvantage of the British system, however, is that, while some local authorities provide substantial transfer payments for the carriage of elderly riders, others provide very small payments

35. Sumner Myers, "Compensatory Transportation," *City* 6 (Summer 1972), pp. 17–21.

36. Great Britain, Department of Transport, The Welsh Office, *Survey of Concessionary Bus Fares for the Elderly, Blind and Disabled in England and Wales*, Local Transport Note 1/77 (London, 1977).

or none at all. Thus, fares for older people vary widely from one jurisdiction to another. A system might be designed to incorporate the benefits of current American and British policies if it were to provide transfer payments on the basis of older riders carried, with the nature and amount of these subsidies determined as an element of national policy.

Mobility for the Suburbanized Elderly of the Future: The Role of the Automobile

This research has pointed to the emergence of a new generation of active, comparatively affluent elderly, including many residing in dense suburban areas. In the areas developing at the urban fringe, the predominant mode of travel will continue to be the private automobile. This will undoubtedly be the case for the future elderly populations of those areas, who will have depended primarily on automobile travel as they age. By the year 2000, some 25 percent of Los Angeles County's total elderly population will reside in those areas now occupied by the new suburban lifestyle group identified in this study. It has also been projected that the largest increase in travel among the six elderly lifestyle groups will occur within the new suburban group. Similar patterns can probably be expected in other metropolitan areas.

In the suburban settings occupied by this group, conventional bus service was of the lowest quality among the six lifestyle groups. In addition, the common orientation of bus service in outlying suburban areas toward the central business district during peak hours reduces the usefulness to the elderly of even the minimal available service. Taxi service to the new suburban elderly was also found to be of the poorest quality. Specialized transit service was similarly found to be infrequently available to this segment of the elderly population, especially in comparison with its less recently suburbanized counterparts. In areas of low residential density, the normally high costs of providing specialized services are likely to become exhorbitant. Costs per rider borne by conventional transit operations are also likely to be high, making expansion of such service possible only at enormously increased levels of public subsidy. The travel needs of this lifestyle group will be difficult to meet through any combination of conventional transit and paratransit services. While many aging suburbanites will continue to drive as they become elderly, a number of them will become physically incapable of operating a conventional automobile or will not be licensed to operate one.

A Role for New Automobile Designs

The travel needs of the elderly of the future living at low densities might be most effectively served by policies which would accelerate the current trend toward smaller, lighter cars. One possible result of this trend may be a small personal vehicle designed primarily to serve local travel. Such a vehicle would be light in weight, relatively inexpensive to own, physically less demanding to operate than a conventional automobile, and able to accommodate the physical characteristics of elderly drivers. Such a vehicle could take effective advantage of the short distances, combined purposes, and off-peak scheduling which characterize much travel by the elderly. Light weight in the design of such vehicles is dictated by the desire to retain operating economy and ensure adequate maneuverability. However, this may involve some sacrifice of safety in the event of collision, a tradeoff which requires exploration during the design and testing phases. For example, such a vehicle could be designed to seat two adults, with some additional space for parcels. Using either gasoline or electric power, it could operate at low speeds, up to 25 miles per hour, while featuring low power and acceleration. Higher power or performance would be unnecessary for travel at the local or neighborhood scale if suitable right-of-way arrangements could be made to accommodate such vehicles. Several such arrangements are possible. Simply, these vehicles might share existing roadways with conventional automobiles, or agreements for shared use of the expanding system of bicycle lanes in suburban areas might be possible. Special lanes, similar to those now designated for bicycles, might be created on existing roadways for exclusive use by the smaller, low-powered cars. Alternatively, such vehicles might be granted exclusive use of some part of the existing roadway during off-peak travel hours. It might even be possible to construct exclusive rights-of-way for use by smaller vehicles over the long run. Such an approach does, however, appear to have extreme disadvantages because of cost, when compared to arrangements which would involve sharing existing roadways.

If produced inexpensively, with simple controls and specialized design characteristics, the vehicle could improve the mobility of the elderly as well as the handicapped and other population groups who currently may not qualify for standard driver's licenses. Both the Stanford Research Institute (SRI)[37] and Garrison[38] envision the licensing of Class B drivers who cannot operate conventional autos nor drive on freeways, but who may be trained to drive these special vehicles, at a maximum speed of 15 miles per hour, on designated paths.

Manufacture of these vehicles appears technologically feasible at this time. A system similar to the Public Automobile Service described by SRI has been recently developed in Amsterdam. Although the vehicles are publicly owned and are not operated in suburban settings, the Amsterdam case shows that a small, electric, short-range vehicle can be developed.[39] As mentioned earlier, three-wheel, one-passenger autos are available to handicapped drivers as part of an ongoing national program in Britain. These vehicles are mass produced and are available with

37. Clark Henderson *et al.*, *Future Urban Transportation Systems: Descriptions, Evaluations, and Programs* (Menlo Park, Ca.: Stanford Research Institute, 1968).

38. W.L. Garrison and J. Fred Clarke, Jr., *Better Neighborhood Transportation: Interim Report* (Berkeley, Ca.: University of California, Institute of Transportation Studies, 1976), p. 59.

39. Terence Bendixson and Martin G. Richards, "Witkar: Amsterdam's Self-Drive Hire City Car," *Transportation* 5 (1976), pp. 70–72.

either electric or petroleum power plants. There are currently at least fifty companies throughout the world that engage in the manufacture of electric passenger cars; thirty-one of these produce cars weighing less than 2,000 pounds. Of the fifty companies, twenty-three are based in the United States.[40] The technological capability therefore appears promising, and the evolution of vehicle design may be accelerated if demand for them increases.

Public demand for these vehicles may not materialize in sufficient quantity if the potential hazards of driving such a vehicle are not taken into account. The perceived lack of safety is a major impediment to their widespread use. The study by Garrison points to the need to coordinate three entities in order to bring about the development of localized travel using small vehicles. These entities are governmental institutions which control and regulate the roadway system and its users, private firms which supply the vehicles, and local communities which will use those vehicles. Garrison argues that public policy should be committed to adapting the roadway network to provide a safe operating environment for these vehicles. The commitment would start on a small scale in local urban settings to allow for experimentation and testing. These demonstration projects would be useful in refining system design, spreading technological ideas, and determining the cost-effectiveness of various types of systems.

There are likely to be two concurrent roles for government policy in a technological approach to improving mobility among this segment of the elderly population. On one hand, the federal government might seek funding authority to contract for the development of small motor vehicles designed to accommodate the characteristics of the aged driver. This research would have three phases. First and probably most important would be research on the design and operational features of such vehicles necessary to accommodate the physical characteristics of elderly drivers which impact upon their use of conventional au-

40. "Directory of the Electric Vehicle Industry," *Electric Vehicle News* (1977), pp. 41–54.

tos. Second would be the integration of these characteristics with existing small, lightweight motor vehicle technology to produce operational design prototypes for actual testing. Following this phase would be the commission of small-scale demonstration projects such as those envisioned by Garrison. These would be directed toward refining vehicle design features and operating characteristics, as well as publicizing the new application of motor vehicle technology.

Concurrently, federal and local levels of government would need to cooperate in determining suitable modifications of traffic control regulations and drivers' licensing restrictions to accommodate widespread use of the smaller vehicles. This would probably entail federally commissioned experimental programs to test and evaluate alternative right-of-way arrangements for use by such vehicles. Pilot programs to test the levels of safety and participation resulting from licensing standards of varying stringency, as well as from differing restrictions attached to vehicle use—maximum speed limits, confinement of use to off-peak or daylight hours only, etc.—could also result from coordinated federal and local sponsorship of experimentation involving the new technology. One further application of small vehicles which might be explored through federally sponsored experimentation might be their use as an individualized feeder system serving existing conventional transit networks. In any case, there is a large role for public policy in meeting the mobility needs of a large segment of the future elderly population through the application of emerging motor vehicle technology.

A Role for More Innovative Use of Automobiles

Whether or not it proves feasible to design new automobiles matched to the special needs of the elderly, whether or not institutional changes are possible to provide appropriate rights-of-way to accommodate such vehicles, and whether or not a sufficient market emerges to permit their large-scale production, the increasing suburbanization of the elderly and the rising cost of providing traditional transit or paratransit service require that the automobile play an important part in solving the transportation problems of the elderly. Low population densities and high operating costs for paratransit as well as conventional transit vehicles will increasingly preclude publicly supplied transit service from areas which will house a steadily increasing proportion of the elderly. With proper recognition of this phenomenon and appropriate advanced planning, it should still be possible to meet the travel needs of senior citizens.

It is important to recognize that the vast majority of older Americans who now live at lower population densities are living in family settings, and the majority of these families do possess automobiles. Each year some people living in such situations will, of course, lose their mobility through the death of a spouse who has done the driving, or through illness or advanced age which ultimately reduces their physical ability to drive. When this happens, if alternatives to public transit are not available, older persons might be forced to relocate to other neighborhoods in which social services or public transportation systems are available. Because relocation in old age is itself a traumatic experience, a preferable solution might involve effective organization, at the community level, to provide matching or car-pooling among senior citizens. The increasing numbers of suburban elderly who do possess automobiles might well be called upon to provide rides and deliver goods to other suburban elderly persons who have lost their access to automobiles. The organization of such an effort, under the auspices of existing social service organizations and senior citizens' clubs, might well be more cost-effective than the provision of paratransit service or dial-a-ride systems, because both capital costs and staff costs would be significantly lower. Present obstacles to such efforts lie in such institutional barriers as insurance and licensing restrictions.

If senior citizens were permitted to collect small fees for driving fellow elderly persons to the doctor's office, the grocery store, or a senior citizens' center, several desirable results could be achieved simultaneously. There would be a clear advantage to the nonmobile citizens of low density suburban areas. Through a personal arrangement with an older person they would be assured of the capability to travel, while having the company during the trip of a person of similar age and, it would be hoped, relative understanding and compassion. If a small transaction of money were allowed, the person providing the ride would be ensured some contribution toward the upkeep of his or her automobile, and would thus have a higher probability of maintaining his or her mobility for a longer period of time. The person paying for the ride would consider the service as a business transaction and would not feel that he was imposing upon fellows for charity or for the granting of a favor. In the case of a low-income passenger unable to provide the fee, social service agencies might reimburse the driver for this cost. Tickets or scrip which have been advocated as part of a user-side subsidy program could easily be extended to cover such a ride-sharing arrangement among senior citizens. To ensure that those providing the rides are in good health and able to drive safely, and that their vehicles are in safe operating condition, the local senior citizens' transportation authority advocated earlier could also function as an authority which grants simple licenses or certificates of operation to those wishing to offer rides under this program.

Ultimately, such a system of sharing rides is not an appropriate substitute for public transportation in low density areas among all age groups. Institutional barriers, such as insurance problems and opposition by franchised operators and transport workers' unions, have been regarded as preventing such a general solution to the need for greater mobility in low density communities. The adoption of this solution might be feasible, however, on a more limited basis to provide for the needs of a specific group of clients with common interests.

Conclusion

The principle of public responsibility for the provision of mobility to the elderly is now well established. It is derived from the political salience of this population group, and from economic, social, and ethical factors which combine to heighten the concern of Americans toward particular needs of the elderly. The nature of programs designed to accommodate the transportation needs of the elderly is, however, likely to change significantly during the next few years in response to lessons learned during the early years of practice under existing programs. While programs implemented to date have been aimed at starting the delivery of essential services as quickly as possible and reaching clients in dire need as directly as possible, these programs have been relatively uncoordinated at the local level and have resulted in high operating costs and low levels of efficiency. Such results were tolerable during the early phase of national programs for the elderly but they cannot be supported indefinitely. Failure to coordinate accessible public transit service with specialized paratransit operations is no longer acceptable, nor is the presence of overlapping and similar operations catering to clients of different social service agencies and supported by separate public budgets. During the next few years elected officials will be seeking systematic evaluations of transportation programs for the elderly. Such evaluations might show tremendous progress toward meeting the needs of groups previously left isolated. Another dimension of these evaluations will undoubtedly be more harsh, however, showing that the administrative complexity of existing efforts far exceeds any reasonable overhead which should be expected of such modest and small-scale programs. The costs to taxpayers per rider and per seat-mile are unacceptably high, while service levels remain too variable and often far too low.

The challenges ahead are clear. An increasingly diverse and increasingly suburban elderly clientele, requiring a wider variety of services, will have to be provided with transportation at a reasonable cost and without the burdens of expense and administration which have characterized such programs to date. The major purpose of this book, revealed in the first seven chapters, has been to document the extent of the emerging diversity and suburbanization among older people and to present a methodology for doing so which planners can employ in other metropolitan communities. In this final chapter, some important policy implications of the social and demographic trends have been discussed, admittedly without the benefit of the kinds of rigorous empirical data which characterized the earlier parts of the study. Three major approaches are likely to be productive in meeting the future travel needs of the elderly. First, existing programs could be coordinated to supply specialized demand-responsive travel. This could be accomplished through the creation of local transportation authorities which combine the functions and resources of the myriad suppliers of specialized service currently operating in most urban areas. By integrating funding sources as well as the production or purchase of travel services, this organization could contribute to meeting more effectively the travel needs of the elderly. A second approach would involve subsidies which would be paid directly to elderly persons to encourage their use of existing alternatives to specialized transportation. Such a policy might offer taxi service at reduced fares to elderly groups residing in areas currently well served by taxi operators. Subsidies for these plans could be administered through the proposed local transportation authority. Finally, the mobility of many suburban elderly of the future could be improved by the development of new motor vehicles and by efforts to utilize automobiles more effectively through an organized system of shared rides for senior citizens.

Bibliography

Abt Associates. *Transportation Needs of the Urban Disadvantaged.* Report No. DOT-FH-11-7808. Washington, D.C.: U.S. Department of Transportation, Federal Highway Administration, Socio-Economic Studies Division, 1974.

Andersberg, Michael R. *Cluster Analysis for Applications.* New York: Academic Press, 1973.

Ashford, Norman, and Holloway, Frank H. "Transportation Patterns of Older People in Six Urban Centers." *The Gerontologist* 12 (1972), pp. 43–47.

――――. "Variations of Urban Travel Characteristics with Age." *Transportation Engineering Journal of ASCE* 98 (1972), pp. 715–32.

Automobile Manufacturers' Association. *Automobile Facts and Figures: 1971.* Detroit: Automobile Manufacturers' Association, Economic Research and Statistics Department, 1971.

Baltes, Paul B. "Longitudinal and Cross-Sectional Sequences in the Study of Age and Generation Effects." *Human Development* 11 (1969), pp. 145–71.

Battle, Mark, Associates. *Transportation for the Elderly and Handicapped.* Prepared for the National Urban League. Sponsored by the U.S. Department of Transportation, Urban Mass Transportation Administration, Grant No. DOT-UT-53. Washington, D.C.: U.S. Government Printing Office, 1973.

Bell, William G., and Olsen, William T. "An Overview of Public Transportation and the Elderly: New Directions for Social Policy." *The Gerontologist* 14 (1974), pp. 324–30.

Bendixson, Terence, and Richards, Martin G. "Witkar: Amsterdam's Self-Drive Hire City Car." *Transportation* 5 (1976), pp. 63–72.

Bengston, Vern L. *The Social Psychology of Aging.* Indianapolis: Bobbs-Merrill, 1973.

Berechman, Joseph, and Paaswell, Robert E. "The Impact of Car Availability on Urban Transportation Behavior." *Transportation* 6 (1977), pp. 121–34.

Blanchard, Robert D. "Lifestyle and Travel Demand of the Elderly: A Case Study of Los Angeles County." Ph.D. dissertation, School of Architecture and Urban Planning, University of California, Los Angeles, 1976.

Brail, Richard K.; Hughes, James W.; and Arthur, Carol A. *Transportation Services for the Disabled and Elderly*. New Brunswick, N.J.: Center for Urban Policy Research, 1976.

Brunso, Joanna M. *Transportation for the Elderly and Handicapped: A Prototype Case Study of New York State Experience in Activating an Element of a Federal Grant Program*. Research Report No. 75-5. Seattle: University of Washington, Departments of Civil Engineering and Urban Planning, Urban Transportation Program, 1975.

Butler, Robert M. *Why Survive? Being Old in America*. New York: Harper and Row, 1975.

Butler, Robert M., and Lewis, Myrna I. *Aging and Mental Health: Positive Psychological Approaches*. St. Louis: C.V. Mosby, 1970.

Cain, Leonard D., Jr. "Age Status and Generational Phenomena: The New Old People in Contemporary America." *The Gerontologist* 7 (1967), pp. 83–92.

——. "Planning for the Elderly of the Future." In *Planning and the Urban Elderly: Today and Tomorrow*. Summary of a Two-Day Workshop. Los Angeles: University of Southern California, 1971.

Cantilli, E.J., and Shmelzer, J.L. *Transportation and Aging: Selected Issues*. Washington, D.C.: U.S. Government Printing Office, 1970.

Carp, Frances M. "Automobile and Public Transportation for Retired People." *Highway Research Record* 348 (1971), pp. 182–91.

——. "Walking as a Means of Transportation for Retired People." *The Gerontologist* 11 (1971), pp. 104–11.

——. "The Older Pedestrian in San Francisco." *Highway Research Record* 403 (1972), pp. 18–25.

Crain and Associates. *Transportation Problems of the Transportation Handicapped*. Report No. DOT-UT-60063. 4 vols. Washington, D.C.: U.S. Department of Transportation, Urban Mass Transportation Administration, 1976.

DeBenedictis, J.A., and Dougherty, E.J. *A Directory of Vehicles and Related System Components for the Elderly and Handicapped*. Prepared for the U.S. Department of Transportation, Urban Mass Transportation Administration, Grant No. PA 06-0031. Philadelphia: Franklin Institute Research Laboratories, 1975.

"Directory of the Electric Vehicle Industry." *Electric Vehicle News* (1977), pp. 41–54.

Falcocchio, John C., and Cantilli, Edmund J. *Transportation and the Disadvantaged*. Lexington, Mass.: D.C. Heath, 1974.

Garrison, W. L., and Clarke, J. Fred, Jr. *Better Neighborhood Transportation: Interim Report*. Berkeley: University of California, Institute of Transportation Studies, 1976.

Gillan, Jacqueline, and Wachs, Martin. "Lifestyles and Transportation Needs of the Elderly in Los Angeles." *Transportation* 5 (1976), pp. 45–61.

Golant, Stephen M. "Residential Concentration of the Future Elderly." *The Gerontologist* 15 (1975), pp. 16–23.

———. *The Residential Location and Spatial Behavior of the Elderly*. Research Paper No. 143. Chicago: University of Chicago, Department of Geography, 1972.

Hartgen, David T.; Pasko, Mark; and Howe, Stephen M. *Forecasting Non-Work Public Transit Demand by the Elderly and Handicapped*. Research Report No. 107. Albany: New York State Department of Transportation, Planning Research Unit, 1976.

Havighurst, Robert J. "The Future Aged: The Use of Time and Money." *The Gerontologist* 15 (1975), pp. 10–15.

Henderson, Clark, *et al. Future Urban Transportation Systems: Descriptions, Evaluations, and Programs*. Menlo Park, Ca.: Stanford Research Institute, 1968.

Hillman, Mayer; Henderson, Irwin; and Whalley, Ann. *Personal Mobility and Transport Policy*. London: Political and Economic Planning, 1973.

Hoel, Lester A., and Roszner, E.S. *Impact on Transit Ridership and Revenue of Reduced Fares for the Elderly*. Pittsburgh: Carnegie-Mellon University, Transportation Research Institute, 1971.

Hoel, Lester A., *et al. Latent Demand for Urban Transportation*. Pittsburgh: Carnegie-Mellon University, Transportation Research Institute, 1968.

Institute of Public Administration. *Planning Handbook: Transportation Services for the Elderly*. Washington, D.C.: Institute of Public Administration, 1975.

Karash, Karla. "Analysis of a Taxi-Operated Transportation Service for the Handicapped." *Transportation Research Record* 618 (1977), pp. 25–29.

Kirby, Ronald F., and McGillivray, Robert G. "Alternative Subsidy Techniques for Urban Public Transportation." *Transportation Research Record* 589 (1976), pp. 25–29.

Kirby, Ronald F., and Tolson, Francine L. *Improving the Mobility of the Elderly and Handicapped Through User Side Subsidies*. Report No. UI 5050-4-4. Washington, D.C.: The Urban Institute, 1977.

Los Angeles Regional Transportation Study. *LARTS Base Year Report*. Los Angeles: State of California, Division of Highways, District 07, 1971.

MacQueen, J.B. "Some Methods for Classification and Analysis of Multivariate Observations." *Proceedings of the Fifth Berkeley Symposium on Mathematical Statistics and Probability* 1 (1967), pp. 281–97.

Markovitz, Joni K. "Transportation Needs of the Elderly." *Traffic Quarterly* 25 (1971), pp. 237–53.

Mason, William M.; Mason, Karen; Winsborough, H.H.; and Poole, W. Kenneth. "Some Methodological Issues in Cohort Analysis of Archival Data." *American Sociological Review* 38 (1973), pp. 242–58.

Michaels, Richard M., and Weiler, N. Sue. "Transportation Needs of the Mobility Limited." Evanston, Ill.: Northwestern University, Transportation Center, 1974.

Miklocjik, Jacob L. "Mobility and Older Americans: An Analysis." *Transit Journal* 2 (May 1976), pp. 41–50.

Miller, Joel A. "Latent Travel Demands of the Handicapped and Elderly." *Transportation Research Record* 618 (1977), pp. 7–12.

Morlok, E.K.; Kulash, W. M.; and Vandersypen, H.L. *Effect of Reduced Fares for the Elderly on Transit System Routes.* Research Paper No. 36. Washington, D.C.: U.S., Department of Health, Education, and Welfare, Social and Rehabilitation Service, Administration on Aging, 1971.

Myers, Sumner. "Compensatory Transportation." *City* 6 (Summer 1972), pp. 17–21.

National Cooperative Highway Research Program. *Transportation Requirements for the Handicapped, Elderly, and Economically Disadvantaged.* Washington, D.C.: National Research Council, Transportation Research Board, 1976.

National Council on Aging. *Developing Transportation Services for the Older Poor.* Senior Opportunities and Services Technical Assistance Monograph No. 4. Washington, D.C.: National Council on Aging, 1970.

Neugarten, Bernice L. "Age Groups in American Society and the Rise of the Young Old." *Annals of the American Academy of Political and Social Science* 415 (1974), pp. 187–98.

———. "The Future of the New Old." *The Gerontologist* 15 (1975), pp. 4–9.

Neugarten, Bernice L., and Havighurst, Robert J. *Social Policy, Social Ethics, and the Aging Society.* Washington, D.C.: U.S. Government Printing Office, 1976.

Nie, Norman H.; Hull, C. Hadlai; Jenkins, Jean G.; Steinbrenner, Karin; and Bent, Dale H. *Statistical Package for the Social Sciences.* New York: McGraw-Hill, 1975.

Norman, Alison. *Transport and the Elderly: Problems and Possible Actions.* London: National Corporation for the Care of Old People, 1977.

Paaswell, Robert E., and Recker, Wilfred W. "Location of the Carless." *Transportation Research Record* 516 (1974), pp. 11–20.

Perloff, Harvey S. "Lifestyles and the Environment: The Future Planning Game." *Planning* 39 (June 1973), pp. 19–23.

Rechel, Ralph E. *Contemporary Issues and Problems in Financing Services for the Transportation Disadvantaged.* Washington, D.C.: Institute of Public Administration, 1977.

Revis, Joseph S. *Background and Issues: Transportation.* Background paper for the 1971 White House Conference on Aging. Washington, D.C.: U.S. Government Printing Office, 1971.

———. "Transportation and the Aging: Some Directions." In *Transpor-*

tation and Aging: Selected Issues, an Interdisciplinary Workshop on Transportation and Aging. DHEW Publication No. (OHD)74-20232. Washington, D.C.: U.S. Department of Health, Education, and Welfare, 1970.

———. *Transportation for Older Americans—1976: Progress, Prospects, and Potentials.* Washington, D.C.: Institute of Public Administration, 1976.

Revis, Joseph *et al. Planning Handbook: Transportation Services for the Elderly.* Sponsored by the Administration on Aging. Washington, D.C.: Institute of Public Administration, 1975.

Revis, Joseph, *et al. Transportation for Older Americans: A State-of-the-Art Report.* Prepared for the Administration on Aging. Washington, D.C.: Institute of Public Administration, 1975.

Rummel, R.J. *Applied Factor Analysis.* Evanston, Il.: Northwestern University Press, 1970.

Ryder, Norman, "The Cohort as a Concept in the Study of Social Change." *American Sociological Review* 30 (1965), pp. 843–61.

Saltzman, Arthur. "The Benefits of Cooperation Among Human Service Agency Transit Operators in Rural Areas." Ph.D. dissertation proposal. University of California, Irvine, 1977.

———. "Coordinating Transportation for Human Service Agency Clients." Paper presented at the International Conference on Transport for Elderly and Handicapped Persons, Cambridge, England, April 1978.

Schness, John B. "Public Transportation and Transportation Needs of the Elderly and Handicapped." *Transportation Research Record* 516 (1974), pp. 1–10.

Sheldon, Henry D. "The Changing Demographic Profile." In *Handbook of Social Gerontology,* edited by Clark Tibbetts. Chicago: University of Chicago Press, 1960.

Shmelzer, J.L. "Elderly Ridership and Reduced Transit Fares: The Chicago Experience." In *Transportation and Aging: Selected Issues,* by E.J. Cantilli and J.L. Shmelzer. Washington, D.C.: U.S. Government Printing Office, 1970.

Skelton, N.G. "Travel Patterns of Elderly People Under a Concessionary Fares Scheme." Newcastle-upon-Tyne, England: University of Newcastle-upon-Tyne, Transport Operations Group, 1975.

Sobin, D.P. *The Future of the American Suburbs.* Port Washington, N.Y.: National University Publications, Kennikat Press, 1971.

Southern California Association of Governments. *Short Range Transit Plan,* vol. 2. Los Angeles: Southern California Association of Governments, 1977.

Taves, M., and Shmelzer, J.L. *Mobility, Transportation and Aging.* Washington, D.C.: U.S. Department of Health, Education, and Welfare, 1970.

U.S. Congress, Senate, Select Committee on Aging, Subcommittee on

Federal, State, and Community Service. *Senior Transportation —
Ticket to Dignity: Report by the Subcommittee*, 94th Cong., 2d sess.,
May 20, 1976.

U.S. Congress, Senate, Special Committee on Aging. *Older Americans
and Transportation: A Crisis in Mobility.* Report No. 91-1520.
Washington, D.C.: U.S. Government Printing Office, 1970.

———. *Transportation and the Elderly: Problems and Progress.* Report No.
34–273, 93rd Cong., 2d sess., 1974.

U.S. Department of Health, Education, and Welfare. *Facts on Aging.*
Washington, D.C.: U.S. Government Printing Office, 1970.

———. *Transportation for the Elderly: The State of the Art.* DHEW Publication No. (OHD)75-20081. Washington, D.C.: U.S. Government
Printing Office, 1975.

U.S. Department of Transportation, Federal Highway Administration.
Trip Generation Analysis. Washington, D.C.: U.S. Government
Printing Office, 1975.

U.S. Department of Transportation, Urban Mass Transportation Administration and Transportation Systems Center. *The Handicapped
and Elderly Market for Urban Mass Transit.* Washington, D.C.: U.S.
Government Printing Office, 1973.

U.S. Department of Transportation, Urban Mass Transportation Ad-
ministration. *Transportation Assistance for Elderly and Handicapped
Persons.* Washington D.C.: Public Affairs Office, Urban Mass
Transportation Administration, 1977.

U.S. Executive Office of the President, Office of Management and
Budget. *1975 Catalog of Federal Domestic Assistance.* Washington,
D.C.: U.S. Government Printing Office, 1975.

Wachs, Martin, ed. "Transportation Patterns and Needs of the Elderly
Population in Los Angeles." Mimeographed. Los Angeles: University of California, School of Architecture and Urban Planning,
1975.

———. "Transportation Policy in the Eighties." *Transportation* 6 (1977),
pp. 103–19.

Wachs, Martin, and Blanchard, Robert D. "Lifestyles and Transportation Needs of the Elderly in the Future." *Transportation Research
Record* 618 (1977), pp. 19–24.

Weaver, Vaun C., and Herrin, Moreland. "Transportation Needs and
Desires of the Elderly Residing in a Medium-Sized City." *Transportation Research Record* 516 (1974), pp. 28–34.

Windman, Jean. *A Look at the Elderly Driver.* Ann Arbor: University of
Michigan, Institute of Gerontology, 1973.

Designer: Dave Comstock
Compositor: Viking Typographics
Printer: Braun-Brumfield, Inc.
Binder: Braun-Brumfield, Inc.
Text: VIP Palatino
Display: Univers 56, 66, 76
Cloth: Holliston Roxite C57590
Paper: 50 lb. P&S Offset Vellum